Make 'Em Laugh

Famous Comedians and their Worlds

MAKE 'EM LAUGH

Famous Comedians and their Worlds

ERIC MIDWINTER

LONDON
GEORGE ALLEN & UNWIN
BOSTON   SYDNEY

First published in 1979

GEORGE ALLEN & UNWIN LTD
40 Museum Street, London WC1A 1LU

© Eric Midwinter, 1979

British Library Cataloguing in Publication Data

Midwinter, Eric
    Make 'em laugh.
    1. Comedians, English
    I. Title
    791'.092'2   PN2597

    ISBN 0-04-792011-4

Designed by
Malcolm Smythe

Special illustrations by
Safu-Maria Gilbert

Typeset in 10 on 11 point Century by
A. Brown & Sons Ltd, Hull, England
and printed in Great Britain
by Unwin Brothers Ltd, Old Woking, Surrey

To Ack

(posthumously, and of whom more on page 88)

Contents

Billy Bennett

George Formby

Jimmy James

Max Miller

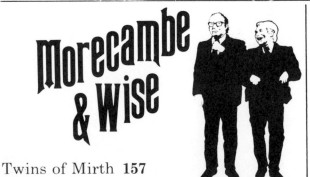

Morecambe & Wise

Les Dawson

Author's acknowledgements

An author's repayment of debts by brief acknowledgements must be one of the least expensive forms of reimbursement. These are certainly paid in genuine currency. My first thanks, then, to some of those whose work has been of immense value. In particular I found John Fisher's book *Funny Way to be a Hero* (Frederich Muller, 1973) of the utmost help, with its perceptive portrayals of dozens of comedians over the last half-century, and Raymond Mander and Joe Mitchenson's *British Music Hall* (Gentry Books, 1965) has proved an excellent guide and mentor. At an individual level, Freddie Hancock and David Nathan, *Hancock* (William Kimber, 1969), John Fisher, *George Formby* (Woburn Futura, 1975), Frankie Howerd, *On the Way I Lost It* (W. H. Allen, 1976), Eric Morecambe, Ernie Wise and Dennis Holman, *Eric and Ernie* (W. H. Allen, 1972) and Les Dawson, *The Spy who Came* (Wyndham, 1976) are but a few of the books upon which I have drawn.

I have listened carefully to recorded material, as this seemed the most valid base for the analysis of the comedian at work. The records I have discovered to be of most help – and I am most happy to acknowledge the fact – are as follows:

'Stars Who Made the Music Hall' (Ace of Clubs, Treasury Series, Mono. ACL 1170)

'Music Hall to Variety' (World Record Club Ltd., Mono W9292)

'The World of George Formby' (Decca, Mono PA50, Stereo SPA50)

and these BBC Records, as ever a most useful source:

'Vintage Variety' (BBC, Mono, REC 134M),

'50 Years of Radio Comedy' (BBC, Mono, REC 138M), and

'It's Morecambe and Wise' (BBC, RED 128M)

I am pleased to acknowledge the various permissions that I have been granted to quote briefly from the extensive George Formby canon:

'In My Little Snapshot Album' (J. Harper, W. Haines, H. Parr-Davies)

'When I'm Cleaning Windows' (H. Gifford, F. Cliff, G. Formby)

(cc) 1973 Lawrence Wright Music Co. Ltd. for World. (Used by permission.)

'My Little Ukelele in My Hand' (J. Cotterell – by permission of Harrison Music Co. Ltd.) and

'Leaning on a Lamp-post' (N. Gay – by permission of Cinephonic Music Co. Ltd.)

I am delighted to say that Billy Bennett's sister, Mrs Margaret Galletly of Brighton, has kindly allowed me to quote liberally from her brother's splendid monologue, 'The League of Nations'. Similarly, I am happy to record my appreciation of Mrs Miller's kindness in allowing me to use some of her late husband's material.

Where I have extracted and used scripted material at some length, as opposed to 'review-type' quotes, I have, of course, sought copyright permission, and, in each case, it has been generously and freely given. My gratitude, therefore, to Ray Galton and Alan Simpson for the Tony Hancock piece; Eddie Braben for the Morecambe and Wise pieces; Alick Hayes, Max Kester and Rex Diamond for the Will Hay pieces, and Frankie Howerd for the use of a piece of his own material.

I am pleased to mention that, in granting permission, Alick Hayes took the trouble to write with shrewd insights into the comic talent of Will Hay, which have helped my interpretation. Indeed, I have been in general much cheered by the heartening response of script-writers, agents and comedians who have read and welcomed those parts of *Make 'Em Laugh* which concerned them.

Jimmy James's son, James Casey, Senior Light Entertainment Producer with the British Broadcasting Corporation, responded nobly to my call for help. He not only provided me with a splendid piece of comic dialogue, but he also read my chapter in draft, and his highly relevant and delightful comments have been enthusiastically incorporated. The Ken Dodd chapter, and many of the general points throughout the book, owe much to some fascinating discussions in as appropriate a place as Knotty Ash itself and with that admirable district's leading citizen. These led to an article in *New Society* (The Geography of Ken Dodd, 24 June, 1976) and this book springs in particular from those occasions, as it reflects, in general, an abiding and lifelong obsession with British comedians.

However, my chief source has been a memory which has endeavoured to reach back some forty years. Much of the descriptive and a substantial amount of the quoted material in the book emanate from that effort of recall, and, sorrowfully, it does not guarantee complete accuracy. Should I have inadvertently misquoted phrases or used published quotations without obtaining permission – despite the strenuous attempts to trace copyrights – then I apologise unreservedly for such transgressions.

Lastly, special thanks to my publishers and particularly to John Bright-Holmes and Anne Wood. Murray Pollinger has also given much valuable assistance, for which I am very grateful, while Michael Radford, John Rennie and Maggie Redfern read and commented on the book in preparation and, each in his or her distinctive way, left it that much the better. Wendy Morgan magically created ordered typescript from out of inchoate manuscript, and grappled courageously with some of the problems of illustrations.

So much for the payment of debts, save that the acknowledgements with regard to illustrations are numerous and are listed on p. 206. Pleasing though it is to rally a fine register of people as supports for this enterprise, eventually (and perhaps it is a poetic justice after presuming to describe great comedians who, by and large, stood alone) I must, of course, accept full responsibility for *Make 'Em Laugh,* and urge the point that those acknowledged are in no way to blame for any errors or infelicities.

Introduction
The People's Jesters

I remember tutoring a teacher-student in the north-east of England who had prepared a project on the history of Newcastle United for his class of nine-year-olds. 'This isn't history', said the head teacher; 'do the Vikings.'

The same objection applies to comic entertainers. Over the years their impact on social life must be enormous, yet invite teachers to conduct a study of Ken Dodd from the standpoint and in the depth that they would appraise Dostoevsky or Beethoven and you get, as I know to my cost, very, very old-fashioned looks. This refusal to accept only a narrow confine of artistic genius is doubly galling. Not only is it a form of intellectual snobbery (which is often disastrous for the cultural items deemed to be in need of state protection) but it gives children, and thus adults, little opportunity to sharpen their critical faculties for those fields where they are going to seek out leisure and amusement. With television the art form of the nation, it is outrageous that so few schools directly assist their pupils to become more sensitive, critical and perceptive in their treatment of the medium. An O-level 'Television' subject, with *Playschool, Kojak* and *Panorama* as its set programmes, might be an exhilarating innovation.

The late Sir Neville Cardus was a superb exponent of the links of genius and of the integrated culture. He could embrace the spirit of Haydn, Don Bradman and George Robey with grace and vision. He once told the tale of Mozart waiting patiently in heaven for the opportunity not of exchanging notes with some mediocre composer but of popping a few questions to Bobby Charlton about the sweet parabola of his enormous cross-field ball or his unerring instinct for the liberties of space.

Like cricketers or footballers, comedians have not been blessed with much academic, as opposed to critical, acclaim, and perhaps they should be thankful. The interlock of comedians with their society has not had so profound an analysis as, for instance, that of poets with society, or politicians with society. This is so much more important, however, when one recalls the necessary engagement of the comic entertainer with his or her audience. There are no lonely garrets or leafy glades, as for the aspiring painter or versifier. Comics must do or die in public. In patois and reference, they must be understandable to that public. Their funniness must be of the popular culture. I shall not argue that comedians create society, or that, by some sort of sociological spontaneous combustion, society creates comedians in its own image. But a relationship does exist. Part of being a great comedian lies, consciously or unconsciously, in being attuned to the refrains of society, in hearing its melodies, in orchestrating them, and in playing them back.

To put it another way, the comedian, like other artists, feeds on yet feeds his host society. One can think of a hundred examples of comic situations or jokes being, as the saying goes, true to life. Eventually, the comedian's work is absorbed into the culture – the catch-phrases, the caricatures and so on – and, once more, the circular argument rolls on. Eventually, it is not easy to separate them. Do we laugh at mothers-in-law because they are basically funny or because comedians for many years have implied that they were?

Recall the sensitive ear of Al Read. We laughed because, to borrow Wordsworth's phrase, he recollected in tranquillity emotions we are heir to or acquainted with. The next time we heard similar phrases in real life the funny side of them was emphasised because Al Read had used them – 'that sounds just like Al Read'. Consider his classic line supposedly uttered by a Mancunian housewife recording a family quarrel: 'There was enough said at our Billy's wedding.' It hints darkly at a compendium of everyone's domestic feuds, and yet tells us nothing.

The successful comedian reflects the society in which he works and lives. In turn, society reflects his work in itself. Thus comics often sit better, historically, in one period than in another, and because of this they are valuable touchstones for social historians. As well as observing the qualities of the 1930s in George Formby and Will Hay, it is also possible to observe lots of George Formbys and Will Hays in the 1930s. The practice and development of their craft carries them perhaps closer to the general public than any other artist, popular or classical. Their routes are neither the populist freeways of the singing and football heroes nor the highroad escapes of the actor or composer. They must ever keep step with the pedestrian pace of everyday circumstance.

That does not mean that they do not offer escape. They do, but it is not the vicarious thrill of the romantic film or pop star, nor the yearning to emulate Lester Piggott or George Best. They speak to us on our own terms about the foibles and quirks of our own lives. It is an escape *into* reality, but a realism usually tempered by their often kindly consideration of its incongruities.

It has its danger. As I have tried to study these comedians, my warm affection and admiration for them has grown beyond bounds. Of course, it is a self-indulgent list, introducing the entertainers who have brought me most comic pleasure over the years. Yet, at the same time, I have become increasingly aware of their value as lightning conductors as I have endeavoured to locate them in their social context.

It is arguable that comedians defuse the angry responses of people. By grinning at Man's condition, by softening the edges of his aggressive efforts to have wrongs righted, by channelling his energies into the mill-race of laughter, by, paradoxically, keeping his pecker up, comedians may have helped resist the correction of legitimate grievance. That suggests one political vantage-point; from another it could be argued that they help preserve the status quo, the unrocked boat and the stability of the social fabric.

In this regard, comedians are a sophistication of bread and circuses. They do not distract you from the issues of the day; they highlight them only to make you laugh at them and possibly take them less seriously. Cast an eye down my twelve apostles of humour: Billy Bennett, George Formby, Will Hay, Robb Wilton, Jimmy James, Max Miller, Tony Hancock, Frankie Howerd, Eric Morecambe and Ernie Wise, Les Dawson and Ken Dodd. The social style of their presentation lies somewhere between neutral and lower middle-class, and those relatively few who seem fundamentally working-class (George Formby, for instance) are aspiring to some kind of improvement and advance, even if, on stage, this means no more than outsmarting someone or getting the girl. That is to say they accept and operate within the conventional social confines. The anti-system comedian is rare indeed.

One suspects that, in private, many of them might take the same political reading. A somewhat naïve patriotism sweeps through the work of many of them, and perhaps into their own lives. So many of them have triumphed, single-handed, over the adversities of show-business that it would be surprising to find them representing anything other than principles of self-reliance and the glories of individual initiative. The exception, perhaps, is Tony Hancock. Eventually destroyed by those adversities, he was much less prone to conventional political postures. Most, to their credit, are indefatigable in their charitable efforts, and this is itself a traditional counterpoint to a belief in vigorous private enterprise. They are fundamentally honest *commercial* men, however warm the cockles of their hearts.

Here is another way in which mutual reflection is illustrated. It would be difficult to conceive of, for instance, a Marxist comedian treading the boards of one of the private theatre circuits, not just because the management would object, but because the audiences would feel uncomfortable. His standpoint would be too antithetical. Comedians stay within the restraints of the state and its generally accepted norms: they rail a little at its institutions – its government, its matrimonial units, its workplaces, its police, even its royalty – but it is an affectionate sniping, and of menace to those institutions there is none. In fact, it may be that they are strengthened by their show of sporting good fellowship in graciously allowing themselves to be used as butts.

In this comedians are veritably the people's jesters. The jester's role was to amuse and – in a literal sense – divert. In the vast democratic court of this century the jester goes about his task in much the same way. Of course the twentieth-century comedian does not consciously commit a political act. That is merely one of the outcomes. Simply, comedians are reflectors rather than reformers.

Their means of reflection vary as considerably over time as their formulae for entertainment. This is the concept of the changing motley, the adjustments, large and tiny, that clowns must make to their methods as well as to their material. This book, part theatre criticism, part social analysis, tries to pick up this tale as, in the aftermath of the Great War, along with much else the old music-hall tradition was giving way to newer approaches.

Programme

MAKE 'EM LAUGH

Billy Bennett

THE RAUCOUS PARODIST

He said, 'Where has the kidney bean; what made the
woodbine wild?
Is red "cabbarge" greengrocery? And tell me friends,'
he smiled,
'Can a bandy-legged gherkin be a straight cucumber's
child?'

After the 1914–18 war, everyone – returning soldiers, workers on a war footing – had to adjust to peace; but the problems peace brought with it appeared insoluble. And the tale begins here because the attempted answer – an end to *laissez-faire* at home and abroad and a switch to a more controlled and more concentrated economy – was envisaged then. The leftist challenge to this solution was muted and frail, and thus modern society, like it or lump it, was under way.

The new style consumer market changed domestic life, as it changed industrial organisation, for, as mining and textiles declined, the food and drink, electrical, engineering, vehicle, and other consumer durables industries raged ahead. By 1931 only 5 per cent of households had resident servants but, as convulsive as the disappearance of servants, was the arrival of the internal combustion engine. There were only a million buses, lorries, cars and motor-cycles in the early 1920s; there were nearly two and a half million in 1930. But the major change and harbinger of a leisured future was cinema and radio. With talkies first available in the late 1920s and the BBC established by Royal Charter in 1927, Britain numbered 3,000 cinemas and some five million wireless licences by 1930. The audio-visual immediacy of the former and the private indulgence of the latter would shortly combine to form that most comprehensive of leisure activities, the television.

The comic entertainer was to the late Victorian and Edwardian music hall what the pop group or popular singer is to television now. In brief, they normally topped the bill. Where, over the last twenty years, we would include the Beatles, the Rolling Stones, Tom Jones and Shirley Bassey among the great crowd-pullers, for that golden age one would scarcely look beyond the likes of Marie Lloyd and Gus Elen. But, of course, the music-hall artist integrated song and comedy. The prototype of the comic entertainer was one who developed a character through songs particularly associated with him or her. Star, character and song had combined in a unified approach to popular culture, but in the post-war years this now was to be dispelled.

A major effect was the partial separation of comedy and music. In future when comedians broke into song it was often as a demonstration of versatility and to give balance or borders to their performance. The tradition of comics 'ending with a song' became established. On the other hand, singers sometimes deigned to play the fool – Bing Crosby, for example, with some success – but, on both sides, it was a kind of self-imposed *lèse-majesté,* almost as if the artist were asking for admiration for being good-humoured and broadminded enough to adopt the opposing role. Some artists – it is perhaps not too unkind to name Max Bygraves as an instance – remained between the two extremes, not fully satisfying the more astringent taste of either school of appreciation.

And, for me, the most attractive comedian straddling the end of the music hall and the beginning of the mixed bag of variety, radio, records, cinema and television, was Billy Bennett.

Billy Bennett was billed as 'Almost a Gentleman', but that was a major exaggeration. He was far from being a gentleman either in manner or content. A burly, awkward figure, he sported a mixture of military and 'masher' garments, all ill-fitting and reach-me-down. There would be floppy trousers, dropping concertina-like over cumbersome army boots, along with a shrunken tunic and sometimes a tartan beret. His starched shirt front or dickey would curl; his tiny drum would be slung from a distinctly female suspender; his watch would be held by a lady's garter.

His was a bulging face: the eyes bulged beneath the black quiff, the cheeks bulged, the lips bulged, even the adam's apple bulged, as well it might given the stout neck garrotted by that tight tunic top or stiff collar and messy bow. Under a snout-like

The opening of the Oxford 'Electric' Theatre in 1911 was a harbinger of the decline of the music hall and of the development of the comic entertainer, with his songs and comedy, into the stand-up comedian of whom Billy Bennett was one of the first.

nose bristled an 'old Bill' moustache: perhaps the modern generations could best visualise Billy Bennett by imagining a toothbrush imperial moustache on an angrier Charlie Cairoli face.

In one respect he represented the tradition of the gentlemanly tramp, a knight of the road who had known aristocratic days. It has Dickensian echoes – Micawber or Vincent Crummles, the actor-manager in *Nicholas Nickleby* – but on the music halls the most celebrated version was Ella Shields's portrayal of 'Burlington Bertie':

I'm Bert, Bert: I haven't a shirt,
But my people are well-off you know.

To visualise Billy Bennett, imagine a toothbrush imperial moustache on an angrier Charlie Cairoli face.

Another example was 'I live in Trafalgar Square':

> It may be a trifle draughty, but I look at it this way, you see
> If it's good enough for Nelson, then it's quite good enough
> for me.

In the United States it was a typically Runyonesque characterisation (Nicely-Nicely Johnson) while Fred Astaire and Judy Garland immortalised the image with 'We're a Couple of Swells' in the film *Easter Parade*. Rather lamely for some tastes, Dick Emery attempts nowadays to feature the gentleman tramp in his television shows, while some years ago Arthur Haynes played the worldly-wise hobo on television.

From another angle Billy Bennett was simply sustaining the

Albert Whelan, noted for 'his smile, his gloves and his whistle', joined with Billy Bennett on the radio in a double act called 'Alexander and Mose'.

red-nosed heritage of the comedian. He compounded some of the shabby gentility of Jimmy Edwards with the straightforward clowning of Charlie Cairoli. He was, however, a verbal clown. His act was oral slapstick. The voice gave little or nothing away of his Liverpool origins. Its most noticeable quality was its resonant hoarseness. Billy Bennett bellowed monologues: he attacked audiences with a trumpeting verve, albeit that the trumpet was somehow beset with a touch of laryngitis. It was Billy Bennett who first utilised the device of the sharp double-beat on the base drum – 'boom boom' – to accentuate the already sledgehammer blow of his comic couplets. It has enjoyed a recent vogue, not least with Basil Brush.

He had several standards, normally somewhat obvious parodies of late Victorian and Edwardian monologuists, such as George Sims, author of perhaps the most famous title in English verse, 'It was Christmas Day in the Workhouse'. Billy Bennett's version was 'It was Christmas Day in the Cookhouse'. He also did 'The Green Tie of the Little Yellow Dog' ('There's a cock-eyed yellow poodle to the North of Gongapooch') and 'The Sailor's Farewell to his Horse'. Sometimes he sang, songs like his signature tune 'She was Poor but She was Honest' performed with raucous sentiment; and he also did, oddly enough, a 'nigger minstrel' duo – Alexander and Mose – with Albert Whelan. Albert Whelan was the Australian singer, with his smile, his gloves and his whistle, to say nothing of 'the Jolly Brothers', usually regarded as the first officially recognised signature tune. But it is the monologue which sustained Billy Bennett in a lengthy career as a top flight comedian from the time of the First World War (he was born in 1887, son of Bennett, of Bennett and Martell, a comic double act) until his death during the Second World War in 1942.

Staring defiantly across the footlights he would grip his audience as the ancient mariner gripped the wedding guest, lulling them into attentive awe with the urgency of his persistent rhythms. He declaimed like a Roman orator, albeit one risen from the ranks, a plebeian play-acting patriarch. One of his introductory speeches echoed that senatorial tradition: 'Friends, Romans, Countrymen, lend me your ears; I have a story to tell. Lend me your ears; if you've not got them with you, your noses will do just as well

This prefaced his mock narrative of the League of Nations, that well-intentioned effort at international control which struggled on through the main phase of Billy Bennett's career:

> The League of Nations met at Berwick Market
> To discuss on which side kippers ought to swim.
> There were Hottentots and Prussians playing honeypots on cushions
> and a Greek with Bubble and Squeak upon his chin.

Billy Bennett, 'Almost a Gentleman'. His act was oral slapstick. He bellowed monologues: he attacked audiences with a trumpeting verve.

Gus Elen, above, and Marie Lloyd were two great crowd pullers of the golden age of music hall.

Some rolled up in taxis that were empty.
Some arrived to say they couldn't come.
The Hindus had their quilts on; the Hebrews had their kilts on.
A Scandinavian rose and said 'Bai Gum' . . .
He said 'Where has the kidney bean; what made the woodbine wild?
Is red "cabbarge" greengrocery? And tell me, friends,' he smiled,
'Can a bandy-legged gherkin be a straight cucumber's child?
That's what Crosse and Blackwell wants to know today.' . . .
A Turk said 'We want work and not much of it;
A job like giving gooseberries Marcel Waves.'
A Zulu most courageous said 'Brothers, it's outrageous
Black puddings should be treated as white slaves.' . . .
The Rajah of Slamozzle got up and blew his nozzle;
He had these few well-chosen words to say:
'Can a sausage keep its figure if its burberry is slack?
If a duck has had its tonsils out, where does it keep its quack?
We know a hen can lay an egg, but can it put it back?
That's what Levy and Franks are fighting for today.'

In the early 1920s Billy Bennett was on the threshold of a fine career. He had been an entertainer in the army during the 1914–18 war, and had then sought a stage livelihood as what, after 1945, was known as 'stars in battledress'. The story goes that, playing the Dublin Theatre Royal in mock army garb, the theatre manager suggested that his appearance might provoke some political hostility. Hurriedly he adapted to a more civilian appearance, his customary eccentric's guise. As the nation went through the throes of adaptation, so did Billy Bennett similarly adapt and entertain it vigorously.

When my father claimed Billy Bennett as his favourite comedian, he was referring to that age, not to all time. The latter honour fell to George Formby senior, who indeed was, apart from Gus Elen, the only artist whom Marie Lloyd could bring herself to watch. The difference was that, essentially, George Formby senior portrayed, through song and style, a comic character. Billy Bennett had taken the step towards being a comedian rather than a comic singer. The comic entertainer of the last fifty years has generally been a stand-up comic, standing up alone or, occasionally, in duo to the theatre audience, radio and recording microphone and, eventually, the television camera.

It was a short step that Billy Bennett took. In a sense he bridges the gap between the Harry Lauders and the Frankie Howerds. George Formby senior raspily croaked songs like 'John Willy' or 'I was standing at the Corner of the Street'; Billy

Apart from Gus Elen, George Formby senior was the only artist whom Marie Lloyd, left, could bring herself to watch.

Broadcasting's natural emphasis on words meant that a largely visual music-hall sketch, like Harry Tate's famous 'golf' and 'motor-car' sequences, lost much of its effect.

Bennett recited monologues with some melodic gusto, normally to an orchestral accompaniment. He more or less forswore the comic song, but, although he quipped between times with less than tasteful glee, he remained usually within the confines of the monologue. He never stood and merely served up jokes.

A corollary of the change in the comic process was broadcasting's natural emphasis on the verbal. The pictorial depiction of a music-hall star was lost on the wireless. The largely visual sketch also suffered. Harry Tate's motor-car sequence was perhaps the most famous of these, and its antics were lovingly repeated by Duggie Wakefield and his confrères in the thirties and forties; but now the concentration was on the *spoken* word, the story-teller and the cross-talk acts. Billy Bennett, his eccentric garb apart, lost little by transfer to the wireless, especially when, as often was the case, he broadcast 'live' before studio audiences in programmes like *Music Hall*.

The monologue itself has a history on the popular stage, and its trembling serious tones are redolent of the Victorian thespian. It had a political and social function. George Sims's narrative of the workhouse Christmas was a virulent anti-poor law tract; into their eighties my maternal grandmother and my great-aunt Bertha recalled effortlessly the lengthy monologues of their Band of Hope girlhood – the versification of the temperance movement, it must be added, having proved stronger than its injunctions. Several entertainers – most notably Nosmo King – retained the heart-rending morally righteous poem well into the 1940s.

So Billy Bennett was mocking a well comprehended cultural phenomenon. Equally, the lines burlesqued were known to all. Rudyard Kipling came in for a fair amount of verbal stick:

> There's a double-jointed wop-wop doing tricks in who-flung-dung,
> And you're a better man than I am Gunga-Din.

The Road to Mandalay witnessed another of Billy Bennett's oral journeys. His explorer burlesque, with its hideous colonial costume, was to inspire Ken Dodd in a similar lampoon a generation later. There was a soldier with the map tattooed on his skin:

> On his back he's got Calcutta,
> Lower down he's got Bombay,
> And you'll find him sitting, peacefully,
> On the Road to Mandalay.

Robert Service was another victim. His quickfire stanzas of life in barrack-room or Yukon gold-rush – the shooting, for instance, of Dan McGrew – used exactly the metre frequently chosen by Billy Bennett. Another identifiable target was the Scottish balladeer, William McGonagall, wellnigh infamous for his banal rhyming accounts of such events as the Tay Bridge disaster.

It might be argued that parodying such versifiers was the literary equivalent of running down an old lady at a zebra crossing. What is interesting is the subject-matter as well as the formula utilised. There is an energetic satire of the militaristic and imperial attitudes with which writers like Service and Kipling were associated. By adopting precisely their same bounce and scansion Billy Bennett caught something of the anti-war, anti-colonial mood of the twenties. As the twenties aged towards the thirties, there was growing disenchantment with the League of Nations, and Billy Bennett's assault on it was always a favourite. Not that he was conceiving of any shrewd political comment: what is meaningful is the public's willingness to guffaw with him at its frailties.

Less attractive was the mildly xenophobic treatment, which apparently found a ready ear among the distrusting Britishers of the twenties. The chauvinist overtones of novelists of that era such as Sapper or W. E. Johns (respectively the progenitors of Bulldog Drummond and Biggles) are well rehearsed, and certainly there was no unease as Billy Bennett paraded geographic grotesques at his League of Nations Assembly.

His strident, bellicose attack on his audiences echoed figures as well as moods of the twenties. There was something of the raucous sergeant-major, feelingly remembered by many of his watchers, and Billy Bennett sustained the military and colonial line throughout his career. There was also something of the tub-thumping street-corner orator about him. Soap-box oratory was in vogue by the late twenties, as both left and right prepared for the bitter contests of the next decade. Billy Bennett often played the insincere, jargon-bound politico:

> 'What we would want today', he would cry, 'is social reform, tariff reform and, more than likely, chloroform. What did Gladstone say after '99? Why, a hundred of course – and he was right!'

Thus Billy Bennett had the type of act, and cut the kind of figure, which fitted the twenties well. There was nothing savage or subtle about his guying of sentiments and ideas suspected of being false. His chief reliance was upon the surprise appeal of nonsense, but the inverse logic of his nonsense rang answering chords in his listeners' minds.

Like perhaps the best of dealers in absurdities, he was essentially a parodist. It might have been coarse, even vulgar, but part of the effect lay in the hearer's recognition of the original. Although a cultural and intellectual gulf away, the

He parodied Kipling and Robert Service in particular. He also did 'It was Christmas Day in the Cookhouse' and 'The Green Tie of the Little Yellow Dog' ('There's a cock-eyed yellow poodle to the North of Gongapooch').

closest literary association with Billy Bennett lies with Lewis Carroll. Lewis Carroll made nonsense of what, in the first years of his success, would have been moral poems, easily recognisable by his readers. 'You are old, Father William' is after Robert Southey's 'The Old Man's Comforts'; 'The Lobster' is after Watts's 'The Sluggard'; while 'Twinkle, Twinkle, Little Bat' and 'How doth the Little Crocodile' are parodies (instantly perceived as such today) of Jane Taylor's 'The Star' and Isaac Watts's 'How doth the Little Busy Bee'.

The application of a sensible solution to a ludicrous situation was Bennett's approach as well as Carroll's. Lewis Carroll is the pre-eminent, the classic, reducer of the conventional to the ridiculous, but an excerpt from his charming 'Mad Gardener's Song' seems not too far removed from the compositions of his more boisterous disciple.

> He thought he saw an Elephant,
> That practised on a fife:
> He looked again, and found it was
> A letter from his wife.
> 'At length I realise', he said,
> 'The bitterness of life.'

Parody has a raunchy folklore thread, of course, as well as a skilled academic bent. Both rugby club and barrack-room ring to many an unprintable and obscene parody. As with Carroll's more polite works, they have sometimes earned the supreme accolade of outliving their models. The tattooed soldier of Mandalay was one of the forces' favourites of that genre. The plaintive song 'My Home in Tennessee' received the same treatment, but this time it was the tattooed girl:

> Underneath her kidney is a bird's-eye view of Sydney
> But what I like best underneath her vest
> Is my home in Tennessee.

Many of Bennett's monologues did a kind of literary double-take. Gunga-Din and Dan McGrew and the Green Eye of the Little Yellow God and the Bookmaker's Daughter may all have provided pure and undefiled lambs for Billy Bennett's oratorial slaughter. But each had maybe several impolite versions – poetical wolves in sheep's clothing? – to act as a juicier *aide-mémoire*. Thus Bennett's 'Christmas Day in the Cookhouse' reminded all of the workhouse and many also of what, in parliamentary language, might be called 'another house'. Seemingly so frankly unabashed, Billy Bennett was still, by what might be called common lore standards, bordering on the euphemistic.

Nevertheless, his immediate appeal was in the juxtaposition of apparently unrelated items and forms. It might have been rugged, but it was surreal.

> The little sardines had gone into their tins
> And pulled down the lids for the night.

is a celebrated couplet, rejoicing in a veritable reversal of the rational, which appears in the monologue whose title – 'The Sailor's Farewell to his Horse' – is itself the quintessence of irrelevance.

The surprise of the association of such overtly alienated matters is underscored, as in all comic doggerel, by the easy facility and keen-edged snap of the rhyming. The fun arises not only from the meaning of the lines but also from the predictably neat closure of the rhyme, rather like a bolt ramming home or a creature's jaws locking together. Although no comedian since has depended so utterly on rhyme for his effect, plenty of comics have thrown in the occasional crazy or rude verse. Max Miller and Eric Morecambe have done this admirably. Arguably George Formby, in song, maintained the tradition, relying on the cheeky tidiness of his rhymes. Certainly the surrealist element, with its anatomical curios, has been gleefully embraced by Ken Dodd.

At the end of the day, however, the very nonsense, two-dimensional and plain dotty as it frequently was, was perhaps the truest bench-mark of the late twenties. It was a madcap era, even a disastrous one. It had its shallow, trivial, short-term craziness; it also spawned some longer-running nastier crazinesses.

Billy Bennett acted as a second-string relay sprinter, accepting the baton of popular comedy from music hall and handing it over to variety. He made his own success by compounding fantasy and earthiness for a public whose mood was tuned to something like that bizarre mix of escapist notions and downright rawness; he helped usher in a half-century of comic performers who spoke, rather than sang, of humorous happenings. He accomplished this in years of troubled minds and consciences, when foundations, good or ill, were laid, and the social dimension was brittle and nervy at the top and disillusioned and acrid at the bottom. Possibly the Einsteinian paradox of his own couplet is not an unfair epitaph of the time:

> Think of what we have done in the future –
> Shall we do our duty in the past?

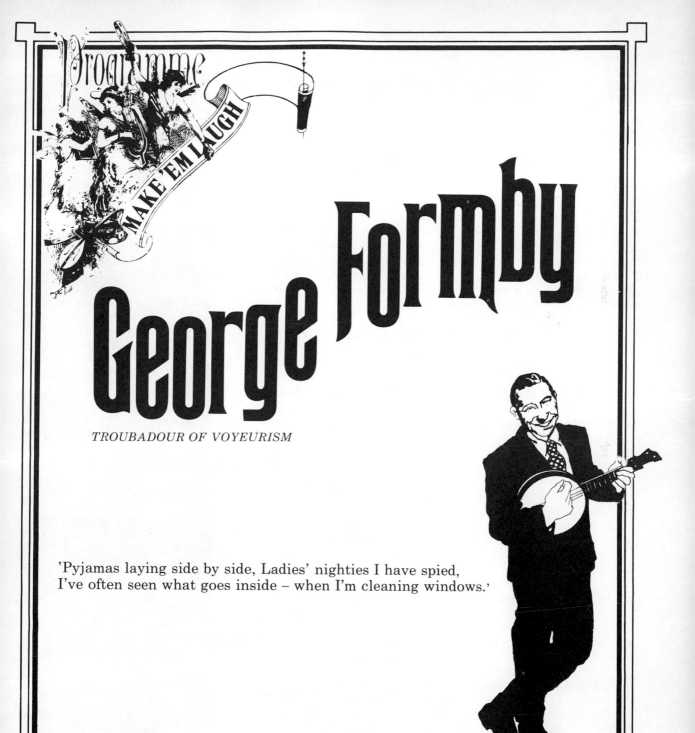

George Formby

Programme

MAKE 'EM LAUGH

TROUBADOUR OF VOYEURISM

'Pyjamas laying side by side, Ladies' nighties I have spied,
I've often seen what goes inside – when I'm cleaning windows.'

The last time I saw George Formby was in the autumn of 1955 at the Palace, Manchester. He had, as he admitted, put on weight, and his hair was greying. Untypically, it was a forgettable play.

It may have been about a railwayman's family and it may have been located in Scotland. George Formby played the quiet, put-upon father, who gave homespun advice to his daughter. One moment alone was memorable. Towards the dreary end of a drab plot, he found himself on stage alone except for a banjolele he found hidden somewhere. Suddenly, as a lighted window in the night heartens a fatigued wayfarer, it was momentarily a lively and buoyant occasion. He sang one of his songs, accompanying himself with long-practised skill, and a Saturday night audience stiffened, lifted itself and gave itself over hugely to simple enjoyment. He ended, and the audience, quite physically, sat back and hunched itself for the tepid remainder of the play. It could have been a verse such as:

> I've got a picture of a nudist camp – in me little snapshot album
> All very jolly 'though a trifle damp – in me little snapshot album
> There's Uncle Dick without a care, discarding all his underwear,
> But his watch and chain still dangles there – in me little snapshot album.

Water in the desert, some might say; anything to alleviate the tedium, and, confessedly, the competition was not brisk. But something of the same becomes evident when one sees those familiar films again on television. There were twenty of these, made between 1934 and 1946, and re-watching them, I normally asked the children to call me in when he came to a song. Interestingly, the children – between five and seven years old – stayed throughout, and I remembered that, at much the same age, I had laughed excitedly at those films, indeed maybe saw the songs as intrusions.

The humour is childlike. It appeals to the child and the childishness in adults. George Formby himself had the mischievousness, the shyness, the terrors and the wide-eyedness of a youngster. The cinematic images that really stick are the chases: the airman in the runaway plane; the jockey in the all-important race; the policeman and, elsewhere, the TT rider on the motor-cycle; on the bus; on the ice; as a sailor; all crazy, zig-zagging jaunts, punctuated by George Formby's frightened squeal of 'ooh, mother'. In the end his simple goodness, sustained by good fortune favouring the naïve, outwitted all the smarty boots and he won the favours of the heroine, never any more sensual than a panto principal girl. Indeed, each film was a rehash of 'Cinderella', with Prince Charming unmasked as a

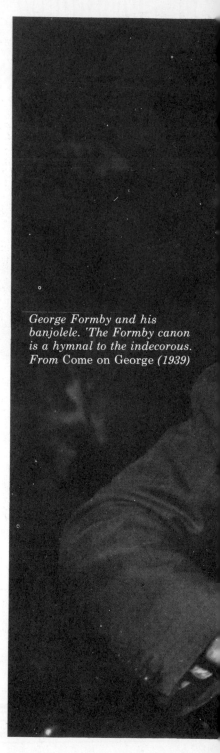

George Formby and his banjolele. 'The Formby canon is a hymnal to the indecorous. From Come on George *(1939)*

George Formby, senior, 'The Wigan Nightingale', perhaps Lancashire's greatest ever character comedian, with his raspily croaked songs. Here he is seen in 1919, and (opposite) shortly before his death in 1921 at the age of 41.

villainous impostor, and Buttons and Cinders consolidating their kitchen dreams. But the films, with their obvious contests of goodness and badness and those manic sequences, are more reminiscent of the cartoon. Where Mickey Mouse or Tom and Jerry are animals adopting human properties, George Formby assumed a sort of cartoon character. He forcibly reminds one of Donald Duck. Both had eyes which popped with wonderment or fear on demand; George Formby strutted with agitated feet asplay like Donald Duck; there was something of the same flustered shows of exasperation alongside the gibbering timidity. Both seemed to have necks on swivels, capable of enormous nervous gulps or of underscoring meanings – a jut of that ventriloquial dummy's neck emphasised most of Formby's coarser punch-lines. The chasm that was George Formby's mouth was not unlike the flat gorge of Donald Duck's beak, both of them able to express radiant wideness, outraged wideness and terrorised wideness. Truth to tell, Donald's cackling address hinted of George's rather babyish whinny, his squawks of despair as well as his chortles of diffidence. One thinks, again, of the ventriloquist's doll.

But thoughts of Arthur Prince's Jim or Buttons or Donald Duck fade abruptly away when, on film, on stage, on radio or television, or on record, George Formby armed himself with his banjolele, sometimes known as the ukelele-banjo. It liberated him; in a sense, it humanised him. Amateur psychologists tell us of the shy man turned to fierce assurance at the wheel of a fast car, or the tame man turned to blatant aggression with a gun in his hand. Certainly George Formby lived in another dimension when he played and sang, and it is an amazing feat that his *élan vital* was and is communicated via every known medium. Despite serious drawbacks in his academic grasp of music, his technical virtuosity is still admired by experts, not so much for the slightly unambitious chord-play of his left hand as for the bewildering dexterity of his right. The insistent metallic tinkle of that rhythmic, high-speed syncopation was to jangle its persistent way on to the memory-tapes of popular culture. From 1925, with his first successful performance in Newcastle, to his untimely death, after some years of marital difficulty and ill health, in 1961, he retained an unflagging following, and, today, he is something of a cult figure, with many artists – Alan Randall especially, Lonnie Donegan, Ken Goodwin, Roy Hudd – happy to trade on the nostalgic aftermath of a career which made George Formby the highest-paid entertainer and the most popular film star of his era.

There were almost four hundred songs; nearly half of them have been recorded. The weary music-lover might sigh that there is only one tune, and the sensitive librettist claim that there is only one lyric. The cheeky ragtime melodies are certainly not elaborate, but their familiar structure was part of the secret: a generation on and they are recognisable by all. Similarly with the lyrics, many of them reliant on the listener's anticipation of the heralded arrival of the repetitive closing line. The pleasure lay in the expected. The resonant tattoo of the banjolele normally escorted a couple of choruses, then alone it would assert its own tinny impertinence, before rounding up the last chorus. Where one might wonder with what curious rhyme Billy Bennett would disconcert, with George Formby everyone knew – his grandad's flannelette nightie, his auntie Maggie's remedy, his little stick of Blackpool rock, a little blast on his whistle, his sergeant-major. Like a Lear Limerick, the final line was triumphantly predictable. Recall the evidence:

> When she said 'what is it, dear?'
> Then I whispered in her ear,
> 'It's me grandad's flannelette shirt.'

> He said there was trouble brewing,
> 'You've been overdoing,
> Your auntie Maggie's remedy.'

> A lady smiled and stopped
> And then she nearly dropped
> When I blew a little blast on my whistle.

The theme was likewise open to forecast. A category of softer domesticated and sunnier cheerful numbers apart, the Formby canon is a hymnal to the indecorous, a musical version of the *News of the World,* that broadsheet of the working man of the thirties. The comparison with Donald McGill's garish postcards has often been made, and there is the same obsession with the private parts and a procession of uncluttered word-plays alluding thereto. One must, however, invoke the schoolboy again. It is juvenile humour, no less funny nor any less scintillatingly presented for that; but it is the mildly prurient humour of the pupil, discovering and giggling over the absurdities of exposed extremities, covert sex-play, semi-nudity and underclothing.

In another sense he stood in the tradition of the old music hall, founded as it was on the comic song. The songs of the music hall – Marie Lloyd's, for example – carried their share of innuendo, but George Formby was, in the Lancashire adjective of that age, 'warmer'. Like Max Miller, he occasionally had troubles with the establishment over the indelicacy of his material. His father, born in Ashton-under-Lyne in 1880, and developing as probably Lancashire's greatest ever character comedian, was gentle, mournful and bronchial, the rasping cough, which eventually killed him in 1921, acrid but no less a trademark than the goofy optimism – 'it's turned out nice again'

– of his son. They shared the same gauche provincialism, but the father was reflective and sad while the son's assault was gaudier, if shallower, in content and approach.

The unsubtle hues of the holiday postcard and the toothsome drive of George Formby found their natural habitat in Blackpool. He was himself born (in 1904) in Wigan, and it was his father – billed as 'the Wigan Nightingale' – who invented that maligned town's pier and thereby created the *locus classicus* of English comedy.

George Formby operated on the Wigan–Blackpool axis, selling his melodic line in phallic symbolism from 'The Wigan Boat Express' to 'Sitting on the Top of Blackpool Tower'. Not surprisingly, the banjolele itself was phallic. The appropriate chorus, aligned with the brash seaside resort, provides a synthesis of the Formby attack:

> While walking down the prom last night as peaceful as can be,
> This bird from Wales said 'How about a stroll down by the sea?'
> She said her name was Gert and that she'd just come for the day,
> She looked so young and harmless that I couldn't turn away.
> And with my little ukelele in my hand,
> I took a stroll with Gert along the sand.
> We walked along for miles without a single care or frown,
> But when we reached the sandhills she said, 'Come on, let's sit down.'
> I felt so shy and bashful sitting there,
> For the things she said I didn't understand.
> She said 'Come on, big boy, get busy; your love just turns me dizzy.'
> But I kept my ukelele in my hand, oh baby,
> I kept my ukelele in my hand.

Put aside for a moment the undoubted professional acumen of George Formby. The question must be raised about the expansive appeal of his performance, an impact which carried him out of the thirties to become a genuine hero of wartime entertainment (last out before Dunkirk and first in after D-Day, entertaining three million servicemen), before a further fifteen years of varied stardom. His career was, however, rooted in the Gaumonts, the 78s and the Radio Luxembourg of the pre-war decade. Was his Wigan–Blackpool axis so correctly aligned with the mood of the masses in the thirties as to allow him wellnigh comic domination?

Some periods are serene but grey; others are unpleasant but exciting. The thirties managed to be both brutish and dull. The 1929–32 slump was the brass plate on the coffin of the Victorian

Gracie Fields used to mix, like George Formby, the comic – 'The Biggest Aspidistra in the World' – and the cheerful – 'Sing As We Go' – and the sentimental – 'Sally'.

economy, already heavily nailed, blow after blow, since the turn
of the century. The million or more unemployed of the twenties
shot to almost four million in 1932, that is approaching seven
million – nearly a sixth of the nation – living on the dole.
Despite a brief respite, it was two million in 1939, when only the
onset of war, it is said, prevented a renewed slump.

The twenties bequeathed to its succeeding decade the staid,
unheroic partnership of Baldwin and MacDonald, stolid in their
rather outmoded yearning for financial strictness, civilised in
their reliance on national unity, over-cautious in their fear of
radical departures. A static duo, they were non-decisive rather
than indecisive; sedate, humane but uninventive. Chamberlain
followed them, brusquer and more businesslike, but equally
unimaginative. Nonetheless, the Baldwin–Chamberlain line
represented the nation's mood, sheering away from abrasive
facts and indulging in a lukewarm pacifism.

Yet it is hardly surprising that the working classes were not
disposed towards a cocky belligerence. Gruesome memories of
Great War carnage were now joined by the acute misery of
unemployment and its deprivations: Chamberlain's description of
the German–Czech problem as 'a quarrel in a faraway country
between people of whom we know nothing' has the authentic
ring of the Birmingham commercial mind, but it might also have
echoed the sentiments of the harassed housewives and depressed
menfolk of the Welsh mining valleys or the shipyards of the
North-East, where the means test was replacing the workhouse
as the symbol of proletarian oppression, with a similar mix of
fact and lore to colour it.

It was George Orwell who delineated that low-water mark of
pre-war impoverishment of mind as well as of matter. Borrowing
Formby senior's discovery, he published *The Road to Wigan Pier*
in 1937, describing 'the frightful doom of a decent working man
suddenly thrown on the streets after a lifetime of steady work'.
His evocation of such dismal scenes must be seen against the
background of an age of immobility. The thirties were inert
years. And one of the most static features of that immobility was
the social isolation of the working class. Orwell's message from
Wigan (like Dickens's message in *Hard Times* about the Preston
he labelled Coketown) was not just about the iniquity of its
conditions but the fact that they were unknown to the middle
and upper echelons of society. If anything, the increased size of
the workplace made social contact between management and
labour more tenuous, while housing development, particularly
the development of the municipal estate, intensified residential
segregation. It was exactly where the depression struck most
cruelly – epitomised by Jarrow, the Rhondda and George
Formby's Wigan itself – that this socio-economic coherence was
most pronounced. Up and down the country embittered blocs of
working people resented what they felt to be their exploitation

In his films George Formby always outwitted the smartie boots and won the favour of the heroines.

at the hands of the middle classes.

This part-segregated working class developed an institutionalised frame all of its own. It had its own markets and shops, with the co-operative societies well over a thousand in number and with nearly five million members. Alongside the trade unions and political clubs, there were other social foci, sometimes religious, sometimes recreational. The working-class pub differed distinctly from its middle-class counterpart. There were also the friendly societies, with three million members in orders such as the Oddfellows and, significant soubriquet, 'the poor man's Masons', the Buffaloes. Since my birth in the early thirties and to this day, my mother has conscientiously given a penny a week to the Foresters for my burial.

The general low level of prices meant entertainment was cheap enough for those who had money at all. With corned beef at sixpence (6d) a quarter and cabbages a penny apiece, for those in work there was perhaps something to spare for the cinema or the gramophone. Twenty million cinema tickets were sold each week in the thirties and in the bigger towns there were plenty of variety theatres: places like Bolton or Gateshead could boast of half a dozen theatres. The radio had become ubiquitous: there were nine million homes with radio sets in 1939. Ironically, George Formby, seemingly springing from the traditional culture, was delivered back by all those media external to it.

But perhaps the most interesting form of working-class escapism was the holiday. In the mid-thirties between five and eight million enjoyed paid holidays, and the 1938 Holidays with Pay Act more than doubled this. Most typical was the emptying of the textile, engineering and other industrial centres for the annual 'wakes' weeks. Like some species of migratory bird or herd animal, entire populations were carried to the coast by motor car, charabanc and cheap railway excursions.

For my own 1937 summer holiday at Rhyl it was bed and board at Mrs Beard's, which meant we bought the food and Mrs B. cooked it for us. There was a pier and paddling and a funfair. Carrying a copy of the *Daily Mail* I disturbed a number of sleeping holiday-makers in the hope that they were Colley Cibber or Lobby Ludd or whoever it was whose identification would that day be rewarded with a prize of a few shillings.

Each evening we watched an open-air show, standing round the fence which enclosed the deck-chairs. There were sketches, a little dancing, a duet or two, and a comedian called Hal Blue. I heard from his saucy lips my first rude joke, which my father carefully explained to me. It was about a thirsty Red Indian staying at the Midland Hotel, Manchester, and, God forgive me, I still occasionally relate it. There was a lucky programme, with a letter cut out, and one night we won a shaving kit, rather grudgingly presented to us 'outsiders' who did no more than drop a coin in a collection box, avoiding the exorbitant expense of the actual seating.

Blackpool was a veritable Mecca for those pilgrims adhering to their shahada in an annual seaside holiday. They looked to the variety stars (especially, in the thirties, the comedians rather than the singers, who tended to be supporting acts) to lead them in their devotions. Twice nightly, with matinees on Wednesdays and Saturdays, the faithful turned stagewards at the call of the muezzin of George Formby's ukelele.

George Formby was not, of course, alone. Gracie Fields had something of the same effect on the working-class north. She was born, aptly, over a Rochdale fish and chip shop. Pushed initially, like Formby, by her mother, she also achieved success across the media – film, records and radio as well as stage. The feeling that she may not, unlike George Formby, have given her all to the war effort tarnished her popular image somewhat,

Even wartime Blackpool carried echoes of 'wakes' week and of the entertainment of the working-class north which nourished George Formby.

but memories remain fond of her. Like George Formby, she mixed the comic (for example 'The Biggest Aspidistra in the World'), the cheerful ('Sing As We Go') and the sentimental ('Sally') in her songs, although, for the discerning critic, a croaking 'Following the Rochdale Hounds' and a shriller 'Ave Maria' were perhaps never entirely successful.

Gracie Fields was, so to speak, George Formby's elder sister at Variety's family party. He had several younger brothers, who, like him, based their theatrical security on the grand double of a long pantomime and a long summer season. George Formby, for instance, often played Idle Jack in *Dick Whittington* in one of the cavernous theatres of the northern cities. My first ever theatre visit was as a four-year-old to see *Mother Goose* at the Prince's Theatre, Manchester. It starred the genial Albert Modley, comfortingly droll and always ready to transform his drum kit into a tram. He would probably have spent the summer at Scarborough or Morecambe. Sandy Powell was another. Where Albert Modley was 'Lancashire's Favourite Yorkshireman', Sandy Powell was a native of Rotherham. His 'cod' ventriloquial and conjuring acts are still well liked, but it was his radio catch-phrase 'Can You Hear Me, Mother?' and his recorded sketches such as the 'Lost Policeman' ('Our Herbert's fallen in the river') which helped make his simple, kindly appeal so popular.

Others who spring from my infant memory are Wee Georgie Wood, Tessie O'Shea, brassy songstress, Formby-like with the banjolele, Arthur Tracy ('The Street Singer' with that other favoured instrument of the thirties, the accordion), and Tubby Turner, with his stuttering catch-phrase, 'If it's h..h..hokay with you, it's h..h..hokay with me.' Many of these were great northern stars, and, in the south, other lights were shining. They included Max Miller, and the Crazy Gang. The Crazy Gang were much more visual than George Formby, but they shared something of his physiological obsessions in their comedy. The placid friendliness of Flanagan and Allen is a pleasing thirties memory, and the whimsical drawl of their 'Underneath the Arches' offers a Londoner's unacrimonious view of the Depression. Interestingly, they first performed it during a Southport summer season.

But their wistful response to the slump was only occasionally echoed by George Formby in numbers scarcely recalled now like 'The old kitchen kettle keeps singing its song'. It is arguable that, with radio and records, a huge proportion of the population must have heard something of George Formby every day during those pre-war years. And much of what they heard, and what thousands saw on screen and stage, was much chirpier and brasher.

By common consensus he gave temporary cheer to a hard-pressed people. In the popular phrase, he took them out of

Albert Modley, 'Lancashire's Favourite Yorkshireman'; and Sandy Powell – 'Can You Hear Me, Mother?'

themselves. By no stretch of the imagination could he be cast in the role of satirist or of fomenter of social unrest. Rather the reverse: it would be easier to see George Formby and his fellow artists as social firemen, dampening any flames of flickering disquiet. He was assuredly a highly patriotic figure, proud of being known as Queen Mary's favourite comedian, and, as his wartime exploits and propaganda broadcasts showed, he believed in an undiscriminating nationalism. But it is unlikely that he ever saw his task in any political form beyond the laudable objective of cheering up hard-working artisans and weary soldiers.

Yet the respite he offered was so close to the original. It was not the other worlds of Shirley Temple or Flash Gordon. A curious element in escapism is the desire to perceive the shadow of reality. Some of these strange over-identifications on radio and television are notorious. Dan Archer gets orders for turkeys every Christmas. A welter of layettes and baby ducks was sent in for a new-born babe down Coronation Street and there were dozens of people who, when the baby's parents were supposed to have emigrated to Canada, wrote asking if they could have the vacant house, some saying how homesick watching the programme had made them.

If the public was searching for the familiar as, paradoxically, a retreat from its very pressures, then George Formby was a ridiculously easy figure with whom to identify. Though not, like 'Our Gracie', of impeccable plebeian stock, given the relative security provided by his illustrious father, he was recognisably out of the bottom drawer. His flattened vowels and thickened twang, his pancake of a face, with its rather soggy features – it all created a studied impression of immense ordinariness. George Formby was the bloke next door. He told silly jokes and sang smutty songs in a humdrum heavily Lancastrian accent; he ostensibly was not very bright, but he kept his pecker up and tried hard to please. In every film part and in each actual entrance on to the stage he appeared as Wigan's equivalent of the Man on the Clapham Omnibus – slightly out of his depth, a trifle perplexed but willing to make an honest effort to outwit the villain on the screen or amuse the crowd in the theatre. His one overt and unmistakable gift was for banjolele playing, but, in an era of mouth organs, accordions, pianos in most parlours, brass bands in every works, spoons-manipulators, whistlers and yodellers, even this was not too exotic. And, of course, as a finished and supreme professional, George Formby never let them, those who identified with him, down.

George Formby poked unpretentious fun at the back streets, underwear and eating habits of his public, and it may have purged them of some of their self-doubts, humiliations and distresses. There seemed to be a funny side to it after all. Alan Bennett, in one of his crustier revue items, lambasted modern

plays for their concentration on rape, incest and murder. 'You can get all that stuff at home', was his irascible comment. George Formby gave them all that stuff from home as well, and his home brew was to most people's taste. Then there was the other angle on that same feature. George Formby cut a very definite dash. It was not just his quite well-publicised trail of motor-bikes, expensive cars and boats. He was turned out nice again on stage, with his greased, sleeked hair and its defiantly thirties parting, and with his good-looking dinner jacket. His principal theatrical image was akin to that of the successful dance-band leader.

I once read how a down-at-heel West Indian was observed spotting a luckier compatriot, extravagantly dressed, driving by in a pricey car, accompanied by a lissom blonde. The former gave a huge grin and a grandiose thumbs-up salute in celebration of his fellow immigrant's success. That delight in another's triumph, that frank lack of envy, is a pleasing human trait, but it has its slightly negative aspect, in that it can mean an inadequacy of aspiration, as well as an example to emulate. The holiday-makers and panto-goers gave George Formby their unstinting applause on much the same basis. They enjoyed his

'Leaning on a Lamp-post at the corner of the street...' has more of Flanagan and Allen in it than is usual for George Formby. The whimsical drawl of their 'Underneath the Arches' offers a Londoner's unacrimonious view of the Depression.

achievements vicariously. It warmed them, but, at the same time, perhaps it saved them from the problem of making that extra endeavour. Sportsmen were among their other heroes. One could pretend that one could kick a ball like Cliff Bastin, wield a bat like Herbert Sutcliffe or ride a winner like Gordon Richards. Having pretended, having identified, it was possible, it was bearable, to return to lathe or loom; in some regard it made it too tolerable.

The humour, broad and remorselessly obvious, gave substance to the identification. It was the humour of the workbench and the factory canteen, with nudist camps, knickers and night attire always likely to raise a grin or a leer. The bombardment of innuendo was not, of itself, novel, nor is it outmoded: where would the irreverent clowns of *Monty Python's Flying Circus* be without the 'naughty bits'? But the sexual and anatomical emphasis of George Formby had a characteristically provincial tang. Needless to say, there was nothing camp about the Formby repertoire. He was a family entertainer, and the sexual allusion was conventionally heterosexual.

This was in keeping with the tenor of his cultural approach. If a couple of hours on the football terraces was the event of the week and a week at Blackpool the event of the year, marriage was the event of the lifetime. Although permissiveness is not exclusively modern, a nexus of features – the desire to leave home, social as well as moral strictures, and birth control still at an unsatisfactory level – placed a weighty premium on the wedding as the central watershed of each person's life. In a bleak era it created many distractions: the playing out of a ritual with the mill girl acting princess for the day; the excuse for an immoderate party; the sheer change of routine and the excitement of starting afresh; the unfolding of the sexual mystery, be the consequence pleasurable or disappointing.

Many of George Formby's songs relate to this phenomenon. Two of his three most popular songs refer directly (and the third, 'When I'm Cleaning Windows', indirectly) to courtship. 'Chinese Laundry Blues' featured that far from inscrutable laundryman Mr Wu, so besotted with his beloved that 'his laundry's all gone wrong; all day he'll flirt and scorch your shirt'. In a standard Formby trick, Mr Wu had 'a naughty eye that flickers, you ought to see it wobble when he's ironing ladies' blouses', with a tell-tale pause and glance before 'blouses'.

A second favourite was 'Leaning on a Lamp-post', with George Formby, lovelorn at a street corner, 'in case a certain' (he made it sound like 'shertain') 'little lady comes by'. Most males, of all classes, have found themselves anxiously in that hopeful situation. Its plaintive quality has more of Flanagan and Allen than is usual for George Formby, and yet, from another angle, it is not uncharacteristic. As his films demonstrate, he was the hero for whom the leading lady eventually fell. While some might have regarded marriage in stressful times as an improvident undertaking, there were those who, after Walter Greenwood, saw love on the dole as resilient human spirit in the ascendant. A touching ballad, 'Leaning on a Lamp-post' is arguably one of the half-dozen most appealing popular love songs in the language:

> I'm leaning on a lamp; maybe you think I look a tramp:
> Or you may think I'm hanging around to steal a car.
> But no, I'm not a crook, and if you think that's what I look,
> I'll tell you why I'm here and what my motives are.

A friend of mine told me of his parents' wedding in Manchester in the early thirties, with the bridegroom's father's last shillings cajoled out of him for a jug of beer, and an aspidistra on an orange box behind curtained windows the only furnishing for their parlour. The father-in-law, forbidding and glum, offered his new son-in-law mordant advice. 'Marriage is a lottery, Fred,' he opined. 'And with our Edie you've drawn a bloody double-blank.'

The double-blank view of holy matrimony was common in George Formby's England. The chance mixture of affection, hope and sex drive which led to the altar was frequently to deteriorate into, at best, a reasonable comradeship, and, at worse, unfettered hostility. Many were, of course, prepared to enjoy the wryer moments, and George Formby unceasingly fed the public appetite for the absurdities and embarrassments of inhibited male–female relationships.

The ancient northern adage has it that marriage is two becoming one, with forty years to decide which one it is. Sometimes it was the Andy Capped male of the species, but George Formby reflected the matriarchal supremacy of many north-western households. Significantly, his chief music-hall sketch throughout a longish career was the honeymoon cameo, with George Formby as the stuttering, nerve-wracked groom and his wife, the ex-clog dancer Beryl Ingham, as the keener spouse. George Formby would have made an excellent Willie Mossop, the sheepish cobbler in the comedy *Hobson's Choice,* reluctant and timorous on his wedding night.

It was so often the predatory and indeed carnal female who caused the discomfort and provoked George Formby's stream of unseemly insinuations. The suggestiveness is paramount. Rational analysis frequently reveals nothing improper in his lyrics: only context and delivery can make vulgarity out of 'my little snapshot album' or 'under the blasted oak'. George Formby evoked a mood in which swimmin' (with the 'wimmin'), ice-skating, the Maginot Line and keeping fit immediately grew suspect, so that any mention of the body or clothing could become uproariously rude.

In most comedians' work it matters little if one man's merriment is the result of a happy childhood or another's sorrowful commentary the fault of a miserable one; what matters is the upshot in the actuality of performance. George Formby's marriage is an exception to this simply because it figured so largely in his public life. His wife Beryl was also his manager, some would say his gauleiter; she ruled his every move, public and private, with an 'iron petticoat'. She appeared with him on stage and, even when she no longer performed, she would take a majestic bow at the end of her husband's act, acknowledging applause like a successful authoress or choreographer.

So much was common knowledge, and perhaps was intended to be. It certainly added a piquant flavour to the performance, with George, ostensibly the henpecked husband at liberty for half an hour or so, indulging himself in some frivolous improprieties. It is difficult to gauge how contrived this was, and to what extent George Formby connived in this deployment of a merciless hatchet-woman in order to preserve his own cheery front. There is surely no doubt that, throughout his career, he was personally a very competitive and ambitious artist.

Equally, there is no doubt that the ogress, however much part natural and part invented, grew, as ogresses will, disproportionately, until her dominion was rancorous and corrosive. After Beryl's death and when, just before his own, George Formby announced his engagement to a younger schoolteacher, it became apparent that the legend of a woman competently but affectionately handling her unworldly but gifted partner, as Hobson's eldest daughter did for Willie Mossop, had soured somewhat.

Oddly, a similar tale is true of another, contemporary, man and wife team, noted for their stage, radio and film work. This was Lucan and McShane, better known as Old Mother Riley and her daughter Kitty. The stresses of sustaining the cantankerous relationship on stage of an antiquated Irish laundress and her uppity daughter helped to destroy their marriage.

Thus nature proceeded to mimic art. Voyeurism, however, is generally thought to be a result of sexual frustration. One thinks of the proxy sexual appeal of striptease and pin-ups, and the less glamorous, if earthier, skulking on canal banks and in copses for salacious glimpses of underwear and nether limbs. It now seems so meaningful that verse after verse of George Formby's most famed number, 'When I'm Cleaning Windows', narrates an episode in such voyeurism. George Formby was the Peeping Tom's piper.

Some years ago a police investigation in the Stockport area revealed the curious information that voyeurs forgather in clubs, organise coach parties to particularly inviting venues, such as especially rewarding sand-hills at Morecambe, and even keep minutes. The bikini watchers on the Costa Brava today are

'George Formby under Fire' 1943. Plenty of good-natured, knuckle-close fun; but many of those who laughed with him at the discomforts of marital consummation would – as he himself gave the constant impression on stage or film – have run a mile if faced with a full-blooded sexual encounter.

The stresses of sustaining the cantankerous relationship on stage of Old Mother Riley and her daughter Kitty helped to destroy the marriage of Arthur Lucan and Kitty McShane.

the descendants of those in the 1930s on Blackpool's Golden Mile titillated by the sighting of a thigh or better as the girls prepared for bathing. And window-cleaning for the voyeur is akin to making an alcoholic the landlord of a pub.

First featured in 1936, 'Windows' revealed girls undressing, blushing brides, pyjamas and nighties, girls in baths – a regal collection of Godivas and their consorts for Lancashire's Peeping Tom of song. George Formby was the troubadour of voyeurism.

Pyjamas laying side by side,
Ladies' nighties I have spied,
I've often seen what goes inside – when I'm cleaning windows.

The blushing bride she looks divine,
The bridegroom he is doing fine,
I'd rather have his job than mine – when I'm cleaning windows.

But it was genial and aboveboard. By a happy paradox, the phenomenon was out in the open. Whatever else, George Formby's bawdiness was more wholesome than the lonely, secretive furtiveness of the truly sexually thwarted. The question of his success, of his identification with the common culture of his day, is one of such balance. The emotional and other impediments of the thirties somehow led to private parts and their coverings being the readiest material for coarse jesting. Some of the response must have been genuine guffaws of amusement; some of it must have been defensive just as, it is sometimes argued, the homosexual is persecuted by those fearful of homosexuality's latent hold on themselves. What is sure is that many of those who laughed with George Formby at the discomforts of marital consummation or the espying of bountifully filled nightdresses would – as he himself gave the constant impression on stage or film – have run a mile if faced with the prospect of a torrid and erotic full-blooded sexual encounter. There was a safety and a stability in admiring lasciviously or chuckling knowingly from a distance.

In a cautious, prurient age, George Formby, through a combination of skill and upbringing, was the comic representative of that viewpoint. There was plenty of good-natured, close-to-the-knuckle fun, but a compound of solid sense, sincere regard, basic diffidence and downright fear dropped the bar before reality needed to be faced. It is not too dramatic to contend that George Formby, beaming impudently from behind his compulsively persistent banjolele, helped nurse an enormous family clientele through a harrowing socio-economic experience, before tending their menfolk in the military trials of a different but vicious reality.

Will Hay

TUTOR TO THE THIRTIES

Will Hay:	Oh, good morning, boys.
Boys:	Good morning, sir.
Will Hay:	Let's start lessons with a will.
Smart:	Why, are you gonna make yours?

In my grammar school classroom about the end of the Second World War a thirteen-year-old pertly gave an exhaustive and erudite answer to some elaborate mathematical poser. After a suitable pause one of his form-mates said 'Thank you, d'Arcy', and the entire class collapsed in mirth. It was an expert borrowing from the current Will Hay radio series. This time he was Dr Muffin, and d'Arcy was the precocious know-all. Each week he embarked on a lengthy, polysyllabic explanation of some abstruse point. Outgunned and bamboozled, Dr Muffin reflected for long seconds before saying, lamely, painfully, 'Thank you, d'Arcy.'

These three short words were like a motto for Will Hay. He was, of course, the inadequate, shiftless schoolmaster beset by pupils both bright and cunning. The grudging, icy civility of the 'Thank you', no less than the aristocratic ring of the surname, said it all. It was the schoolmasterly evasion in schoolmasterly terms, polite, cool, and – as was then normal – 'distancing' the relationship emotionally by the use of the surname. Will Hay had overreached himself; he was the ineffectual teacher, and the pupils knew it, and they happened to be considerably more academically inclined than he; but, by tactical deployment of teaching clichés, he endeavoured to hold the fort. Of all British comedians he has been most successful in creating a prototype character, almost to the point where his name and the type are co-identifiable, like Kelloggs and cornflakes or Oxo and meat extract. Several times in my own teaching career do I recall people being described as 'a Will Hay figure', and, even today, few would fail to grasp the meaning. Other comedians might be used for comparisons – he talks like Frankie Howerd; he looks like Eric Morecambe – but no one has quite so completely created a fictional character for the variety stage which has survived so remarkably.

His films and their recent revivals on television mean that another generation now recognises the wispy hair, the slightly slack mouth and the snub nose of Will Hay. But the recognition is primarily due to the pince-nez. The bespectacled comedian – Sandy Powell, Arthur Askey, Harry Worth – is not unknown, neither, as Eric Morecambe reminds, is he slow to make a prop of his glasses. Has, however, anyone other than Will Hay so emphatically created a comic personality around his eyeglasses? Pinched, seemingly cemented, to his nose, they gave no hint of precariousness, although their tumbling off would have offered an obvious gag to many less subtle comedians. Rather did they remain the constant inseparable of his never still, devious face.

The lenses acted as a two-ring circus for his acrobatic eyes. Peering through them or, more typically, peeking over them, his eyes performed a trapeze act of the emotions: dismay, greed, irascibility, smugness, foxiness and, above all, suspicion, with the optical arena ensuring the focus was sharp for all watchers.

Each changing darting glance was underpinned with its own nasal and vocal accompaniment, with the deprecating cough and the disapproving sniff to the fore. His voice had a rusty, gravelly, slightly husky intonation, and he was second only to Robb Wilton as a 'timer' of material. But where Robb Wilton's timing was principally oral, Will Hay's was chiefly visual. For instance, no one has managed double takes of such inordinate length. He would gaze absently and vacantly over a precipitous edge or at an impending disaster, turn back with intense attention to his prior task for long seconds, until, eventually, realisation, snail-like, crawled across his features, and, heavily shaken, he would look once more for dread confirmation.

On the stage he was invariably 'the schoolmaster comedian', but, wisely, he rang the changes on ineffectual authoritarianism in his films, so that, as well as the headteacher threatened with eerie homicide in *The Ghost of St Michael's,* he was, in turn, fire chief, police sergeant, prison governor and station master. Like another bespectacled film comic, Harold Lloyd, he often found himself in hair-raising situations, on the sails of a windmill or on the hands of Big Ben for instance. The antics, in schoolroom or on railway station, were sometimes hilarious, and the manic railway journey in *Oh! Mr Porter* bears comparison with the classic rail chase in *The Marx Brothers Go West.*

On stage or on film, the dialogue was unsubtle and straightforward. Much of it was based on uncomplicated ambiguities and misunderstandings of language, not often above the level of the schoolboy howler, although occasionally – 'a martyr is a pile of wood with a man on top' – showing a little spark of inspiration. A typical example is from *My Learned Friend*, when, as diffident prosecuting counsel, Claude Hulbert found Will Hay, accused of sending begging letters, in complacently pedantic vein. He demonstrated that each phrase of the letter was absolutely true – 'I am an orphan. I have no mummy or daddy' or 'I am writing this letter with my back to the workhouse wall'.

Even more typical is this extract from Will Hay's classroom:

W. Hay: Oh, Good morning, boys.
Boys: Good morning, sir.
W. Hay: Let's start lessons with a will.
Smart: Why, are you gonna make yours?
W. Hay: Eh? Make my what?
Smart: Make your will.
W. Hay: Listen, I'm talking about the conscious mental effort to profit by my teaching.
d'Arcy: Oh, jolly good, sir.
W. Hay: What's jolly good?
d'Arcy: That explanation, sir.
W. Hay: Oh, thank you, d'Arcy. I've been reading those

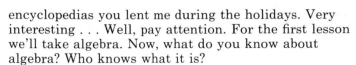

Will Hay, 'ringing the changes on ineffectual authoritarianism' in one of his stage sketches and below Good Morning Boys *(1936).*

encyclopedias you lent me during the holidays. Very interesting . . . Well, pay attention. For the first lesson we'll take algebra. Now, what do you know about algebra? Who knows what it is?

Beckett: Please, sir.

W. Hay: Yes, Beckett?

Beckett: I've seen one but I don't know what it is.

W. Hay: *Seen* one?

Beckett: Yes, sir.

W. Hay: Oh. I've heard of people seeing pink elephants but I've – I never – What do these look like?

Beckett: Please, sir. It had stripes.

W. Hay: Stripes?

Beckett: Yes, sir.

W. Hay: You're not thinking of a sergeant, are you?

Beckett: No, sir. This had more than three stripes, and it had long ears like a donkey.

W. Hay: Ohh, that sounds like you, Smart, doesn't it?

Smart: I know what he means.

W. Hay: Yes?

Smart: He means a zebra.

Beckett: Yes, sir; isn't that what you said, sir?

W. Hay: No, no, no, no, no. That's a different thing altogether. Algebra is – er – er – well – it's er – er – anybody like to tell Beckett what algebra is?

d'Arcy: Certainly, sir, I would.

W. Hay: Yesss, I hoped – I mean I thought you would. Well, carry on, d'Arcy, carry on.

d'Arcy: With pleasure, sir.

W. Hay: Yes?

d'Arcy: Algebra is a method of calculation which, reduced to its simplest terms, substitutes alphabetical symbols for known and unknown quantities and thus enables us, by a series of equations, to adduce the actual numerical content of the unknown quantity, generally denoted by the alphabetical letter 'x'; in other words –

W. Hay: Well, never mind about the other words. You've used quite enough words as it is. So, that's – er – that's algebra, is it?

d'Arcy: Yes, sir.

W. Hay: And I've been teaching it all this time and didn't know. I'm cleverer than I thought.

The interplay of these conversations is not easily conveyed in script form. Listening to it on record, it sounds, in fact, highly conversational, with overlaps of interrogative syllables and snorts, exactly as if the quartet were chatting about algebra among themselves for the very first time.

Alick Hayes, a notable Will Hay scriptwriter, relates how

profoundly Will Hay thought about the characters he played. Each line had to be real. He would say 'No, Alick, that line's funny, but it's not *true*.' And then he might embark on a lengthy digression about Dr Muffin's ancestry and career and how he had been haunted by frustrations and disappointments as he had plied his trade as a mediocre schoolmaster. This shows a remarkable depth of interpretation for what was essentially a music-hall cameo.

What mattered most to Will Hay, then, in situation or dialogue, was the interplay of each with characterisation. He always claimed (rightly) that his performance was no burlesque, but merely a sharpening of the outline of the truth, an exaggeration but not a distortion of genuine schoolteaching. What was more important than either the tomfool activity or the simple script was the relation with the 'boys'. 'Good morning, boys,' said Will Hay crisply as he entered his classroom, setting the mood immediately for the ensuing contest between pupils attacking with impertinent sharpness and teacher defending from behind a barricade of teaching platitudes. The relationship was much the same in the fire station or the prison, with Will Hay still clinging incompetently to the trappings of authority and the 'boys' as full of cheek and bravura.

There were two stereotypes of this boyhood. There was the fat saucy one and the old one, seemingly witless but sporadically acute. These were played originally by Will Hay's son and Gordon Saunders, but the most famous of these duets, because of their cinematic partnership with Will Hay, was Graham Moffat as the fat boy, Albert, and Moore Marriott as the ancient loon, Harbottle.

Indeed, Will Hay never failed, on stage, radio or screen, to surround himself with fine character actors, and, without doubt, his own high standards were most frequently attained when he was working with such talented confrères. His grand career, while centring, in attitudes and main thrust, in the thirties, spanned many years, with his consistent top billing illustrated by royal command performances as far removed in time as 1925 and 1945. Like Robb Wilton, he preferred to see himself as a comedy actor, and it is as such that his influence has been greatest. It is otiose to reflect that television comedy thrives on actors rather than comedians, that some massive talents – Jimmy James and Ken Dodd among them – have never quite caught on the television the imperishable mastery of their stage persona. Television's comic accolade must go – Tony Hancock and Morecambe and Wise always excepted – to the legitimate actors. Arthur Lowe, John le Mesurier, Wilfred Brambell and Harry H. Corbett, Ronnie Barker and Warren Mitchell would stand at the heads of most people's lists. Much the same is true of cinema, and even Tony Hancock and Morecambe and Wise would ruefully recognise the reality of that comment.

Will Hay led those character comedians who, through the days of variety and early radio, kept alive for popular culture the tradition of comic acting and bequeathed it to television. Radio has been able to sustain itself upon, in fact has been the stimulus for, verbal humour, not only in providing showcases for comedians per se but in its notable lineage of *ITMA, Take It From Here,* and *The Goon Show.* Will Hay also added his cinematic gift. Almost alone of British stage comedians he used film as something profounder than the demonstration of his stage performance. George Formby, Lucan and McShane, Frank Randle, Tony Hancock, Morecambe and Wise – whether their films be regarded as successful or not they added little to our basic appraisal of their comic roles. The cinema merely gave us another chance of seeing them in familiar action. Because of his insistence on the interplay of characterisations and because this allowed the use of a firmer story-line, the cinema showed a wider range and a different emphasis in the case of Will Hay. With the other film-star comedians, the accompanying casts are completely forgettable, mere stage props for the main act. Moffat and Marriott, Claude Hulbert as the chinless stuttering accomplice, John Laurie's doom-laden caretaker in *The Ghost of St Michael's,* and several others are almost as memorable as Will Hay himself.

This is perhaps the finest tribute one can pay him. The characters around him were not anonymous straight men, nor did they overwhelm him. One suspected occasionally that Tommy Handley, for example, was little more than a stalking-horse for the *ITMA* characters, his own comic personality rather submerged. Will Hay thought deeply and worked hard to maintain a much more balanced relation in which the nuances of everyone's characterisations were realised as richly as possible.

Will Hay reversed the aged saw about the buffoon aspiring to play Hamlet. He was (like George Robey) a trained engineer, born in Aberdeen in 1888, and he was a noted astronomer, with the discovery of a white spot on Saturn to his credit. He sometimes appeared, in this serious vein, on the BBC *Brains Trust* programme. Like many of his contemporaries, he entered the profession via the concert party, and until some two or three years before his death in 1949 he remained deservedly popular.

His main success came in the thirties, and he was, essentially, a thirties character, albeit in different fashion from George Formby. Both developed a huge following across the social categories, but they began, in their professional approaches, from quite dissimilar points on the sociological and cultural spectrum. Indeed, this was also true of them personally, with Will Hay the learned astronomer and George Formby the self-confessed semiliterate. Where George Formby began as a largely working-class comedian who, with dinner jacket and ukelele,

The public school and varsity tradition in Variety: (a) Ronald Frankau;

(b) 'Play the game, you cads'—The Western Brothers;

conquered Queen Mary and the West End, Will Hay expanded from the suburban seaside clientele of Douglas to embrace admirers in all parts of the country.

It is noteworthy that, just as George Formby was the triumphant representative of a low comedy tradition, Will Hay was the standard-bearer for a fascinating group of middle-brow comic performers. In a sense they were the inheritors of George Robey's mantle. Himself a well-read man, he took a mock severe line with audiences, adopting a circumlocutory style and using the sharp, single command 'desist' to rebuke and quell his heartily laughing fans. During the thirties and forties there were a number of well-modulated, well-mannered comedians on show. As well as Claude there was Jack Hulbert; and there was the Coward-like cabaret style of Ronald Frankau, who on radio joined sometimes with Tommy Handley as Murgatroyd and Winterbottom. Quintessentially, there was Gillie Potter, 'speaking to you in English', with his whimsical and correct narrative of rural life in mythical Hogsnorton. Another savant, he retired in horror as the crooners and bobby-soxers moved into the theatres of the fifties, and from the leafy shades of Bournemouth wrote letters to *The Times* and articles on heraldry and archaeology. There was Oliver Wakefield, that gifted raconteur who always left out the crucial words, and there was Claude Dampier, beaming and twittering over his genteel friend, Mrs Gibson, and there was Vic Oliver, classical violinist and married into the Churchill family. Like George Leybourne alias 'Champagne Charlie' and Charles Coburn alias 'The Man who Broke the Bank at Monte Carlo' before them, they all represented a middle- and upper middle-class tradition, sometimes racy, sometimes refined, often in their private as well as their public lives.

The universities nurtured this tendency with Claude and Jack Hulbert, Richard Murdoch and Jimmy Edwards all initially members of the Cambridge Footlights. By the fifties the cycle turned once more, and higher education spawned another brood of comic sophisticates, first Michael Flanders and Donald Swann, then the *Beyond the Fringe* quartet of Jonathan Miller, Alan Bennett, Dudley Moore and Peter Cook, and thus to a shining series of radio and television satire shows, culminating in *Monty Python* and *Fawlty Towers* of the ineffable John Cleese.

But perhaps most notable in this regard would be the Western Brothers, Kenneth and George, whose drawled, public school fruitiness was a singular cameo of British variety in the thirties and forties. 'Play the game, you cads' was their constant refrain, nonchalant and imperturbable, with their satires mild and unmalicious. With George at the piano and Kenneth leaning elegantly against it, they observed life's cares and the day's news with Harrovian detachment. I saw them at the Winter

Gardens Theatre, Blackpool, during the war, when the railways slogan, in a period when transport was under pressure, was 'Is your journey really necessary?' This they adopted for the punch-line of one of their slowly unfurling commentaries: 'As the doctor', drawled Kenneth, 'said to Hitler on the day that he was born', then in duo, 'was your journey really necessary?' A member of the audience visited the lavatory during their act, and, as he returned, Kenneth very civilly posed him the same query. Monocled and white-tied, one might have expected them to be defiantly ordinary in real life, but, unbelievably, they did have aristocratic connections, staying in stately homes while their colleagues skulked in the hideousness of squalid theatrical diggings. They were both badly hurt in a motor accident on the way to one such mansion. The one recovered consciousness and hazily observed in the next hospital bed the other (in actual fact, cousin not brother), equally heavily bandaged and splinted. 'Well,' he drawled languidly, 'at least we won't have to follow Lucan and McShane.'

The unmistakable public school and varsity traditions of this celebrated line of artists, leaning heavily toward the revue and cabaret rather than the variety stage, is a piece of social history of its own. What is interesting is that Will Hay probably enjoyed a wider range of support than any of these, and this may have been because he chose to play the aspirer to elitism and not the elitist himself. Where the Western Brothers or Gillie Potter were incontrovertibly ensconced by birthright and breeding in the stage positions they assumed, Will Hay was the parvenu and the pretender, his accent suspect and the angle of his mortarboard ill assumed. Indeed it was often accident which jettisoned him into his authoritative positions, as prison governor in *Convict 99* or as sacked teacher turned master spy in *The Goose Steps Out*.

There was something of the harlequinade or the Elizabethan masque in the way he reversed roles. Like Mr Bultitude in Lord Anstey's novel *Vice Versa,* where son and father change places magically in a prep school context, Will Hay often deliberately suggested that kind of alteration as he adopted his stage headships of Narkover College or St Michael's.

The lower middle class aspiring for the middle – the theme is redolent of the thirties and Will Hay epitomised it. This was the other aspect of George Formby's thirties, the era of the Depression and its attendant miseries. The slump hit hard and squarely but not consistently; great tracts of Britain were left untouched, particularly the criss-crossed estates of suburban clerks and commuters. Here were the growth points of pre-war Britain. Light industry thrived as coal mining and cotton tumbled. During the thirties the output of electrical goods and motor cars doubled, while production of aircraft and artificial textiles multiplied over and over. The supply of electricity doubled. The selective incidence of the cruelties of the slump

(c) 'Mr' Gillie Potter 'speaking to you in English';

(d) Claude Dampier.

must again be stressed: in fact industrial output per head rose
by a third – one of its greatest increases in our history –
between 1924 and 1937.

The mass production of consumables lead to a striking
expansion in retail outlets during the thirties. The co-ops, the
multiple shops and the department stores gained ground, but the
small-time tobacconists, confectioners, chemists, and furniture
and hardware retailers increased rapidly as well. These were not
yet the major durables – the characteristic purchases were cheap
cosmetics, fountain pens, electric irons, vacuum cleaners and
bicycles. The Americans outbought us in refrigerators at the
ratio of twenty to one in the thirties. But, in order to focus on
Will Hay's achievement, it is important to note another aspect
of that development, namely the introspective and defensive
response of the British economy in the depression. The
government protected the home market as much as it was able,
and this flourished as the export trade withered. Such an
introverted posture was in line with many of the thirties
attitudes. On all sides there were ostriches desperately seeking
to hide their heads in economic, political and social sands. What
David Thompson has called the 'incorrigible *immobilisme*' of the
thirties pervaded the whole of society. To some degree it
expected its entertainers to contribute their share of escapist
routes, just as the Youth Hostels Association, formed at the
beginning of the decade, offered three hundred hostels to its
eighty thousand members by the time war came. In their homes,
in their leisure, in their nation, men and women sought domestic
– if necessary, blinkered – snugness. George Formby played the
working class down; Will Hay played the middle class down.
Both assisted their followers to resign themselves to their
ascribed lot in life: the miners and spinners laughed
disparagingly at their slight yen for the exotic; the suburban
mortgagees grinned at their anti-hero's blundering efforts to
improve himself. Both seem to be hinting to their cohorts of
listeners and watchers: stay where you are and don't run the
risk of wanting too much.

Will Hay's thirties were more, therefore, a decade of
steadiness, unpretentious consolidation and comfortable
advance. Between 250,000 and 400,000 private houses were built
each year, with family after family moving into the three-
bedroomed semis, festooning the country with their ribbons,
sometimes untidy but giving quiet pleasure to their occupants.
'Safety first,' pronounced Baldwin, and his moderate, avuncular
line was well received around the Bush wireless sets in the
living-rooms of this new suburbia. The Depression had, in
relative terms, left them untouched; it was slowly passing in any
event. The Great War was a generation away, and it seemed, to
many, possible to settle for a cosy, limited, not too exciting
contentment. And perhaps the frenzied nastiness of Hitler and

Will Hay – 'his lenses acted as a two-ringed circus for his acrobatic eyes' – in The Goose Steps Out (1942) with Peter Ustinov and Barry Morse; in The Ghost of St Michael's (1942) with Charles Hawtrey and Claude Hulbert; in My Learned Friend (1944); and with his two famous partners, Moore Marriott and Graham Moffat, exhibiting respectively the artless rapacity of old Harbottle and the lazy crapulence of Albert, in Oh! Mr Porter (1938).

rumours of another war would fizzle out.

One must search, I believe, for some psychological explanation for the strange and powerful place which the boarding school has held for so long in British culture, and perhaps most emphatically of all during the 1930s. Will Hay became the most potent personification of that tradition, but he would hardly have managed so complete an ascendancy unless that tradition had existed. Although the number of children attending independent boarding and day schools has never been high (over the last years about one in sixteen of England's children) there was an immediate connection made by millions for whom a midnight feast in the dorm was as alien as a foreign legion fortress under Arab assault.

The appeal of the school in fiction owes a lot to its attraction for the children themselves, but their parents and other adults also seem always ready to revisit in fiction those childhood experiences. Yet the state day school has little or no place in the canon. The residential school offers the literary device of the completely enclosed society, within which the classical unities of time, place and action may be validly observed. But that is only part of the explanation.

Perhaps the static, unchanging character of so fully integrated and sheltered a society was attractive to millions who were enjoying or who yearned to enjoy a serene and stable life. The public school on stage and film and in book form represents a piece of mass wish-fulfilment. It has its snobbish overtones, for the shelter craved was class-ridden. It was at the opposite pole to the equally mythical and equally class-ridden solidarity and security of George Formby's artisan communities.

But many people did, often at some sacrifice, and many more doubtless would have preferred to, place their children in such schools. It was, in part, a desire to immerse them totally in a well-ordered educative experience, and talk of character building was, if anything, louder than talk of academic prowess. The wish to mould character according to a well-defined pattern was and is often pre-eminent, and perhaps the most important aspect is the disciplined schedule and nature of the proceedings. It is the fear of unpredictable outcomes which bends, particularly at times of public stress, many minds toward a hearkening after good order and a just regimentation.

So if the proletariat could escape from their miseries to the naughty jingles of George Formby, the bourgeoisie could put aside their fears of internal strife and external hostility with a temporary registration at St Michael's. It remained respectable, even at its seediest. George Formby sailed close enough to censorious winds to have songs banned by the BBC. Will Hay, whatever lies he told or frauds he negotiated, rarely strayed from the course dictated by middle-class taboos. In a sense he was the conventional left-wing prototype of the petit bourgeois, a coating of rectitude hiding the deviousness within. A slight confusion of 'Cheltenham' and 'Gentlemen' on the platform signs in *Oh! Mr Porter* was his greatest concession to vulgarity. Whatever else, the good name of the school must be preserved, like the good name of Acacia Avenue for its polite inhabitants.

Maybe they even, unconsciously, considered our island home as one huge public school, with Stanley Baldwin its benign head teacher, and George V the revered chairman of its board of governors. Alan Bennett's play *Albion House* hinted at this. Interestingly, when the old school did suffer attack the argot was transferred bodily from school to war yarns, with the Germans playing boorish, crass 'town' to the English 'gown', sprightly and honourable and triumphant in every martial scrape. A less kindly, harsher instance might be Lindsay Anderson's film *If,* where the public school offers a self-contained metaphor for an authoritarian pseudo-fascist state under vain revolutionary attack.

It has been a lengthy tradition. *Tom Brown's Schooldays* and Kipling's *Stalky and Co* set it in train, with Talbot Baines Reed's *The Fourth Form at St Dominics* as the next chief landmark in public-school fiction. Indeed Will Hay's *The Fourth Form at St Michael's* was a play on that title.

The man who really put the public school on the map of popular culture was Charles Hamilton alias Frank Richards, of *Gem* and *Magnet* fame. He died an octogenarian in 1961, having become reputedly the most prolific writer of all time, with a record word-count of a hundred million (80,000 words a week at the height of his amazing powers). His major achievement was the invention of Billy Bunter. Neither a likeable villain such as Long John Silver nor an honourable hero in the Wren or Buchan genre, Billy Bunter is yet a part of our common heritage and language. Will Hay's greedy and corpulent Albert borrowed avidly from Billy Bunter, although Albert enjoyed a pertness where Billy suffered a crassness.

Around that central figure and most notably within the cloisters of Greyfriars, Frank Richards wove a spell and captivated a nation with his cheerful narratives of public-school life. As well as its values, its patois became generally known. The chirpy slang of Harry Wharton, Bob Cherry and company is still easily recognisable down to the last jolly wheeze, and a nation which had usually left school at the same age as the new boys rolled up at St Jim's was comfortably conversant with fags, the remove, prefects and prep. Mr Squeltch was for the comic paper what Will Hay was for the stage: an overtly stern, capped and gowned figure, but one vulnerable to the impudent pranks of his pupils.

During the thirties, and apart from the significant volume of school story-books for girls as well as boys, every comic had its minor public school, each in pursuit of the same themes of last-

EVERYTHING HE TOUCHES EXPLODES

Hotspur's *Red Circle and its housemaster, Mr Smugg, was the comic magazine equivalent of St Michael's and Will Hay.*

'The inheritor of the Will Hay stage mortarboard has been "Professor" Jimmy Edwards'.

minute sporting reversals, feared canings, thwarted bullies, detested swots, and, above all, sullen and doltish teachers outflanked by pupils displaying a merry intelligence. *Rover, Champion, Skipper, Wizard* – each advertised its equivalent of St Michael's and of Will Hay, with the *Hotspur's* Red Circle and its housemaster, Mr Smugg, probably the most memorable. It is unlikely that Will Hay could have so successfully cultivated his caricature had it not been against that vivid backcloth of a culture wellnigh saturated with his fellow pedagogues. One might, alternatively, ponder whether he, in turn, made the fictitious portrayal of the school that much more acceptable.

It has continued. The inheritor of the Will Hay stage mortarboard has been Jimmy Edwards. His hearty, bucolic approach is much less subtle and much more hyperbolic than Will Hay's. On stage he utilised the audience as a mock class with some effect, but relied on highly coloured interpretations of questions like 'Why did the Australian go in the bush?' for boisterous laughs, where Will Hay was more intent on conveying the nuances of beleaguered schoolmastership. One of Will Hay's schools was Narkover, based on Beachcomber's log of its activities in the *Daily Express,* and Jimmy Edwards with Chiselbury in his television show *Whacko* followed that prison-like nomenclature. *Whacko* implies the overt nature of the Edwardian academy, with wining and wenching priorities on the headmaster's own curriculum. He is as disreputable and as lacking in erudition as his more profoundly characterised mentor, but the overall effect is of burlesque rather than satire.

The penitentiary labelling of both comedians' schools is interesting, for the prison, like the boarding school, offers the artist another closed and static arena in which to operate and one in which, conventionally, the inmates resent their incarceration and channel their frustration into the outwitting of authority. Will Hay himself was to play, in *Convict 99*, a prison governor, and the BBC television series *Porridge* gives Ronnie Barker as the astute convict Fletcher an opportunity to accomplish apropos of prison warders what Albert, perhaps more primitively, put across Will Hay. Billy Bunter himself has appeared on television, while more recently *Please Sir* attempted, without undue success, to present the modern state school. It was probably not stylised sufficiently, relying on a rather flabby realism. Its mainstay was Deryck Guyler as the caretaker, and, in his characterisation, surly and watchful, one saw the descendant of all those janitors and porters, those ancient and eccentric retainers, who have figured in school yarns way back to Tom Brown's Rugby.

One must consider the wider base. The anti-authoritarian troupe, as represented by Harry Wharton and Co. or Will Hay's scholars, were and are to be found throughout children's culture in the United States as well as Great Britain. On film and television and in comics the Dead End Kids and Our Gang, lengthily featured in the *Dandy,* are cases of transatlantic imitation. Lord Snooty and his Pals in the *Beano,* one of several influences on Ken Dodd's Diddymen, are another example, and there are several more minor illustrations. They obey an all but ritualistic order of command. There is the leader-figure – Harry Wharton, Lord Snooty or Spanky MacFarlane; and there is often a loyal lieutenant – a Bob Cherry; a greedy fat boy – a Porky Lee in Our Gang; a 'brains' – an Alfalfa Switzer, also in Our Gang; and several others. Richmal Crompton's William, for instance, gains in stature and interest in the company of his diverse pals, Henry, Douglas, and Ginger. They have internal adversaries with whom to contend – the bully, with his sadistic lineage as old as Flashman, and the sneak especially – but their chief contest is with authority, normally the schoolteacher.

Is it a tradition blessed by the ages? Consider Robin Hood and his outlaw band, enclosed within the well-defined confines of Sherwood Forest. They are carefree and daring, and only the trappings of venison under the greenwood tree and quarterstaff jousts as against the tuck shop and ten to win and the last man in separate the two. Little John plays devoted Bob Cherry to Robin's Harry Wharton, with Friar Tuck the prototype for Billy Bunter and Albert. Insecure in his false title and bamboozled by the antics of his light-hearted foes, the Sheriff of Nottingham is practically Will Hay's double.

It is precisely at that point in what seems to be an eternal combat that Will Hay pulled a shrewd master-stroke. In many of his films and sketches a working rapport was established between Will Hay and his erstwhile antagonists. Much as they argued and complained among themselves, a sense of shared confidence frequently emerged. It was another aspect of his parvenu status. He assumed official roles undeservedly, sometimes by accident and sometimes from the company of the godless and delinquent: the dunce made head, the convict made governor, the unsuccessful teacher made secret agent, the petty crook made police sergeant. As one of his early film titles pronounced: 'Boys will be Boys'. Will Hay was always the ex-ranker, and he never shook off the spirit of his previous incarnation. Small-time theft, fraud and deceit, plus a staple addiction to gambling, these were the features of his recent past he could never put behind him, and it was through such stratagems that he was exposed as no better than those over whom he sought to administer power. And no worse. Eventually it was in the interests of the pupils or the convicts or the inefficient firemen or the incompetent policemen or the indolent porters to protect his position. They never wittingly let him perish; it was against their instincts of self-preservation. A leader who shared their weaknesses and foibles was distinctly preferable to one who would have censored and scolded in

Well-balanced team work was the essential ingredient of Will Hay's success just as it was of the Marx Brothers.

unpleasant earnest. Thomas Arnold, even Mr Chips, would have resolved the difficulties of Narkover in moments, just as, in fire, police and railway stations, their equivalents would have put to rout the lazy crapulence of Albert and the artless rapacity of Harbottle.

Ultimately, it was a conspiracy. The frantic squabble between teacher and pupils was ceaseless, but, beyond that, if a greater danger – such as the headless coachman in *Ask a Policeman* – or, more compellingly, a higher authority – the railway company, the Home Office and so on – threatened, then a sulky truce was uneasily sustained and an unsteady coalition formed.

In artistic terms it meant that Will Hay never became divorced from his purported underlings. He was never left, devoid of sympathy, with all the amusement directed *at* him, locked in the audience's stocks, pelted by the Alberts, Harbottles and d'Arcys. By this device he was able to remain in much closer, tighter relation with the rest of the team, and, at the same time, it enabled him to retain a valid two-way communication with them, thereby widening the scope of the interplay of character.

We come full circle to the essential ingredient of Will Hay's comedy – the well-balanced team work. At the other extreme from Tommy Handley, little more than a maypole around which other clowns festooned their gaudy ribbons (and none the worse for that professional reticence and underplaying), there have been those who have dominated and diminished their team-mates. Harry Tate, in his celebrated 'motoring' sketch, was a potent and accomplished wag who remained ever the centre of the comic attention. Other groups – the Marx Brothers are a classic example and the Crazy Gang another illustration – have been bands of co-equals, each member contributing his peculiar and specialised talent. Will Hay attained another kind of distinction. He formed the golden mean between retaining his proper status as lead performer and ensuring that his comrades were never ciphers.

Each of Will Hay's cabals formed a complicated mesh of intercommunion. Compared with the more conventional double act, the permutations of a Will Hay trio progressed geometrically, not arithmetically. With the twosome there is sometimes only a one-way connection, with the straight man providing nothing; in the better duos he does, and there is two-way contact. With three the possibilities accumulate, for apart from the series of one to one correspondences there is an additional set of doubles versus singles. Will Hay was the supreme navigator, carefully charting the byways and alleys of this comic journey. And, for those who consciously or otherwise enjoyed the timeless whimsy of Will Hay's world, seeing it, mistakenly or yearningly, as Britain encapsulated in an educative unit, there was the final pleasure. Just as Will Hay and his boys would lay aside their differences to close ranks against an external enemy, so would the nation lay aside its quarrels and concentrate on a common foe.

But the agile scheming of Will Hay's comic inventiveness did not end with such social and quasipolitical analysis. There was a class aspect. Will Hay was viewed as a Johnny-come-lately and, as such, open to scorn. One recalls how, because of his father's trade connections, Billy Bunter was subjected to the good-natured but nonetheless covertly snobbish ragging of the Wharton clique. There was a generational aspect. Cleverly, Will Hay always presented himself centrally as the middle-aged figure, flanked by youth and senility. The witless gaffer, shining occasional beams of sharp lucidity, is another standard of literature and the stage. Sometimes they have been tragic, like Marty South's father in Hardy's *The Woodlanders,* but more frequently they have been amusing, like Newman Noggs's Aged Parent in *Great Expectations* or Old Gobbo in *The Merchant of Venice.* Radio had its examples. Mark Time ('I'll have to ask me dad') appeared on *ITMA.* Television offers the sordid aggressiveness of Wilfred Brambell as Albert Steptoe and the gentler daffiness of Arnold Ridley as Godfrey in *Dad's Army,* both, in separate ways, in the Harbottle lineage.

Thus did Will Hay create and people his own world for the delight of his fellows. Carefully, he assembled the pieces, and his assemblage of social and other features into a delicately interwoven pattern remains one of the treats of British comedy. In its timeless quality and in its fluent interchange of age and class, it resembles another inter-war world, the world of Wodehouse. Certainly they both had the same mellow style. Like many of his contemporaries, Will Hay graduated from the concert party, a less brusque and steely schooling than the music hall. One thinks of Leslie Henson – 'let's all sing the "la" song' – and the Two Leslies. Its proponents tended to be pleasant enough, but leaning toward a twittering effeteness.

Will Hay was much too accomplished to allow his colleagues or himself to suffer that fate, just as he avoided the other extreme of overweening callousness which disfigured some music-hall comedians as they tried too hard to win cheap guffaws. What, in fact, he created was to come nearer the work of the comic novelist than any other comedian. His characterisation was as profound as it was intimate. It lacked perhaps the full-bloodedness of Dickensian comic gallery. Its quieter, more veiled colours were possibly closer to a character sketched by Evelyn Waugh or Angus Wilson, themselves often creators of largely thirties figures. What is sure is that, in that static, rather introverted decade, his controlled portrayal of the groping, overreaching schoolmaster was impeccably located, suited to the times and contributing to them.

Will Hay and the scornful Smart, played by the ageless

Like Will Hay, Leslie Henson – here seen with Cyril Ritchard 'doing' 'The Green Eye of the Little Yellow God' at a wartime bomber station – was a graduate of the concert party.

Charles Hawtrey, summarised the whole relationship in the following characteristic exchange, along with d'Arcy, knowledgeable where Smart was ignorant, innocent where Smart was knowing:

Smart: Well, if you're so clever why do you always correct d'Arcy's book first?

W. Hay: Why do I correct d'Arcy's book fir—?

Smart: Yeahhh. Come on. We know.

W. Hay: Well, if you know there's no need for me to tell you, is there?

Smart: Ah now, don't try and wriggle out of it.

W. Hay: I'm not trying to wriggle anything.

Smart: Oh, yes, you are.

W. Hay: If you must know, I correct d'Arcy's book first, because – er . . .

Smart: Well?

W. Hay: Because he's sitting nearest to me, I suppose; quite the natural thing to do, really . . .

Smart: Yessss, I don't think. You correct his work first because that's the only way you can get to know the answer.

W. Hay: That's absolute piffle.

Smart: Oh, no, it isn't and I can prove it.

W. Hay: Oh, can you?

Smart: Next time you can take my book first and d'Arcy's last.

d'Arcy: I don't think you should accuse the headmaster of cribbing, Smart.

W. Hay: No.

d'Arcy: After all, I'm not always right.

Smart: Well, blimey, when you're not, we all pay for it.

An audience at panto or end-of-pier show will still hoot when the comedian raises his hand, and this classroom signal acts as a cue to grin at the teacher as laughing-stock. I once asked a group of teachers why they insisted on this, rather than permitting the children to visit the toilets whenever they wished. 'If Jimmy Robinson', said one, 'could go to the toilets whenever he wanted, he'd stay there all the time.'

The lesson Will Hay tried to teach teachers was that the classrooms should be as interesting as the urinals for the likes of Jimmy Robinson. He obliquely reflected the arid and unbecoming tricks of their trade, and some, alas insufficient, have heeded the implied warning. That was the specific encapsulation of a character in place and time. That he was able then to set this specific as part of a more general social context of incompetent authority and impertinent underling was the mark of his artistry.

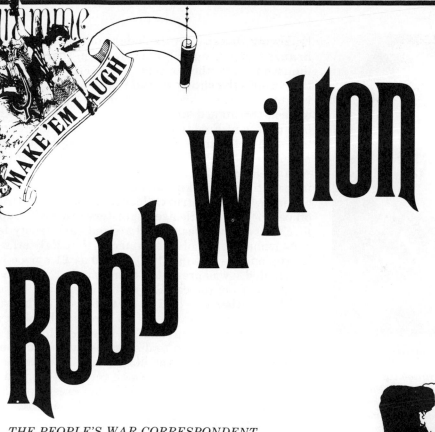

Robb Wilton

THE PEOPLE'S WAR CORRESPONDENT

Then she said, 'Our Harry's sure to be called up and when he's gone there'll only be his army allowance, so what are you going to do about it?' I said, 'I'll just have to try and manage on it.'

Robb Wilton 'spoke like a man shaking his head in mildly bemused exasperation'. He used to say about Jimmy James that he was the 'greatest timer' who ever performed; but Jimmy James's view was, 'There's only one timer in the business, and that's Robb'.

Following Dunkirk, at the height of the blitz in 1940, with Britain facing the peril of an invasion scarce contemplated for a thousand years, the concept of the 'Fire Guard' was enunciated. In a twentieth-century version of the device of 'watch and ward', volunteers were asked to group together to give fire protection to each threatened street. My grandmother, a patriot from the first phrase of Freddy Grisewood's 'Kitchen Front' recipe to the last item of the nine o'clock news, prevailed upon my mother, never the most extrovert of women, to inaugurate such a body. As a fireman's wife, she was told, it was her duty; and, dutifully if hesitatingly, she knocked on the doors of our street and assembled an eccentric collection of two male OAPs and five office-working middle-aged spinsters. An SFP (Supplementary Fire Party) band was wound around each trusty left arm.

As emblem and sole weaponry of that Falstaff's fire brigade, a stirrup pump – by June 1940, 86,000 at £1 apiece had been distributed – was presented to my mother, and, to our delight, men came from the council with white paint and emblazoned S and P on either side of the front door. But, almost before the Luftwaffe could drop another incendiary bomb, a rule came to light which forbade firemen's wives from looking after stirrup pumps. Delight turned to disgust as the stirrup pump, like the ceremonial halberd of the horseguards, was transferred across the road to number 13. The men returned from the council with their paint and crude stencils, feebly erased our S and P (its faint image was visible for years) and the lintels of number 13 were appropriately daubed.

It is difficult to imagine that it was Herbert Morrison, then Minister of Home Security, who deliberated and ruled on this technicality. London was ablaze around him, and, according to some accounts, the East End, legendary aviary of those chirpy sparrows, the lovable cockneys, was on the verge of major discontent. Nearly two in every ten Londoners were made homeless at some time during the blitz, and too many local councils had frequently neither the wit nor the courage to respond adequately. Morrison also had to grapple with fire brigades consisting of pre-war 'regulars' and new full-time auxiliary firemen, tricked out with scores of part-timers, all spread over nearly 1,700 different authorities.

More likely some pettifogging local clerk had invented the rule or over-zealously interpreted some existing statute. But it was a case Robb Wilton would have savoured. Common sense might suggest that a house with a resident fireman was not an inappropriate base for a stirrup pump, but, if some law or decision said otherwise, then with inexorable certitude must that be pursued.

My own first view of him was during the war at a Stretford cinema which every month or so staged a week's variety. Wryly, Robb Wilton's first variety appearance was at a theatre just beginning to show an early movie between acts. In that same cinema I saw several well-known wartime stars, such as Frank Randle, exuding antiquated lechery through an alcoholic mist, and Billy Cotton, with a band whose cacophonic antics threatened eardrums as engagingly as any until the electronic pop groups. I even saw there the ritualistic blooding of Julie Andrews, a simpering toddler hauled on to take a curtain with her parents, the musical duo Ted and Barbara Andrews.

Robb Wilton was a cosmos removed from the plebeian if proficient crudeness of the one, the raucous din of the other, or the refined sugar of the third. On this occasion he was doing a variation of his usual Home Guard theme, as a special constable. In his acts he negotiated much of the legal and civil defence canon, but the substance never varied. He stood quite still, the only movement one perpetually fidgeting hand. It focused the air of unease he cultivated, that one hand flickering inexhaustibly over the drawn face, above a body stationary and looming.

The fingers passed wearily over the forehead and chin, drummed nervily on the teeth and so on, through a well rehearsed series of mannerisms as characteristic as Chaplin's three o'clock feet or Little Tich's elongated boots. But, with Wilton, it was digital choreography, with the entrechat a little finger pensively nibbled at the corner of the vaguely drooping mouth. He was a sizeable man, but, by mid-war and sixty years of age, he had lost the thicker-set proportions of his middle age. On early film and on many photographs, he looks rubicund and roly-poly faced, but his plumpish aldermanic aspect was gone. If anything, this heightened the gloominess of the portrayal, at the trifling expense of a little blandness. He looked gaunt and the dark police uniform added to the funereal depiction. Above all, I recall the pallid white face. He rarely wore make-up, and the harsh chalkiness of the countenance, proscenium arch for Robb Wilton's ceaseless finger ballet, is deeply engraved in my memory.

When he spoke it was in a droll Lancastrian tone, hinting occasionally of his native Liverpool's nasal inclinations, but round-vowelled and with a note of peevish gruffness. He simply related the exchange of views he had recently suffered with his wife, a narrative replete with 'I said's', 'she said's' and 'well, then's', and a gallery of pauses, hesitations and omitted syllables almost impossible to capture in print.

> The day war broke out, my missus looked at me and she said 'What good are yer?' I said 'How d'you mean, what good am I?' 'Well,' she said, 'you're too old for the army, you couldn't get into the navy and they wouldn't have you in the air force, so ... what good are yer?' I said 'I'll do something.' She said 'What?' I said 'How do I know? I'll have to think.' She said 'I don't see how that's going to help you, you've

'Robb Wilton was a special constable that evening at the Longford Theatre'.

never done it before ... so what good are yer?' I said 'Don't keep saying what good am I.'

Now, well then, she said, 'Now our Harry,' then she said 'Our Harry's sure to be getting called up and when he's gone there'll only be his army allowance, so what are you going to do about it?' I said 'I'll just have to try and manage on it.' She said *'You'll* have to try and man—'. She said 'What about me?' I said 'There'll be my insurance.' She said 'I can't get that till you're dead.' I said 'Then you'll have to wait.' She said 'Suppose I die first?' I said 'Well, then you won't want it.' But you can't reason ... she's no brai— ... anyhow, I got fed up and I put my hat on and I went down to the local. Oh, the times that woman's driven me into the local.

The account was invested with such a spluttering, lip-smacking, tongue-clicking, heavily breathing delivery. But it was exceedingly underplayed. One never quite hears the splutter, the clicked tongue, the intake of breath, the sigh, all consequent upon his patient astonishment at the follies of his wife. One merely feels they are there; there is a hint of their existence, rather as when, over the telephone, one sometimes visualises the other speaker's mannerisms. Robb Wilton spoke like a man shaking his head slowly in mildly bemused exasperation. It was from that sure foundation of demeanour and voice in matchless combine that he would expose, through the abrasive questioning of his wife, the foibles of the Home Guard, the special constable or other branch of the 'people's war'.

If there had been no war, Robb Wilton would have had to invent it if he were to become one of England's finest ever comedians. It is worth recalling that, by the day war broke out, Robb Wilton was fifty-eight years old. Like Churchill, who took up the premiership when most start to draw their old-age pensions, he had been a well-known bill-topper since before the First World War.

Billed as 'The Confidential Comedian', he was rated highly enough to have made a London appearance by 1909, and his sketch 'The Magistrate' was featured in the 1926 Royal Variety Performance. By 1940 he was one of very few comic entertainers to be a top-ranking top of the bill. Then the war helped to place him among the handful of comedians who might fairly be termed geniuses.

The Second World War accentuated the administrative momentum of the centralised state. A glance down the legislative shelves of the public archives illustrates the sudden and huge thickening of statutes and enactments after 1939. Dickens may have been able to use the new poor law of the 1830s as a model for Bumbledom, and – with Dodson and Fogg in *Pickwick Papers,* for example – he constantly harried the delays and postponements of an over-elaborate Victorian legal system.

Now the state was to be placed on a total war footing, and, whatever the needs and whatever the eventual triumphant finale, there is no denying the immense accretion of bureaucratic rules and rulers at every level. And this meant massive administrative procreation. Civil servants almost doubled to well over 700,000 by the summer of 1943. In that year alone 300,000 people were prosecuted and found guilty of lighting offences.

Consider the most important aspect of all: food. The Ministry of Food, which ran its £600,000,000 annual turnover through over a thousand local Food Offices, employed 50,000 civil servants. Halfway through the war, with rationing at its most characteristic, these 50,000 clerks and administrators dispensed to each person each week just over a shilling's worth of meat, two or three pints of milk, a couple of rashers of bacon, an occasional egg, a half-pound of sugar and the same of fats.

It is not that rationing was unpopular; rather the government vacillated a little before introducing it, with the public largely welcoming, even demanding, such a device. It was to serve, in the late forties, as the propagandist spectre of the 'anti-controls' factions of the right, but most people accepted the notion of fair shares. Yet the obverse was ever-present in those 50,000 civil servants, just about one for every two hundred households. And fair shares could not avoid the tedium of shortages and queues, and, as a consequence, the black market and that telling wartime phrase, 'under the counter'.

The war evolved a series of public images, each the opposite, less pleasant side of the patriotic coin. Rumour was often responsible, but beneath its smoke the fire flickered luminously enough. There was the serviceman with the 'cushy number' (another wartime coining); there was the civilian column-dodger (there were instances of famous sportsmen being driven by such criticism from the perils of civil defence into the cosy haven of jobs as physical training instructors in the forces); there were the tea-drinking civil servants, thought to be very thick on the ground; there were megalomaniac air-raid wardens and firemen found guilty of looting. The 'bold gendarmes' lived and were fruitful.

Despite efforts to secure a sense of common interest, the middle classes still prospered and the working classes suffered more of the agonies of the civilian war. At the beginning of the war a private's wife received only twenty-four shillings a week, and the improved wages of tradesmen were often the result of exhaustingly long hours. Average weekly earnings rose from just over £4 to just over £6 during the war, but prices rose over 40 per cent during the same period. The top 10 per cent of earners took home 30 per cent of after-tax private income at the end of the war, only a small drop from the 1938 figures. The well-to-do had many bonuses. They found it easier to find accommodation either before or after bombing; their homes were mostly located in less hazardous districts and were usually more strongly erected; and there was even the distinction between the nauseous railway arch shelter and the luxuriously converted baths of the expensive hotel. There is some evidence that the middle classes did not always pull their weight on evacuation schemes.

Food is again a useful example. Bowing to middle-class opinion, restaurants and cafés were provided with regular supplies of food, with the result that the well-heeled were able to dine out and save their rations. Conversely, workers in heavy industry were, on the same diet, less well nourished than professional and clerical workers in sedentary occupations. Despite sincere efforts to create some sense and dimension of social equity, the rich were favoured and the poor penalised when the country was on a total war footing.

So people's wars varied. Being a prisoner of war in Japanese hands involved a terrifyingly different war from being an army unit librarian in the middle of Scotland. But even on the humdrum Home Front, 60,000 people lost their lives in air attacks. Some towns under aerial attack had to be cordonned off completely for a period, while after the Coventry blitz the idea of martial law was seriously considered. Nonetheless, especially after the blitz had stopped and active service apart, the war for many was one of ennui and frustration. It was not that they were anti-war, hostile, so to say, to the idea of fighting Nazism. They approached it in a mood of resigned forbearance, making the best of it, not much enjoying it and rarely glorying in it. If the trench was the symbol of the 1914–18 war, the queue became the hallmark of the 1939–45 war. 'Don't you know there's a war on?' was the half-accusatory, truculent response to complaints or queries of any kind. It was adopted as a music-hall catch-phrase by Hatton and Manners, cast as cockney chappie and Lancashire lass, and she would draw out the broad vowel of 'war' at noisy length.

Light entertainment revealed and fed this mood. It was not a patriotic war in the sense that the 1914–18 war had been. The changed attitude towards the many deserters, psychiatric cases and conscientious objectors was a pleasing indication that the white-feather mood had passed. There was, of course, a wish that trials would be shared, which was understandable enough, but jingoism was much reduced. The Edwardian music hall had spurred on this fevered approach to nationalism, and, in the film of *Oh what a lovely war,* Maggie Smith's cameo of the recruiting songstress brilliantly captures this flamboyant, hollow appeal. The First World War spawned exuberant marching songs and ballads depicting loyalty worn with off-hand bravery – 'Goodbye-ee ... I'll be tickled to death to go'. The second war was not spared these, but Vera Lynn was the typical singer now. She evoked the purer sensibility of private grief and separation, and gave herself strenuously to the cause. One ex-Burma campaigner, although he did not like Vera Lynn's voice, used to travel miles to watch her and pay tribute to her sterling war effort.

If the popular song was less war-oriented (and the war-oriented songs tended towards the clumsy comedy of 'Hanging out the washing on the Siegfried Line') than in the First World War, light comedy reversed that proclivity. The 1919 Royal Command Performance, designed as a tribute to the war effort of the variety artists, starred George Robey, Grock, Harry Tate in his celebrated motoring sketch, Arthur Prince and Jim, his naval dummy, and Clarice Mayne, of 'Joshua' and 'I was a good little girl' fame. They pursued the impeccably etched characterisations of their essentially peacetime Edwardian milieu, while comedians in the early 1940s turned their humorous attention on to the war itself with sudden, sometimes overemphatic, assurance. Radio especially contributed to this, and Tommy Handley, agreed by all to be the acutest radio script reader ever, was in the van. *ITMA* was fast and irreverent. It was populated by catch-phrases personified – 'Can I do yer now sir'; 'I don't mind if I do'; 'I go, I come back'; 'After you, Claud'; and a hundred others. It caught the catch-phrase infection from the *Bandwaggon* of Arthur Askey and Richard Murdoch, and the crackling pace from the American radio comedies of Bob Hope, Fred Allen and others. Tommy Handley, apart from his 'The Disorderly Room' sketch, had never been a first-class stage performer but, come wartime, he had the technical acumen and the breezy good sense to place himself at the centripetal hub of a weekly display of verbal pyrotechnics.

His persona, as Mayor of Foaming-at-the-Mouth or Minister of Aggravation and Mysteries, was, however, invariably that of the trivialising, slightly corrupt, opportunist public figure, surrounded by over-formal officers like Mr Fusspott, the 'Man from the Ministry', and Sir Short Supply, dotty foreigners like Signor So-So, and mildly criminal types, like Ali Oop, the porn postcard pedlar. The essentially semantic attack of *ITMA* thrived on a world of controls and officialese, It preserved and passed on, that much more pickled, the blimpish drunken army officer, in Jack Train's creation of Colonel Chinstrap, while in Dorothy Summers's Mrs Mopp it freshly portrayed the corporation's official cleaner. Many wireless entertainments were for and of the forces. Richard Murdoch joined with Kenneth Horne and Sam Costa to guy the well-mannered futilities of the unduly remote RAF station in *Much-Binding-in-the-Marsh*. In *Stand Easy* Charlie Chester led a troupe of colleagues through a less sophisticated view of the vagaries of army life, whilst Eric Barker and Pearl Hackney poked fun at the senior service from the vantage point of *Merry-go-Round* and *Waterlogged Spa*. The factories had the somewhat contrived

jovialities of *Works Wonders* and *Workers' Playtime,* and ENSA
provided a range of light entertainment from top-class to
unbelievably tawdry. But no one would deny the massive
popularity of *ITMA,* thirty minutes of oral slapping and cuffing
at the bland face of officialdom.

Did the authorities ever worry about the lack of patriotic
fervour in the nation's light entertainment? The answer is that
they were primarily concerned with the intangible quality of
'morale', of which laughter was a chief indicator. At best they
might have argued that freedom to wax satirical about one's
institutions was the objective of British warfare. At worst, they
might have felt that such mild political burlesque was no more
than the pinprick of inoculation against the incipient disease of
rebelliousness. In the middle ground, however, was the belief
that sixteen million people laughing at *ITMA* contributed to
that commonality of purpose which could not be enforced and
without which total war could not be waged.

It was into this atmosphere that Robb Wilton, with his forty
years of acting and comic experience behind him, brought his
art when it was at its greatest; and, as the henpecked Home
Guardsman, he found his own 'finest hour'. Admittedly, he was
well liked enough after the war too, but his 'the day peace broke
out ...' raised nostalgic smiles rather than convulsive laughter.
As a comic entertainer Robb Wilton re-lived a world of small-
town officialdom and public officers. Some commentators have
focused on the haphazard disorganisation of such sketches as
their major theme; his *alter ego,* one of several, Mr
Muddlecombe JP reflected this, and certainly there was an

*ITMA, fast and irreverent
and full of catch-phrases, the most
famous of the Second World War
radio shows. (Right) 'Good
Morning, Nice Day' from Clarence
Wright to Tommy Handley.*

element of that most frustrating aspect of bureaucracy – the missing file, the lost letter – in his portrayals. But more central to him was that massive air of deliberation that surrounds the official mentality.

It was the wrong-headed pondering of a functionless and irrelevant set of administrative data leading painfully to an excruciatingly unwise decision, which, having been made, was to be stalked lingeringly to its final useless and senseless resting-place. Once this respectable frame of reference, with its internal code and inner sanity, was infringed by a real-life occurrence or mundane question, then the framework rocked a little. What is important is that it never fell. The ark of the bureaucratic covenant might be shaken, but it was never shattered. As Mayor, JP, policeman, fireman and, most famously, Home Guardsman, Robb Wilton celebrated that unhappy resilience of officialdom. He never lost his temper or changed his mind radically to accommodate the incoming viewpoint. He would grow exasperated, even peevish, but he would never explode. Robb Wilton would describe himself as 'a comedy character actor', and, having abandoned engineering as a trade when eighteen to become a straight actor, this was a theatrical branch upon which he continually drew. In his monologues it is a conversation with 'Rita', his purported stage wife, which he mournfully records. In his sketches the women who pester him tend toward the hysterical; as he reports his wife she is evidently scornful and sceptical to a degree. But in all cases they are raising sensible and rational issues. The counterpoint of common sense, exhibited tearfully or demandingly, with

'Can I do yer now, sir', from Dorothy Summers as Mrs Mopp. To the left stands Jack Train whose many voices included the German spy 'Funf' and 'Colonel Chinstrap' ('I don't mind if I do').

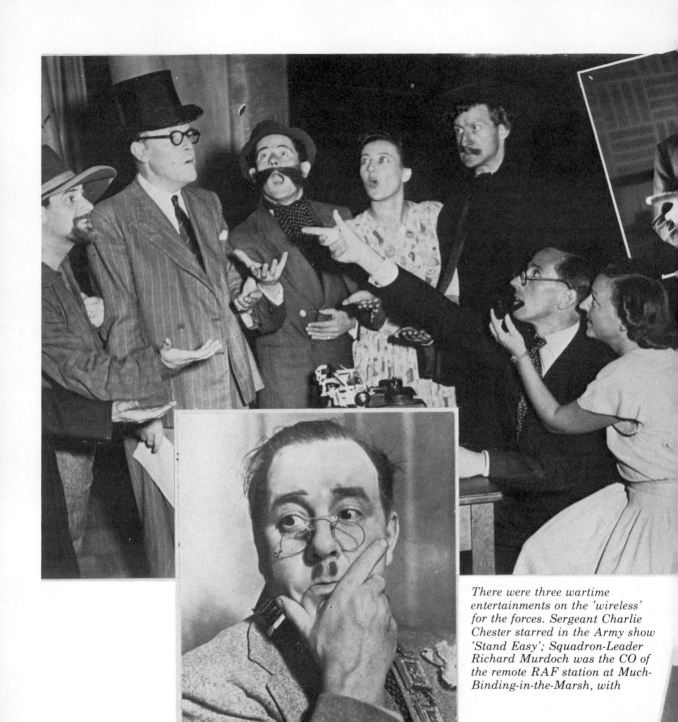

There were three wartime
entertainments on the 'wireless'
for the forces. Sergeant Charlie
Chester starred in the Army show
'Stand Easy'; Squadron-Leader
Richard Murdoch was the CO of
the remote RAF station at Much-
Binding-in-the-Marsh, with

Robb Wilton as Mr
Muddlecombe, JP.

Kenneth Horne as his AOC. For the Navy Lieutenant-Commander Eric Barker and Pearl Hackney starred in 'Merry-go-Round' and later 'Waterlogged Spa'. Here they are seated with, from left to right, Dick Griffin as Digger Dan, Richard Gray as Lord Waterlogged, Humphrey Lestocq as Flying Officer Kite ('I rather care for that!'); Barbara Sumner, the Show's singer, and Jon Pertwee as the clandestine Commander Highprice.

seeming irrationality, stated smugly and without rancour, forms an unfortunate cameo of our age. One might see it in the truculent, ill-at-ease demands of the claimant at the social security office, faced, across the counter, with the bland, incomprehensible clerk, with his unintelligible officialese marshalled and unremitting.

He developed this kind of portrayal over many years. One of his most famed sketches, 'The Fire Chief', is extant on film dating from 1932, while by the 1930s he had also successfully developed the Muddlecombe character. It became a standard wartime radio comedy show, normally Wednesday evening's major show. The persistent demonstration of the truth that the 'law is a h'ass' has nourished literature and the stage for many a year. Robb Wilton, on music hall and radio, puzzled and ruminated his perplexed route through hundreds of court cases and solicitors' briefs. Indeed, the official psyche has long been an artist's butt, with Shakespeare's Dogberry and Gogol's government inspector rather more classical examples than Mr Muddlecombe JP. But the music hall has contributed its own fair share of clerkly caricature. The clipped tautologies of George Robey as a mayor and the sonorous diction of Wilkie Bard as a policeman were also deployed in the exposition of official foibles.

But one can now analyse in retrospect and observe that in a Robb Wilton wartime monologue there was a synthesis of a comic artist and an age unequalled in the story of the light theatre. It would be portentous to conclude that Robb Wilton was so introspective and sociologically aware as to have guessed at all the nuances himself. He had a ready ear and a genuine sympathy and, during the leisured mornings peculiar to his trade, he would listen at police court hearings for the quirks and sounds of his caricatures. He had considerable comic instinct and enjoyed the reputation of being profoundly funny off stage. Compering a charity show at Wormwood Scrubs, he introduced a performer constitutionally incapable of retaining any sense of the lapse of time with the words: 'and by the time he's finished, most of you lads will be out of here'. Or in the Palladium bar, consoling the Deep River Boys at the curt compression of their act, he commented sadly: 'It was hardly worth blacking up for, was it?'

The anecdotes are instructive. Both have a cruel edge but, perhaps above all other comedians, Robb Wilton was warmly lovable and held in the fondest of affection. He never attempted to get away with murder, but his frequent grand larcenies were received compliantly. His measured assaults on legal buffoons on occasion caused complaint but his good-heartedness and what appeared as the essential dottiness of his story lines shone through and the objections fell lamely. Such grievances were as feeble as the trifling conceits of his magisterial scripts.

Both anecdotes demonstrate a preoccupation with time and, without exception, Robb Wilton was music hall's unrivalled master of timing. Recently there have been three fine imitations of Robb Wilton by his great admirer Ken Dodd in his one-man show *Ha Ha* (his Andy Mann voice on radio is also Wiltonesque); in the *Happy as a Sandbag* musical reverie of the Second World War; and by Arthur Lowe (who worked with Robb Wilton years ago) in the stage version of *Dad's Army*. Ken Dodd captures the voice uncannily, and the other two observe the mannerisms and intonations closely. Indeed, every saloon bar has its wireless buff keen to pass a hand over an anxious

Robb Wilton was the henpecked Home Guardsman thirty years before Dad's Army. *(Inset) Arthur Lowe, who impersonated Robb Wilton in the Dad's Army theatre show, and John le Mesurier. Corporal Jones? No, a contemporary Home Guard photograph for instruction in camouflage.*

forehead and mouth 'the day war ...'

None of his imitators, however, can quite catch the timing, either in the phrasing and checking of the sentences or, more especially, the pauses. When listening to him on tape, even imagining the facial massage, there is still a split second of disquiet lest the recorder has broken. He held pauses with the delicacy of a wine taster. His impersonators do not have the nerve – the audacity – to sustain that exquisite timing. 'The wife said "You'll have to go back to work."'' The pause seems eternal. Then, eventually, accurately, bitterly he adds: 'Oh, she's got a cruel tongue, that woman', with 'ker-oo-el' and 'tung-er' gaining an extra syllable apiece as token of his heartfelt sorrow. As Wilf Mannion might have weighed a long pass or Len Hutton leaned effortlessly into a cover drive, so did Robb Wilton time his performance immaculately. Jack Benny deployed the long, muted glance with superb and witty skill. Incidentally, he often utilised the same technique of caressing his face with one exploratory hand. He, however, was the master of 'silences'; the Englishman made the 'pause' his very own.

In brief, the indispensable element of a Wilton performance was that he was a very humorous and kindly person deploying superb technique. With the war his Home Guard monologue became a classic because, that admirable professional method apart, it was poised at the intersect of three basic social and cultural components. They were three love-hate relationships, concerning the individual and authority, social class, and domestic life.

First, Robb Wilton musingly posed the problem of the ordinary individual beset by the critical call to arms: 'I said "There'll be, there'll be munitions ..." She said "Now how can you go on muni—." I said "I never said anything about going on, I said there'd *be* some."' As always, he hammers home the logical rebuff with the ponderous delicacy of the dancing elephant in the circus ring. It is highly personalised. He agrees that he's not the only one to guard our shores against Teutonic onslaught: 'There's Ted Bates, Charlie Evans and seven or eight altogether.' The names are cleverly chosen. It is not the banal Bloggs and Snooks or the Smith and Jones of the run-of-the-mill sketch, nor is it the verbal fantasising of *ITMA* with its nonsense names such as Mona Lott or Sam Scram. It is reminiscent of W. W. Jacobs, whose short tales of dockland and village life earned him minor fame before and after the First World War. His names like Peter Russet, Bill Chambers and Ted Reddish sound uncommonly like Robb Wilton's comradely associates. How carefully chosen was 'Rita' for his wife's name – comically lower middle-class, but slightly obtrusive, with its slight exotic tint borrowed from the movie star Rita Hayworth; yet not obviously outrageous, like Carmen or Gloria. Towards the end of the monologue Robb Wilton plunged, as it were, into the depths of ordinariness, as Rita objects that, if Hitler invaded, her husband wouldn't recognise him. 'Doesn't she know', he plaintively asked the audience, 'that I've got a tongue in me head?'

The British civilian both accepted the need for an authoritarian war regime and resented its surveillance. He did not much like clothing coupons, but realised their justification, yet he was not keen on official 'snoopers' catching out those guilty of trading without them. Robb Wilton caught the sensibilities of this mood with aplomb. Munitions, the Home Guard, the ARP, all the orders and regulations – they were regarded as being both probably essential and also a little pointless. As the Home Guard lance-jack, he was, as ever, setting himself up as authority's Aunt Sally to be pilloried. He was always the police *chief,* the fire brigade *captain*, the prison *governor*. Arnold – another pleasing choice of name – was the unseen subordinate with whom Robb Wilton pretended to communicate on the fire station intercom in a beautifully phrased precursor – along with Jeanne de Casalis and her Mrs Feather character – of those mock telephone conversations which were a cabaret craze in the USA in the 1960s. As Home Guard or fireman, nothing would rush him. When the lady with the burning house remonstrated with his circuitous choice of route for the fire engine, he replied 'Aye, but it's a prettier run.' Robb Wilton sat astride the see-saw of the necessity–futility syndrome, judging it to a nicety.

Second, there is the issue of social class. The Wiltonesque gallery of characters is *petit bourgeois* to a man. It would be very wrong to view the laughter he raised as being directed at quaint, lovable English institutions. His creations were frequently unpopular with working people. The policeman and the special constable of my Stretford memory were regarded with suspicion in many working-class districts. The ARP warden, too frequently hectoring and a wee bit power-crazed, was often decidedly unpopular. The Poujadist image of the Home Guard is accurately reflected in the front rank of *Dad's Army* – a bank manager and two bank employees, a butcher, a funeral director and Godfrey, retired into genteel tranquillity from a career as a gentleman's outfitter. Even the rather more coarse and bellicose greengrocer warden fits the bill.

He had the cautiously chosen pronunciation, with the slurs showing ominously through, of the vaguely aspiring suburban book-keeper or insurance agent, black-booted and wing-collared in arid respectability. No allusion to sex, let alone near-the-knuckle crudity, passed those clerkly lips. But British society distinguishes by class not caste, and Robb Wilton was shrewd enough to benefit from these blurred borders. He was perceptive enough to realise that the work ethic was no less acceptable to the shop assistant and the town hall cashier than to the industrial worker, and that topics like insurance and football were socially binding: 'I see Chelsea drew on Saturday,' he said conversationally to the distraught lady in the fire station as he tried to resolve the tricky business of form-filling relating to her by then incandescent home.

His precarious poise, just above the back-to-backs of Paradise Row, still in touch, but with his status looking upward towards the white picket fence of Laburnum Grove, was superbly maintained. He lived somewhere between Albert Chevalier and George Robey. A neat illustration of this lies in a story told by his social inferior, Billy Russell, who prior to and during the war addressed the nation in hoarse camaraderie 'on behalf of the working classes'. Lamenting the troubles of the black-out ('I ended up in me own 'ouse three times last week'), he was particularly abusive on the subject of 'RIP Wardens'. The black-out, incidentally, was one field in which the Germans acted more sensibly than ourselves, by only insisting on covering or extinguishing lights during the air attack. For all his efforts at blacking-out ('There's not a blanket left on the bed,' he moans) the warden still scolds him for a light under the door. 'You don't expect', demanded Billy Russell belligerently, 'they're coming on their 'ands and knees, do yer?'

Robb Wilton would have been the air-raid warden, never his enemy, never, in social category, the overt jeerer at authority. If, in his sketch, such an argument had arisen, he would have met it with his own pachydermic brand of logic.

Yet it was always soothing and balm-like. It was never Kafkaesque enough to frighten the working classes into a proper realisation of the oppressions of the system, nor barbed enough to make the middle classes fear that he might prove subversive.

Third, and underpinning the unsatirical, non-radical character of Robb Wilton's performances, was its domestic substructure. With a compelling twist, he made the persistent critic of pettifogging officialdom his own wife. Women's libbers may note appreciatively that, however shrilly, it was almost always women who posed the natural reality against Wilton's artificial fabrication. Robb Wilton's antagonists ranged from ladies trying to get their burning houses extinguished to those attempting to confess to murder. Often these were played by his real wife, Florence Palmer, whom he met in Hull in 1903 when both were members of the same stock repertory company.

The comedian's wife is an ever-present target for his jeering abuse. Al Read – 'That's the wife in the kitchen' – presented a similar portrayal of the husband – never less than stoical, never more than niggled. Beyond that, Robb Wilton added the merest soupçon of social comment. During the war many men – and women too – were released from the tawdry restrictiveness of married domesticity to pursue an honourable cause. Right back to the crusades, when all the motivations for flocking to the

Billy Russell used to address the nation 'on behalf of the working classes'.

Robb Wilton and his wife, Florence Palmer, in one of their early 'pettifogging officialdom' sketches.

Robb Wilton 'had the cautiously chosen pronunciation of the vaguely aspiring suburban book-keeper or insurance agent.'

colours – the land hunger, the thirst for glamour and glory, as well as more laudable motives – have been counted, escape from the aching monotony of a miserable job and a broken home still remains. This is not to downgrade the sentiment of Vera Lynn and the White Cliffs of Dover; but Robb Wilton recognised once more the reverse face of a social institution. It was not a violent reaction. It was the resigned, long-suffering response of the female-dominated northerner, rather akin to Les Brandon, in Peter Tinniswood's mordant novels and his television series, *I didn't know you cared.*

Like many a hard-pressed spouse, military or civilian, Robb Wilton fled to the arms of Bacchus – in his case, more prosaically, to the Dog and Pullet. The association of civil defence with public houses was, of course, no coincidence. Robb Wilton's Home Guard 'group', as he termed it, was stationed at the Dog and Pullet. His wife rebuked him stiffly, supposing it to have been his idea. 'Aye', he snapped tetchily, 'and that Charlie Evans is trying to claim it as his.' So he places his non-visible, argumentative wife in the position of both nagging him and insulting the establishment in the dubious shape of the Home Guard. Sympathy is equally distributed in all directions. One's head accepts the wife's chilling analysis; one's heart warms towards Robb Wilton's surly defensiveness – just as one senses both aspects of the necessity–futility syndrome and the incipient class skirmish of a Robb Wilton monologue.

Thus, by a fluent compound of knowledgeable insight, comic flair and – mysterious ingredient – happy chance, Robb Wilton found an integrated formula which was mathematically perfect for the people's war. He died in 1957 after an enormously long career, but it was in and for the war that he reached his zenith.

A celebrated story of his ad lib humour concerns his appearance at the end of a rickety Yorkshire pier during a thunderstorm. He battled on, as the rain rattled on and against the tinny structure, accompanied by frequent claps of thunder, the petulant roar of a disturbed sea and the din of wind-blown walls. A dog howled lustily nearby; a door in the auditorium banged incessantly, and, finally, a flare was released to summon the local lifeboatmen to urgent duty. Robb Wilton paused and stroked his face thoughtfully. 'I think', he paused, 'they're trying to train me as a police horse.'

It is no bad analogy. In the Second World War light entertainment stood turn as a kind of police horse, cajoling and encouraging the crowd, managing both to discipline and to attract affection. During the war morale was in part sustained not by the empty vessels of patriotism but by accepting war objectives and methods as a displeasing, if essential, national vocation, and distilling some of the resultant complaints and grievances through comedy channels. Robb Wilton was the leading exponent of that process.

Programme
MAKE 'EM LAUGH

Jimmy James

PILGRIM OF COMEDY

Hutton Conyers: No, it's an elephant.

Jimmy James: I don't suppose it makes any difference to you whether it's male or female.

Bretton Woods: It wouldn't make any difference to anyone but another elephant.

Jimmy James: I shall have to stop you going to those youth clubs.

About the turn of the 1950s I enjoyed my happiest evening of light entertainment. Appropriately this happened in every comedian's first choice summer spot, Blackpool, and on the Central Pier at that. The two main acts were Morecambe and Wise, on the verge of comic fame, and the nonpareil Jimmy James. Both, as was the practice, did a piece in each half, so that one could savour some ninety minutes of matchless comedy.

As Jimmy James puzzled and chattered through one of his unbelievable conversations, one of the group I was with whispered: 'Christ, he's the spitting image of Ack.' Ack was my father, whose affection for music hall, along with an adherence to Manchester United and a devotion to Lancashire County Cricket Club, formed his cultural bequest to his son. Suddenly a likeness I had never noticed was only too apparent, and, since then, I have not been able to think of them apart. Maybe the similarity is one of the reasons why Jimmy James remains my favourite comedian of all time.

Both my father and Jimmy James were stocky, barrel-chested northerners of late Victorian vintage. Jimmy James was born in Stockton-on-Tees in 1892, son of a steelworker-cum-amateur clog dancer, and himself a singer until in his thirties he turned to comedy. Both had heavy features, like those a child might knead and pummel out of his first piece of clay – deep set eyes, with bulging, baleful eyeballs, dark, full eyebrows, a wide, creased forehead, a snout of a nose, wrinkled pouches for cheeks, protruding, cushiony lips, highly prominent ears and a neck curtailed and thick. There was something canine, too, about the faces. Perhaps it was that compound of gruff, hail-fellow friendliness and brooding, heavy-lidded sadness which some dogs manage to convey.

For many of his sketches Jimmy James appeared to wear my father's suit, one as unpressed as their creased countenances, one redolent of fifty-shilling tailors, demob suits and the utility clothing which made the tailoring of the late 1940s vapid and unflattering. With a bowler hat or a trilby pressed hard and firmly back, both seemed to give the impression of fading, quietly unsuccessful turf accountants.

Then there was the cigarette. Jimmy James used the cigarette brilliantly as his major prop in every sketch, while my father, a lifelong eighty-a-day man, had fingers soaked practically tangerine with nicotine. Neither can be imagined without that unhealthy adjunct, at a time when, in the post-war years and before the health menace had properly been appreciated, smoking was a national addiction. Standing on one side of a football ground, one could note, during a gloomy afternoon, a hundred flashes of match or lighter every second in the crowd opposite, like an urban ignis fatuus, and about as delusive.

It was, however, the similarity of their conversational style which was most striking. Both were excessively anxious to mix,

'Jimmy James was, in legitimate or light theatre, the supreme stage drunk of all time ... His secret was simple. Other actors and comedians perform drunkenness; Jimmy James played the drunken man who believed himself sober.

'He utilised the cigarette brilliantly as his major prop in every sketch.'

to communicate and to socialise. To the point sometimes of
embarrassment, and whomever he happened to find himself
beside, my father, never in other respects the most energetic of
workers, would exert himself manfully as he attempted to build
some conversational bridge, however frail and transient. He
would float an endless series of gambits, eager to uncover some
link, no matter how flimsy and temporary, for a productive
relationship. Likewise Jimmy James. In a literary philosophy
alien to both their gregarious, masculine natures, E. M. Forster,
in *Howard's End,* provided their motto: 'only connect'. Both
endeavoured to reach the other bank and make that connection.
Such keenness to span the chasms meant often that not only did
they put their feet in it but they suffered a few duckings of
discomfiture joyously borne. In his portrayal of the early
morning drunken homecoming, Jimmy James committed a *faux
pas* of gargantuan proportions. Gazing blearily up at the tall,
unimpressed policeman, he asked 'What time are you due back
aboard ship, sailor?'

Jimmy James in the fullness of his career placed this
outgoing, sociable disposition, tricked out with the inevitable
cigarette, at the service of three comic masterpieces. The first
was the intemperate reveller who approached the law in so
cavalier a manner. No one doubts that, in legitimate or light
theatre, Jimmy James was the supreme stage drunk of all time.
From the *Twelfth Night* of Toby Belch and Andrew Aguecheeck
to the Glasgow to which Will Fyffe totteringly belonged,
intoxication has been a theatrical staple, but Jimmy James, so
to speak, outdrank them all. His secret was simple. Other actors
and comedians perform drunkenness; Jimmy James recognised
that the inebriate is unaware of his condition. He played the
drunken man who believed himself sober.

The pit orchestras of the late forties, sometimes no more than
seven or eight assorted violinists and trumpeters, were ideal for
the purpose of Jimmy James's introductory number. 'Three
o'clock in the Morning' wheezed and scraped its shaky tell-tale
melody across the auditorium, and then, just as one supposed
nothing was going to occur, Jimmy James emerged in a trail of
cigarette smoke, stage left. Mysteriously, he found himself in the
foreign rig of full evening dress, with a shiny topper jammed far
back on that broad pate where normally a derby was stuck. One
collar wing had liberated itself. Occasionally he whispered
'shhh' confidentially to the audience. He lurched with the
ponderous precision of the accustomed boozer who thinks he can
handle his liquor; he stuttered with that pedantic emphasis
which betokens the same. The cigarette was, as ever, held in his
left forefinger and thumb, the other fingers delicately bent like
the dowager's at a vicarage tea. He would swing his arm in a
gigantic, swooping arc, attempting, sometimes without success,
to steal an inhalation as the cigarette nose-dived past his

quivering, tobacco-hungry lips. Every few seconds the shooting star of that glistening fag-end would rush into that same spectacularly irregular orbit, all the while his right hand just pushed, with underlined nonchalance, into the pocket of his sagging trousers.

In the main, he used three drunk sketches – 'The Spare Room', when he arrived in the bedroom at 3 a.m., and 'The First Night' which featured the policeman, together with a domestic sketch, 'Sober as a Judge', in which he explained to a suspicious wife why he had been out all night. His second masterpiece, no less funny, requires lengthier explanation because the elements were more complicated. Jimmy James, in his John Collier suit, was flanked by his two sidekicks. One, Hutton Conyers, named after the Yorkshire village, was a mophead with a long coat à la Harpo Marx, while the other, Bretton Woods (after the venue of the 1944 international conference), was a lanky, sorrowful, gangling figure in a tight suit and check cloth cap. The former hectored and carped; the latter stammered diffidently. They were played by a number of people, and, later, the latter figure became better known as Eli, and was played by Jimmy James's nephew, Jack Casey. Rather like the Will Hay trio, they provided the two other sides of the conversational triangle, equal sides but of different qualities, adjacent to Jimmy James's base.

They were introduced as his discoveries, and their discoverer reminded the audience that rain was likely if this pair had travelled so far up the river. They made him uncomfortable, even irritated, but he nursed them along with a kindly sympathy. He was always anxious to connect, willing to pursue manic discussions politely and completely. Hutton Conyers constantly posed him one of the most notable questions in music-hall history: 'Hey, are you puttin' it around that I'm barmy?' Jimmy James countered this belligerent inquiry as disarmingly as he could. 'Why,' he might have asked, 'are you trying to keep it a secret?' Their principal conversation piece concerned a shoe box in which, improbably, Hutton Conyers kept jungle animals. There was, for instance, the giraffe presented to him in Nyasaland. In what I always found one of the funniest possible asides during this bizarre dialogue, Jimmy James would interpolate, with the sincerest conviction, 'lovely people, the Nyasas'. The counterpoint of such ordinary touches with the craziness he accepted with but mild surprise and just a little exasperation, created a pattern of rich humour.

It would be established that Hutton Conyers was the Member of Parliament for Scunthorpe ('Do they know about it?' asked Jimmy James in worried tones) and that it was in the unlikely position as foreign secretary that he had been presented with the giraffe, as company, perhaps, for the two man-eating lions received on similar duties in Egypt.

Jimmy James:	Where do you keep them?
Hutton Conyers:	In this box.
Jimmy James:	I thought I heard a rustling.

(As 'this is going to be a long job', Jimmy James sends Bretton Woods for a couple of coffees.)

Hutton Conyers:	Are you telling him about the giraffe?
Jimmy James:	No, I'll tell him now. *(to Bretton Woods)* He's got a giraffe in that box.
Bretton Woods:	Is it black or white?
Jimmy James:	I'll ask him. *(to Hutton Conyers)* He wants to know if the giraffe is black or white.
Bretton Woods:	No, the coffee I mean.

(The conversation turned to an equally mystical elephant, and Jimmy James stared incredulously at the shoe box under Conyers's arm.)

Jimmy James:	No, it couldn't be. Is it male or female?
Hutton Conyers:	No, it's an elephant.
Jimmy James:	I don't suppose it makes any difference to you whether it's male or female.
Bretton Woods:	It wouldn't make any difference to anyone but another elephant.
Jimmy James:	I shall have to stop you going to those youth clubs.

At last he plucked up the courage to ask Hutton Conyers whether he kept the elephant in the box, and Hutton scoffed at this proposition, on the grounds that there was 'no room', even allowing for Bretton Woods's suggestion that the giraffe might 'move over a bit'. Hutton Conyers claimed that the elephant was in a cage.

| Jimmy James: | Of course. And where do you keep the cage. |
| Hutton Conyers | *(with Jimmy James in immediate echo):* In the box. |

The unhinged air of mystery hanging over this reasonless trio was emphasised by one's ignorance of their origins. When Jimmy James appeared as the late-night reveller, surprisingly clad in his Astaire outfit, there was no explanation of whence he came or how he had acquired his topper and tails. Similarly, Conyers and Woods (often played, which must have contributed to the group's superb teamwork, by James's close relatives) seemed to be voyagers from nowhere. The solid comforts of their manners and exchanges only heightened the question surrounding their identity. It was an injection of mysteriousness into ordinariness which was not unlike some of the themes developed much later and much more sophisticatedly by dramatists like Harold Pinter. Nor is it too pretentious to recall that Jimmy James had a little of their fastidious ear for the half-hidden oddities of everyday language.

Jimmy James – 'dressed like a fading, quietly unsuccessful turf accountant'.

Jimmy James toyed lovingly with every sentence. He enjoyed talking humorously and he never told a joke. In his bluff north-country tones, he prided himself on the rhythms of his language, and it was this comic melodic line, rather than the witty thrust, which captured the attention. Having an abhorrence of scripts, which sometimes left both his colleagues and his producers weak-kneed as he conversed his sunny way without them, he was the prince of ad libbers. His linguistic invention made other purported fast respondents – Tommy Trinder or Ted Ray – look lame or, at best, reliant on computerised memory rather than native wit.

He added two famous visual effects. One was to turn to his right to address Hutton Conyers, who, at that exact second, chose to lean back and look behind him, leaving Jimmy James staring into space. He adjusted rapidly to his left, by which time his henchman had resumed his original position. Each time he turned to speak to one of them, this practised, rapid misjudgement of near-colliding heads occurred. Accompanied by snorts of surprise, it was as if three cockerels suddenly decided to weave and peck about them. Almost as difficult to transmit in words as this was his treatment of his constant companion, the cigarette. As in the toper's cameo, the cigarette, fastidiously held, would, like the arms in the army salute, travel 'the longest way up'. Sometimes its journey was in vain, but when those rubbery lips did manage a swift draw, the exhalation was a moment of wonder. By a lateral shuddering motion of his lower jaw, his tobacco-pouch cheeks released puffs of smoke to left and right and up and down in bewildering quick succession. Like an erratic injun smoke signaller or one of those humanoid Disney railway engines, he punctuated the conversation with bursts of cigarette flak.

Then, to end the seamless robe of their discourse, the threesome turned to song. 'I've got a letter here', Jimmy James would announce, 'from a singing lighthouse keeper in Bootle.' There was anguish in his choking effort to find the note: 'fah, fah, fah, fah, fah,' he would croak and carol at varying pitches, before belting out a chorus of something like 'Oh what a night it was, it really was a night' in what can only be described as pub style and tempo.

I am indebted to Jimmy James's son, James J. Casey, for a wonderful story about this finale which illuminates the whole comic world of his father. Now the BBC's Senior Light Entertainment Producer, he was, as Cass James, Bretton Woods for several years. When Jimmy James tried the note for the song, he would vainly attempt to engage the help of the pianist. 'That piano's damp, isn't it?' he would ask. Or 'Is the pianist playing at a dance?' he would inquire. Turning to the violinist, he would again ask for the note, and it is worth recollecting that pit orchestras in many theatres at that time may not have been over-proficient. Once more he failed to achieve the note, and so he upbraided the conductor.

Jimmy James: That's an old fiddle, isn't it? An old fiddle.
Conductor: It's an old master.
Jimmy James: Pardon.
Conductor: It's an old master.
Jimmy James: He's an old – what did you say?
Conductor: It's an old master.
Jimmy James: He's an old – oh, the fiddle, yes, yes, I see.
(At this point both stooges leaned over and whispered by way of explanation into the master's ear.)
Jimmy James: Yes, so did I at first; no, old master, the fiddle.

A simple enough tale, but on Cass James's first appearance he leaned over and just mumbled anything. Afterwards his father was furious. 'What the hell were you mumbling about in the old master gag?' His son said, 'Nothing; I was just whispering "rhubarb".' 'Don't rhubarb me,' said the livid parent. Cass James then said, 'Alright, I'm supposed to say "I thought he said bastard".' Jimmy James replied, 'Well, bloody well say it in future. How the hell do I know what you're going to say until you say it.' As his son says, this taught him more about timing than any other single thing in his life. Jimmy James was, in his son's phrase, 'the supreme timer' because his reaction could not have been more perfect – it was based on the fact that he didn't know what the stooges were going to say! One final postscript to this anecdote. The 'pardon' to the conductor in that dialogue has, in its timing and pitch, been revived successfully, as all television viewers will confirm, by Eric Morecambe.

Jimmy James died in 1965, having worked to within a twelvemonth of his death in his early seventies. At the prime of his career, just after the war and into the fifties, he enjoyed the commendation of a solitary royal command performance, where he performed the third of his comic masterpieces, now well known, although its origin – and its originator – are often forgotten. His lecture on the cooking of fish and chips revealed those two vocational hazards, the permanently cocked arm of 'batterer's elbow' brought on by long years of sieving and plunging in the sizzling vats; and the fluttering eyelid of the chipster's 'permanent wink', a nervous blink consequent on hours spent at risk from flying splashes of fat. Especially in tandem, the overt manifestations of these two occupational complaints looked excessively camp. And yet the explanation was not only innocent but liable to excite a valid sympathy.

For some of us the immediate post-war years had their innocent aspect and they excited a sympathy, valid or invalid. It was, of course, something to do with moving through adolescence at that point, and, in consequence, seeing answers as well as questions in bold capital print. The 1945 general election, for what is now the middle generation, was the first major domestic political event of their lives, and, after what had in effect been many years of national or coalition government, two front benches of character and gifts faced one another in clear-cut contest.

But surely there was an artlessness about that time, inexplicable in terms of mere youthful aspiration. It was in part the overlap of wartime camaraderie and the delight in well-earned victory. It was not euphoric: there were few of the noisy junketings of 1918. It was more a quiet satisfaction. It was in part the promise of the socialist dawn, the promise brighter for its surprising nature. Despite the villainous problems of peace, here was a Labour government ready to reform society drastically and not revert to the sad practices of pre-war years.

The issues were plain as a pikestaff. The collieries and the railways were to belong to the people. You may love or detest the notion, but there it unavoidably was. Mourn it or celebrate it, the dismemberment of the Empire – especially the granting of independence to the Indian subcontinent – was starkly apparent to all. It was only later that all sides realised that things were not so simple – that mines and trains perhaps had to be nationalised to save them from extinction – when all the sophistries and complexities of public control or national liberations made themselves manifest and when there seemed little difference in working for or being the customer of a public monopoly or a large private company.

It was a time of great public issues and great public activity. British Railways was soon to become a national institution, and, as such, a ready target for comedians, while on New Year's Day 1947 the new National Coal Board took over not only 1,700 pits but lots of other oddities, ranging from 140,000 houses to holiday camps and abattoirs. Even given the material limitations, housing moved on apace. In 1949, against a target of 200,000 houses well over half a million were built, together with another quarter of a million repaired homes or temporary buildings. New private residences were restricted firmly and expenditure on them carefully watched: the emphasis was on the public sector. In the financial field, especially with the severe eye of the puritanical Stafford Cripps on the exchequer, egalitarian policies were in the air. Clement Attlee claimed by 1950 that the gap between the highest and the lowest paid in Britain was narrower than in the Soviet Union.

The whole structure of public finance, public economy and public welfare revolved around Aneurin Bevan's National Health Service. July 1948 was the appointed hour, and, again, it was a straight bout, with Bevan opposed by that doughty champion, Charles Hill of the British Medical Association, who but lately, as the Radio Doctor, had been advising the nation on

Will Fyffe – like Jimmy James he was a great stage drunk.

its earthier physiological practices. Within a year, 40 million had NHS cover, a fifth having dental treatment and an eighth obtaining spectacles. Almost 200 million prescriptions were issued. The undammed surge of pent-up demand demonstrated the need for such a service which, at those prices, cost £400 million annually, and, after defence, was the largest enterprise in the country. It was a gigantic stroke carried out against the spirited opposition of many doctors; it was vivid drama with, according to choice, goodies and baddies.

Some of the comradely mood of wartime survived, and the acceptance of 'fair shares' continued. By 1950 much of this had eroded, with the shining gleam of what Bevan called 'the revolutionary moment' tarnished. Gruesome winters, troubles abroad, strikes, the black market, overplanning, the public exasperated by rationing – the hard blacks and whites of the earlier confrontations gave way to blurred, shifting discolorations.

It was an austere, even dull, time; but its very plainness had, or so many felt, a serene, hopeful and fulfilling quality. One recalled that, historically, eras of a gaudy and riotous character had often been unstable and lacking in harmony. There was a feeling of openness and of fairness. Soon there might be disillusion, scepticism and fragmentation, but, for a while, the tang of social idealism was in the air. This is reflected culturally, at least in the popular arts, where genuine sentiment struggled with gratuitous sentimentality. J. B. Priestley, Graham Greene and others published their novels, and twenty million each week watched British films like *Brief Encounter* and *The Third Man*, the Wilding–Neagle romances and the early Ealing comedies like *Kind Hearts and Coronets*. Right prevailed on the radio, safe in the varying hands of folksy Wilfred Pickles and Buchan-like Dick Barton. A time, then, of jovial greyness, perhaps as near as we shall ever reach to that combination of ingenuous enthusiasm and stoic severity which appears to be the hallmark of revolutionary zeal from Cromwell and Robespierre to Tito and Mao. The ubiquitous headscarf and the sombre suit typified the latter aspect, just as the prevailing urge for decency and fair play in matters like education and health typified the former.

Jimmy James exemplified some of these traits. He had none of the brash assurance of the Edwardian stars, let alone the glitter of a Ken Dodd or a Max Miller. He was more akin to George Formby senior than his merrier son. Neither had he the gloomy cynicism of Les Dawson, nor even the head-shaking minor anguish of Robb Wilton. The late forties, and Jimmy James with them, seemed to say: 'We won't get caught again in overblown, vain aspirations, like the twenties, but where there's life there's hope and it's worthwhile making the effort.' His was a restrained good-heartedness, a determined earnestness to resolve

Sid Field, here seen in his famous 'Address the ball' golf sketch, openly admitted a great artistic debt to Jimmy James.

97

Dave Morris, pebble-lensed manager of Club Night. *Like Jimmy James he was pestered in his acts by northern eccentrics – ''as 'e bin in, whack?'*

the problems beset him by late-night revelry or manic compatriots, but qualified by a proper sense of the dismalness of reality. In the interests of promoting one who eight years running had been champion European chipster ('Beat Joe Davis three times. Of course, he's a fair snooker player, but he's rubbish at the chipping') or of reaching some rational compromise in his interminable debates with Hutton Conyers and Bretton Woods, he would talk garrulously and amiably.

It was a friendly and affable sociability, yet it was tinged with a breath of sorrow, a realisation that things would, perhaps, fail to work out satisfactorily, but that one should not shirk the endeavour. Some commentators have seen in his wellnigh lunatic rapport with his two colleagues a hint of menace. I certainly never picked up that vibration. He was much more the pilgrim, keenly, sadly aware of the limits of the human condition, but valiant "gainst all disaster' – a John Bunyan among comedians – in his attempts to improve man's lot.

The theatres of the 1940s and early 1950s were an appropriate forum for that kind of comic pilgrimage. My father would take me to a main-line Manchester railway station on Sunday mornings to watch the comings and goings of shows and acts booked by the week. One can imagine Jimmy James, on the steam trains with their newly painted BR or in one of those oblong-shaped saloons of the post-war era, travelling slowly and deliberately from Preston to Portsmouth or Warrington to Wolverhampton. In the flaking theatres of towns that read like the roster of the Football League's current divisions, he would assemble, along with a few fellow artists, for 'band call' on Monday morning, offer superb fare for twelve performances, and then onward, ever onward, to Walsall or Oldham. Gaunt theatres for a gaunt age! And Jimmy James's acts needed little of tinsel and sheen to support them. Sometimes he had a simple street backdrop for his drunkard's promenade; otherwise nothing, except the inexhaustible supply of cigarettes.

Such theatres were stark frames for the development of his great gift. He could fantasise seriously within them; it was the near-credibility of his fantasies that was so impressive. It was the instant, solemn quality of his invention which caused his fellows to think of him, to use a possibly misleading term, as the finest ever ad libber. The story is told of his being asked by a television production assistant, rather condescendingly, to say of what exactly his act consisted. 'Now I'm glad you asked me that', he replied, 'because we've been a bit worried about it – well, you were worried, weren't you, Eli? You see, when we open on the trapeze and we're hanging there upside down – in the Chinese costumes, of course – we swing, and as we swing we sing "By a Blue Lagoon She's Waiting" in three part harmony. Now that'll be alright because the camera can move (Eli, it can move *with* you, you see). But it's the finish that has got us worried, sir, when we get the bowls of goldfish on the strings and we spin 'em on our teeth and they go right out – it's what you call centrifugal, Eli, centrifugal – will the trapeze be wide enough. . . . And, by the way, have the Chinese costumes arrived yet?'

In the authentic ring of what, in his obituary, the *Guardian* called 'his voice of Durham Clay' and with what, in an *in memoriam* piece ten years after, the *Guardian* called his features of 'melting rubber', it was all too believable for the shaken listener.

It is interesting to observe the *Guardian* paying him that rare dual tribute. He was not lionised in his day by royalty or by what Jimmy Porter called the 'posh Sundays', nor for that matter did he have the mass following of Formby or Miller. No cult formed around his name, and for many he may be the least recollected of the comedians described in these chapters. It is curious that he was not more appreciated. There are a number of answers, and they each have the insipid taste of the 1940s. First, he was a creature of the theatre, when the theatre was on the turn. Up to the 1930s the theatre was make or break for the popular entertainer. Then, gradually, the cinema, then records, wireless and, finally, television became other, often premier, vehicles of fame. The 1940s marked a kind of halfway house, with the theatre already on its decline into anonymity. Jimmy James was unused to and scornful of the deadeningly strict scriptings of radio and television; the former robbed him of his fine visual appeal, the latter of his creative relationship with 'stooges' or an audience. Possibly even the less pacific atmosphere of clubland would have not quite suited him. He was, indubitably, a theatrical first and last, which meant that his talents were never broadcast as widely as they deserved.

Second, it is likely that his performance was a trifle outlandish for the conventional souls of the 1940s, bred on the accepted traditions of pantomimes, seaside concert parties, cross-talk acts and stand-up comics on the radio. After *ITMA* and until the advent of *Take It From Here* (roughly the immediate post-war period) radio did little more than offer a showcase (like *Variety Bandbox*) for comedians such as Derek Roy or Reg Dixon. One can scarcely use words like 'sophisticated' or 'subtle' for Jimmy James, but the ruminant nature of his meditations meant that he was a little beyond the chance or occasional theatre visitor. While never the stuff of a small minority's cloistered patronage, his admirers, firm in their allegiance, were the regular, almost professional devotees of the music hall.

Third, one wonders how much he sought massive popularity. He was a most serious but jauntily independent performer. His chief interest was really in the actual portraits he painted. These were pastiches worked out each evening, variations on the three running themes of chipster, drunk and stooges,

*'We three from "Happidrome",
Working for the BBC,
Ramsbottom, and Enoch, and me'*

99

Larry Grayson used to study the disjointed rambles of Jimmy James's monologues in order to polish his own style. Tony Hancock was another who adjudged Jimmy James his master – 'the same care with language and the same angle of almost credible pseudo-realism'.

according to the state of his own personality and the personality of the audience. It was not so much an obsession with becoming ever more perfect or – as Ken Dodd envisages the comic muse – extending its range ever farther. It was more the compulsion lovingly, twice nightly and at occasional matinees, to make manifest that comic muse in a highly personalised style. That being the purpose, it mattered little if it was the Palladium (where, as number two to several of the Americans who topped the bill there after the war, Jimmy James enjoyed fine critical acclaim) or first house, Monday evening at the Workington Empire. It was like a painter who, having adopted an individualised approach, fills canvas after canvas in the same distinctive manner. Each night Jimmy James breathed life, a little varied but basically the same, into his characters, irrespective of his whereabouts or his watchers. It might have been L. S. Lowry discovering endless permutations, seemingly unworried as to how they might be received, on the bent angularities of his east Lancashire townsfolk, many of them not far removed in gangling stature from Bretton Woods himself.

Fourth, this spirit of independence typical of the forties was very pronounced. Gone was the forelock tugging of long ago and the servility which was to be found in music hall as well as on rural estate; gone, too, was the surly bitterness of the anti-establishmentarianism of the pre-war years; while the scratchy agitation of the sixties was in the future. It was a defiance, dignified, non-violent and not unfriendly. It was a refusal to be pushed around, but without any hysterical reactions. Jimmy James sometimes fell foul of important impresarios; he never became screechingly twitchy, nor did he ever yield. If it meant working the second-grade halls, he never flinched, but without rancour recognised that a more rickety easel and a less extensive palette made no difference to the consummation of genuine artistry. Such solid intransigence was perhaps part of the early post-war mood, but it ensured that Jimmy James never had the chance to leap nor would he have deigned to crawl into instant stardom. Coupled with that must be his own engaging habit of aligning gigs with race meetings, again a symptom of his refusal to take show business at its own shallow valuation, although it is ironic indeed that while the greatest ever stage drunk was a lifelong abstainer, he surrendered to a compulsive gambling which along with his liberal spirit made him thrice bankrupt.

But as he negotiated his ceaseless round of chain-smoking drollery, Jimmy James was, by the late forties and early fifties, carving significant benchmarks for the future. However slightly or accidentally Jimmy James may have reflected the spirit of those times, in one respect he mirrored them accurately. The years of the 'silent revolution', so-called, proved, in the view of some social historians, an immensely strong formative influence on the years that followed. The 'social evolution' of welfare politics, a mixed economy, relaxed morals and all the consumerism and technology of the atomic age originated in those times. Along with everything else, the next quarter-century of British comedy, planned for its own mixed economy of radio, television, cinema, theatre and night life, began there, too. In the political and cultural family trees it always seems a bit of a back-handed compliment to call people like Chaucer, Robert Owen or Adam Smith the Father of something or other. It credits them with the invention, but implies they were not quite adequate or lucky enough for its full maturation. In calling Jimmy James the Father of Post-war Comedy one recognises the discoverer, and feels that it was fortune rather than insufficiency which led to his lack of top-level recognition.

There were some contemporary imitations. There was 'Happidrome', with its close-knit threesome. Harry Korris as Mr Lovejoy, the theatre manager – 'ee, if ever a man suffered' – stood exasperated betwixt the stage manager, Cecil Fredricks, as Ramsbottom, and Robbie Vincent as Enoch, the idiot call-boy. 'Let me tell you,' announced Enoch weekly, following this with some declaration such as 'I've got blue blood in my veins.' 'What d'you think I've got,' asked an irritated Lovejoy, 'dandelion and burdock?' The formula was a little artificial. More creative were the activities of another scoffer at scripts, the ebullient Dave Morris, pebble-lensed manager of *Club Night*. Like Jimmy James he was pestered by northern eccentrics – ''as 'e bin in, whack?' was the repetitive query of one, not too far removed from Conyers's constant question about the news of his barminess.

Stage drunks by the dozen trod gamely in Jimmy James's unsteady footprints. Drink has always been a mainstream subject of the music hall, with Frank Randle, as the vulgarly aged and besotted hiker, a leading example. 'I'll be glad when I've had enough,' he used to complain between enormous belches. It was Freddie Frinton, however, who more slavishly copied Jimmy James, down to the top hat, tails and the uncontrolled cigarette.

Jimmy James's influence on those who learned from him rather than copied him was the more important. Roy Castle, that warm-hearted if never profound musical clown, gave up his own act for three years in the early fifties to do further education as Hutton Conyers. The plaintively effeminate Larry Grayson carefully studied the disjointed rambles of the James monologue in order to polish his own style. Sid Field, whose intensely brief, perhaps overestimated, contribution to the history of comedy fell precisely into that initial post-war era, confessed a great debt to the master. Morecambe and Wise, in duologue, often pursue a drift, verbal and visual, which is reminiscent of Jimmy, Hutton and Bretton *en salon*. Eric Morecambe is reported as saying that he uses Jimmy James's material for two reasons – as a tribute

Roy Castle gave up his own act for three years in order, as Hutton Conyers, to partner Jimmy James.

101

and because it's very funny, but mainly because it's very funny. On the distaff side, Hylda Baker's trysts with the silent, looming Cynthia are a kind of feminine edition of Jimmy and Eli.

The influence of Jimmy James has spread wider than may at first be apparent. Tony Hancock adored Jimmy James and judged him his mentor. On examination, and allowing for the East Cheam subculture, the flow of the Hancockian subconscious had the same care with language and the same angle of almost credible pseudo-realism. Then there was the moment on a 'Parkinson' chat show, when Michael Parkinson (himself a lifelong admirer of Jimmy James) had as his guest Peter Sellers, who fell into an entranced reverie as he recalled the nights in the wings sitting at the feet of the comedians' Gamaliel. Ken Dodd sees Jimmy James as a meaningful influence, particularly given the acute grasp of his timing. Frankie Howerd watched, learned and graduated; in general, his whole conversational air, at once sociable, world-weary yet defiant, bears the James trademark. Robb Wilton said of Jimmy James that he was the 'greatest timer' who ever performed, whereas, in an interesting and attractive exchange of critical fellowship, Jimmy James would say 'There's only one timer in the business, and that's Robb.'

A few months before he died, his fellow artists presented a gala benefit night for him in London. It was a rare occasion, and, obviously, its intention was to help him through his financial problems. It was also a Festschrift, the token of tribute of the successful students to their tutor. Jimmy James was like the Oxbridge don who never becomes a populariser, telly pundit, or best-selling author, but who has won the respect and affection of his colleagues for the perception and seminal influence of his tuition. Jimmy James is variously known as 'the comedian's comedian' and 'the comedian's teacher'. A connoisseur's comedian, he had both a loyal and faithful public following and the total appreciation of those severest critics, his fellow comedians.

As the Britain of the late forties, recovering from war, stalwartly tried to recreate and send forth notice of its social democratic intentions, so was the entertainment industry realigning and reconstructing. Foremost among the creators of fresh veins of comedy was Jimmy James, and the contorted spirals of his cigarette smoke will drift eternally down the galleries of music-hall memories. I confess to a nostalgic affection in recalling Jimmy James and the post-war period when my father saturated me in theatre (and when the immortal 1948 Manchester United team won the Cup and Lancashire last won the County Championship). But even allowing for such sentiment, Jimmy James was still the Brutus of comedians, the noblest of them all.

Programme

MAKE 'EM LAUGH

Max Miller

COCK OF THE COMIC MIDDEN

She said, 'Will you come up to my flat for coffee and games.'
I said, 'Don't bother with the coffee.' Well it was raining
outside, and there are only two things to do when it's
raining, and I don't play cards . . . 'Ere!

They called Beerbohm the incomparable Max, but his namesake on the halls might have claimed the epithet for himself. However, where the author and caricaturist used his gifts, in his own words, 'well and discreetly, never straining them', Max Miller certainly eschewed such reticence. In his own manner as outrageously witty and as resplendently rigged as Sir Max, he too became a cult figure, but Miller's was a cult of the majority and not of an aesthetic minority.

Londoners seem to make totems of their comedians, as of some of their other artistic figures. George Robey and Marie Lloyd in the earlier generation were lauded, while latterly comedians like Sid Field, Max Wall and Max Bygraves have enjoyed the same peculiar kind of worshipful attention.

There has also been evident an element of pathos in comedians well loved in the metropolis. It is an old tradition. Jack Pleasants delighted London audiences with his nicely modulated rendition of 'I'm shy, Mary Ellen', every syllable tortuously wrapped in embarrassment, whereas, of course, Charlie Chaplin was ever the premier exponent of that finely balanced combine of mirth and sadness. Sid Field apart, the years since the war have witnessed the at times uncomfortable endeavours of Norman Wisdom or Charlie Drake to achieve something of that difficult balance.

It may have been Max Miller's refusal to indulge in that often cheapened sentimentality alongside his humour which endeared him to me. Of all the southern-based comedians I appreciated him the most, chiefly for the dapper economy of his comic attack. Consider extracts from his celebrated assaults on an admiring audience at the Metropole or the Holborn Empire or another of the several haunts where he served up his spicy mix. Poised over the footlights, crouched towards the audience, his delivery was unbelievably rapid, spattering his clientele like a friendly light machine-gunner:

> 'Ere's a funny thing happened to me this afternoon. A girl said to me 'Hello, Max.' I said 'I don't know you.' She said 'It's my birthday; I'm twenty-one today.' She said 'Will you come up to my flat for coffee and games.' I said 'Don't bother with the coffee; I'll come up.' Well, it was raining outside, and there are only two things to do when it's raining, and I don't play cards. 'Ere!

Or, less bawdily, but at breakneck speed:

> I just came back from my holiday and I always have a wonderful time because I've not got one of those wives who says 'Where have you been, how much did you spend, who have you been with?' She doesn't say that: she comes with me. . . .

Jack Pleasants (above) used to sing 'I'm shy, Mary Ellen', in the bathetic tradition often popular in London, but Max Miller never indulged that type of sentimentality alongside his humour.

I went to buy a two-year-old horse, about four years ago. The man said 'Come inside; I've got the horse you're looking for.' So I went inside and there was this horse lying on the floor, with a lot of blankets and sheets covering 'im up. 'E said 'That horse'll cost you some money.' I said 'It's dead, isn't it?' 'E said 'No.' I said ' 'Ow much d'you want for it?' 'E said 'A pound.' I said 'A pound! Blimey, 'e hasn't got any shoes on.' 'E said 'Well, 'e's not up yet.' Well, eventually I got the horse outside and tried to get on, but every time I tried to get on 'e kicked, and 'e kicked so hard 'e got his foot in the stirrup. I said 'Listen, if you're gonna get on, I'm gonna get off.' Well, I got on the horse and it fell down, so I picked it up, 'cos I'm an hefty lad, you see. So I get on again and it fell down again, and I told the man; I was there. I said 'This horse is no good to me; everytime I get on, 'e falls down. You've got some nice horses there; you've got about eight or nine in the string,' I said. 'I'll take the one in the middle.' 'E said 'Don't take the one in the middle; they'll all fall down.'

One must visualise in the mind's eye as well as listen with the mind's ear. He was at the other extreme, sartorially, from his contemporaries, the Will Hays, the Jimmy Jameses, the Billy Bennetts, the Robb Wiltons who all affected a studied unkempt ordinariness if not a seediness of dress. Max Miller dressed like a peacock paying court. His plumage was the blaze of his exotic-flowered suitings, and their tumbling show of oranges and greens. Above that irrepressibly sharp, shrewd and self-confident face was ever the trilby, normally a dazzling white, just a shade too small, perched at the most impudent angle. The audience erupted at his appearance. He would try to quell their excitement with mock discomfort: 'No, come on now, shurrup, shurrup,' he would plead. They laughed not at the outrage of his clothes, as they might have done at the Ugly Sisters grotesquely costumed for the ball; they laughed at the audacity. How dare anyone, they laughed, wear clothes like that? For, in a curious way, he was not overdressed, any more than one could accuse the peacock of being unduly gaudy. In a word from one of his own lyrics, he was 'snappy'.

Given the premise of audacity, there was no denying his smartness. Granted the bravado of his style and material, his dress was as absolutely appropriate as the mute's sombre black at a funeral. The white trilby was reminiscent of his own hero, G. H. Elliott, the chocolate-coloured coon, absurdly enough a native of Rochdale. Several comedians – Ken Dodd is another – revere the memory of a singer or dancer rather than a comedian. Here was another snappy dresser, usually in white to set off the dark make-up of his hands and face, and who with his clear-cut tunes like 'Lily of Laguna' and 'Hello, Susie Green' sang with flute-like clarity and soft-shoe danced with engaging simplicity.

Like G. H. Elliott, who lasted many a long year, dying in show-business harness aged 79 in 1962, Max Miller made no pretence to profundity. He lacked the depth of characterisation of a Jimmy James or a Robb Wilton, but he never acclaimed otherwise. And not for him the clumsy attempts of fellow comedians to switch to sentiment, in a pathetic effort to show (literally and metaphorically) the itty-bitty tear on the clown's mask. He would, correctly, have despised such tawdriness. He was concerned only to amuse his audience with a devastating and twinkling exposition of racy humour, as mouthed by a gleeful and self-confessed lecher. Just as Jimmy James stayed sober as a judge while he performed his stunningly accurate drunk, so did Max Miller remain, off stage, a relatively reserved personality. These make for interesting social comparisons when one recalls the effect of alcohol on Sid Field or Frank Randle, the effect of unhappy marriage on George Formby or Arthur Lucan, and the effects of both on Tony Hancock.

On stage, however, Max Miller took his preening, cockerel stance a step further. He looked like a male bird in mating colours; he dressed like one; he pranced and feinted like one, dodging back to peer into the wings in case of eavesdroppers, shimmying forward to the footlights to exchange his confidences more personally. His voice sustained the illusion. It was chirpy, vain and effervescent, with a slightly shrill, thrush-like note. His exercises in dancing had the same traits. First there was the mating-call of his catchy tweet-tweet of a signature tune:

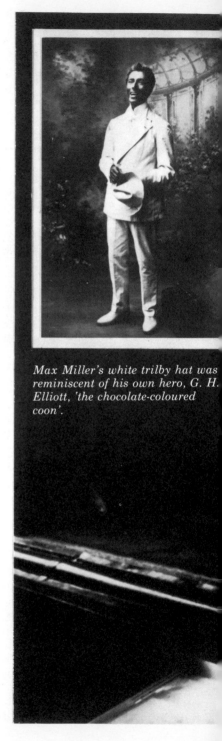

Max Miller's white trilby hat was reminiscent of his own hero, G. H. Elliott, 'the chocolate-coloured coon'.

> I fell in love with Mary from the dairy,
> But Mary wouldn't fall in love with me.
> Down by the old mill stream
> We both sat down to dream,
> But little did she know that I was thinking of a scheme.
> Now on the farm said Mary from the dairy
> We've got the finest cows you've ever seen.
> I don't do things by halves
> I'll let you see my calves
> And they're not the same shaped calves as Nelly Dean.

'Dance,' he would proudly announce, and, softly and effortlessly, he would tap and jig and circle, the intermittent badinage timed musically to a nicety – 'Goin' rahnd, lidy, goin' rahnd; I don't get giddy, do I? I'm gonna do the splits now. 'Ere *(to the drummer),* give me a touch-up with the wire brushes, will you? 'Ere we go.' Then, with legs about a yard or so apart, he would conclude: 'That's all; half tonight, half tomorrow night. Good night, gal.'

His material, of course, was legendary for its blueness, for its deliberate self-advertisement of a massive sexual prowess. It was saloon bar stuff; it ran him into trouble often enough, but more

106

for his brash refusal to conform than for the horrendous nature of his scripts. It was golf and fishing stories applied to the sexual act. It was an unending boast of ceaseless sexual pursuit, rather like the conversation one might, cartoon-style, expect a couple of randy old roosters to be having behind the barn.

But it was at this very point of dispatch of the humour that Max Miller pulled his neatest trick. He talked directly to the women, not the men, in the audience. He completed his unified presentation of the cock robin by concentrating on the hens among his audience. Any recording of Max Miller is liberally strewn with addresses to the ladies. His overt arm beckoning – ''Ere a minute lady, 'ere a minute' – often signals the beginning of another tale. Or ''ere missis', which was his other eagerly repeated call for feminine attention. To complete the birdlike attitude, he used 'duck' repeatedly to make his exhibitionist appeals.

Neville Cardus said George Duckworth was the Chanticleer of wicket-keepers; Max Miller was the Chanticleer of comedians, shocking hundreds of Pertelotes into delighted embarrassment by his suggestive patter. So much was he able to modulate the tenor of this vulgar bravado that he could interlace good clean stuff and still evoke the same response. Listening carefully to his audience reactions on record, it is the slightly high-pitched tone, with a hint of squeal within it, which is most noticeable. The men watch, listen and enjoy, almost as a second-phase response, which now includes the ecstatic discomfort of their own womenfolk.

His real name was Thomas Henry Sergent and he was born in 1895 and died in semi-retirement in 1963. He had several manual jobs, rather removed from the indolent image he eventually exhibited on the stage, and early theatre work included membership of an army concert party in India – shades of *It Ain't 'alf Hot, Mum*. Indeed, his accents always carried the urgent, brassy, half-cockney jangle of the regular soldier.

He was born in Brighton, and worked the metropolitan area non-stop until the late 1950s. He rarely did any other than the stand-up act; it was uncommon to find him in a sketch, let alone in a pantomime. If it seems right that George Formby operated on the Wigan–Blackpool axis, it was equally just to find Max Miller travelling the Brighton–London line. London, the temptations of the wicked, cosmopolitan city; and Brighton, traditional location of the stolen, adulterous weekend – Max Miller gloried in the naughty allurements and connotations of both spots.

He was, first to last, a gold nugget of music hall, his dexterous command and his necessary vulgarness both being of its essence. Others have tried to bear his banner forward. Arthur English, in the fifties and sixties, and more lately Mike Reid have tried to achieve fame as fast-talking cockney comedians. Jimmy

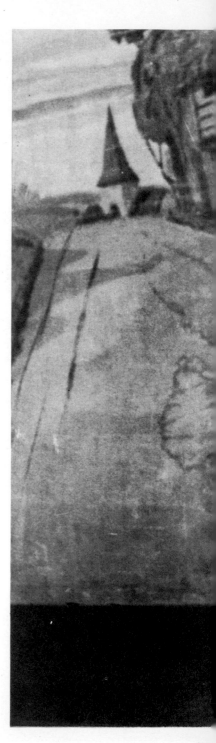

'Poised over the footlights, crouched towards the audience, Max Miller's delivery was unbelievably rapid, spattering his clientele like a friendly light machine-gunner.'

Tarbuck, a great admirer of Max Miller, has tried to adapt urban Liverpudlian to that formula, but, despite his undeniably pleasing disposition, neither he nor the others have quite borne the standard bravely enough.

Perhaps they missed two points. First, that Max Miller's propositions were consciously directed at the women in the audience, whereas many comedians with a tendency towards sexual innuendo endeavour to appeal to the men. Some commentators have seen something a trifle homosexual in the Miller brand (which he imprudently encouraged with lines like 'Well, what if I am' as they giggled at his florid plus-fours) but his pose was much more that of the male on show. He was never really as arch as Sid Field or Larry Grayson.

Second, they have tended to mistake his high-speed approach for volubility. On precise reckoning, Max Miller never wasted a word or a breath. His repetitions and interjections were required to underline the impertinent spirit he so triumphantly conveyed. His imitators have relied on talking a lot at pace, rather like the American Civil War general who spoke of getting there 'fastest with the mostest'. Max Miller's dress, deportment, dance rhythms and delivery were only as extravagant as was minimally indispensable. Again like the strutting bird, each note and movement was the least complex necessary and always in strictest control. If cockney comedians are those who chatter with abandon even to the point of gibberish, then Max Miller is not to be numbered among them. He was an Alfred Jingle, if not a Sam Weller.

In real terms, however, the inheritors are doomed, for Max Miller was the last of the line, rather than the first. He may have been, as Israel Hands said of Cap'n Flint, 'the flower of the flock', but he was the final, if the most exotic, bloom. This is one reason I place him in the fifties; not because he reached his peaks then, for the thirties and forties would then be more relevant, but because he faded then, and with his fading a classification of comedy ended. His own ringing conceit – 'there'll never be another' – was the Cheeky Chappie's wry irony.

There is a personal reason. Because he tended not to intrude on our northern fastnesses, I never saw Max Miller until the fifties, and then it was at the now demolished New Theatre in Cambridge in the mid-fifties. It was already a dying theatre, as the art-form it presented was wellnigh deceased. Dingy, dusty, invariably empty, with brown-grey portraits autographed by old-time stars, it was scarcely fair to watch Max Miller in those surroundings. I remember the cadaverous, lanky bass-player, the fat-fingered pianist, and the severe-looking Miss Mattie on the violin as much as anything from that theatre. But, for Max Miller, some of the crowds returned, and his shining cheek flared and carried the evening brightly.

With a fittingly ironic bitterness, England's variety theatres closed in the decade in which England's role as a world power ended. Britain lost its Empire, quoted the historians; and, as a fifties second-rate funster would have added, not only its Empires, but its Hippodromes and Palaces too. Loss of imperial grandeur was but one element. The two other incisive events of the fifties were the Hungarian Revolution, when the monolithic potency of the new Russian empire could no longer be underestimated, and the Suez blunder, when the new American empire sharply reminded us that Palmerstonian gunboat diplomacy was gone forever. Suez was so feeble and agonised a flick of the old beast's carcase as to be acute in its embarrassment. It proved vividly what was suspected.

There were or seemed to be compensations. At home the consumer boom and rising living standards gradually became more evident, while in the fifties television became the art-form of the national community. The addition of commercial television was linked overtly with the increasing emphasis on material well-being. It was largely a decade of glossy advance in goods and products, and the restrictive self-interest that that implies. These were the years of the hidden persuaders and some called it the age of affluence. Others felt that the comradely co-operative spirit of the forties yielded to a more abrasive and self-seeking motivation in the fifties. Social changes are swings and roundabouts. The greater public-mindedness of the forties perhaps carried grimness, dullness and a certain mediocrity in its wake. The egocentric and hedonistic thrust of the fifties brought frank and unabashed pleasure to millions and the sheer security of pounds in the pocket and products in the home. Rationing vanished; the number of motor cars sprang from just two million to five million over the ten-year period; six times as many new private houses were completed in 1960 as in 1950; expenditure on large durable goods such as furniture, carpets and radios increased over three times in the period; the sunbaked beaches of southern Europe began to exert their appeal; the refrigerator and the washing machine became as indispensable to the newly-weds' semi-detached as the aspidistra and the gas ring had been to the terraced home of the thirties.

It was shallow enough, even where it was unadulterated, and by the seventies that 'live now, pay later' tab had to be picked up by an ailing economy. It was like a huge national hire purchase exercise, with the country seeking a quick pleasurable return then repaying the mounting instalments in sorrowful leisure. Did we gather our rosebuds while we might, partly to hide from the nasty fact of oblivion as a world power? Possibly we did, just as Max Miller might have advised us to do.

Curiously, the worn metaphor of the political stage was more relevant than usual. The Suez debate was arguably parliament's last grand *pièce de théâtre* – a colleague of mine had an uncle, a venerable canon of the established Church, who took his umbrella and smashed his television screen when Hugh Gaitskell's features and anti-Suez sentiments were presented thereon. The fifties were a Conservative decade. With the ponderous dignity and painful gait of the dying Henry IV, Winston Churchill crossed the stage and took his final curtain, whilst that erstwhile Prince Hal, Anthony Eden, lamentably failed to quicken the Agincourt pulse like Henry V.

They gave way to possibly the greatest showman-politician since Disraeli. Harold Macmillan was something between an Edwardian player-manager and an ageing circus ringmaster. He apparently delighted in Peter Cook's skilful send-up of him in *Beyond the Fringe,* in some contrast to Harold Wilson's reported anxieties over *Mrs Wilson's Diary.* With a patrician calm and

The Cheeky Chappie and the Old School Tie. Max Miller sharing a microphone, unexpectedly perhaps, with the Western Brothers at a Foyles' Luncheon in 1940 held in 'honour' of 'Lord Haw-Haw of Zeesen'.

113

imperiousness he dismembered the Empire and provided *panem et circenses,* in retrospect a Nero rather than a Tiberius. He was billed theatrically as Supermac, or, as when he purged his cabinet like a bloody gladiatorial spectacle for the masses, Mac the Knife. Happiest of all, he had a catch-phrase like all the best comedians – 'you've never had it so good', almost a transcription of Tommy Trinder's 'you lucky people'. I remember a wedding banquet at the end of the fifties. It was a buffet – itself a sign of the times – and there was even caviare. There was a touch of the Joe Lamptons about it, with fitter's son marrying director's daughter, and it was the good life in abundance. Toward the end of a convivial evening, a lifelong Labour Party activist grinned blearily at me over his champagne glass and through his cigar smoke. 'We've never had it so good,' he said.

Unluckily, the content has proved to be as theatrical as the style, and at no time in the last century has the light theatre more nearly echoed the sounds of the body politic than in the fifties. Desperate for custom, the theatres turned from twice-nightly variety to the touring revues, usually packed with the standard, if stationary, nudes. The very titles of the shows betoken the extremes of panic and despair, and even their battered punnings are more memorable than the shows themselves – *Fig leaves and Apple sauce, The Bareway to Stardom, Strip, Strip, Hooray, Knights with Eve,* and so on. To be fair, they had that ghastly attractiveness of the third-rate (as opposed to the tedium of the second-rate) which made *Opportunity Knocks* so riveting. Phyllis Dixey was a much less than dumb doyen of that naked brigade, while Jane from the *Daily Mirror* was also on the rounds, a chubby, lisping, strawberry blonde, with Fritz her poodle. I watched her at the Hulme Hippodrome, where now the bingo-caller drones on the spot where she did her global tour – eskimo on sledge, clad only in white muff, then on to Hawaii. With the pit orchestra vamping and pumping brassily, she introduced herself in mincing soprano:

> I'm Jane, and it's plain that I'm only a model;
> I can't dance, I can't even croon.
> And the doggie I coddle is also the model
> You see in the popular strip-cartoon.

Max Miller would have felt at home with such shenanigans, but he would presumably have felt some contempt for the trivialisation of his craft. It was a pitiable effort to add a frenchified note of titillation to the proceedings. There was even an anglicised *Folies Bergère,* absurdly starring Harry Worth. To be fair, it was more entertaining than a Parisian version of the late fifties – a long-drawn series of extravagantly ornate tableaux. If only the British 'girlie' shows, as they were

Laurence Olivier's portrayal of Archie Rice in John Osborne's play The Entertainer *recalled for many people the music-hall figure of Max Miller.*

sometimes called, had emulated the fast-moving gaiety and stylish verve of the *Moulin Rouge*. This had the kind of panache which Max Miller so colourfully personified. But, in the English theatre, it was rather like a failing school which adds a little French to the syllabus in an eleventh-hour attempt to survive.

However, fail it did. It was a grand compensation that one of the most dazzling exponents of the dying art was present at the wake. It was like a firework display in the back garden, when Father carefully retains the most flamboyant rocket to end the night with a blazing cascade.

The metaphor of decaying theatre and declining society was aptly spelled out in John Osborne's play *The Entertainer,* subsequently filmed in 1960 under Tony Richardson's perceptive direction. Laurence Olivier, on both stage and screen, created the central role of Archie Rice, replete with all the banal shabbiness and false hope of the second-rate performer on the

115

downward slope. It is said Laurence Olivier visited several small-time theatres to watch such comics in action, and his was assuredly a bravura performance. The social decadence is underpinned by the counterpoint of Archie both with his father Billie, survivor of a more golden era of music hall, and with his sharp-witted daughter, and, all in all, the play offers a memorable view of life and light theatre in the fifties.

There is a sense in which Osborne's verbal and Olivier's thespian virtuosity made it almost impossible for Archie Rice not sometimes to be a roundly comic figure in the vulgar tradition of the music hall. At these moments it was Max Miller who was most readily recalled. There was the same crispness about some of the patter ('a little song entitled "The village bell won't ring tonight; the vicar's dropped a clanger" '); the same deftness of confidential glance and footwork; the same heavily scored innuendo; the same allusion to homosexuality, along with the unremitting insistence on supercharged sexual athleticism. Of course Archie Rice was, in the stark phrase of American film critic Steven H. Scheuer, 'a showbusiness louse', and both Olivier and, in the play's provincial tour, John Slater always communicated that empty horridness alongside the wheedling catch-phrases. Max Miller was much more happy-go-lucky, perhaps happier because luckier, than Archie Rice, to the point where what on paper sound extremes of conceit and vanity were embraced by audiences as other agreeable aspects of an all-round amiable persona.

The luck lay in standing at a fulcrum of social and moral change. Over the spread of his career, British society had dared sufficiently to cock a snook or two at what Matthew Arnold termed 'strictness of conscience', but it had by no means cast all or even most aside as it was to do in the sixties. That vacillating, occasionally hypocritical, position was ideal for Max Miller. It was a society which could not quite decide whether it was permissive or not. A community which could allow nudes on stage and then refuse to let them move is a compromising, undecided community. Max Miller's shade of blue would have been forbidden by theatre managements and others before the thirties, while in the sixties it would scarcely have been considered 'warm' in the huge theatre clubs of the northern circuit.

Like Oliver Wakefield, a rather more upper-crust but nonetheless uninhibited raconteur, he was banned from radio several times, and that confirmed his unholy reputation. An interesting feature of this stance was the emphasis on marriage. In the Miller canon it was an institution under attack, but it survived. His alliances with the many females who apparently fell for his perky charms were, by definition, adulterous, but there was no hint of marital breakdown, let alone the liberated bacherlordom of the sixties.

The careers of George Formby and Max Miller ran over parallel times. The material of both intrinsically concerned the sexual relation, but where George Formby was forever peeking and shying away from womanhood, Max Miller was gloriously insatiable in its pursuit. It reflected a recognised cultural distinction: the bashful northern lad as the quarry, the unabashed London gent as the hunter. Max Miller acted as everyone, especially the ladies, expected a commercial traveller to act.

In stage terms he treated his wife abominably, cavorting his flirtatious way through dozens of extramarital exploits, many of which she uncovered. The wife, of course, has been a stock butt for comedians since the taming of the shrew and well before, but most comics narrate a rueful tale of henpeckedness. Robb Wilton never mastered the pragmatic Rita, while Al Read, particularly suited to radio, took on some of this mantle in the fifties, feigning a wife of similarly chilling interrogative skills; for example:

Unlike Max Miller, who treated his 'wife' abominably, Al Read used to feign a wife of 'chilling interrogative skills'.

> When are you going to get a latch on that gate? I'm sick and tired of telling you about it. It's been bang, bang, bang, bang all night again. I don't know what's come over you, you've no interest in this house at all. Anything for the easiest with you . . . then when you roped it up nobody could get in or out. All that fuss we had when the men came to empty those dustbins. I won't forget it, I won't. I'll give 'em 'We're bin-men, not mountaineers'.

Dozens of comedians, right up to Les Dawson at the present time, have insisted on their persecution by wives of great unpleasantness and little attraction. 'My wife's a very funny woman . . . ' was a favourite opening gambit of Max Miller and many others since. But, apart from his jaunty transcending of her suspicious observation, Max Miller added another dimension to marital comedy, one rather more the vogue in the media and literature of the fifties than in the pre-war era, and one uncommonly entered by comedians. This was the notion of the unfaithful wife.

He usually made some reference to this infidelity during each of his acts. Not that he was nonplussed by her indiscretions. He apparently found them as light-hearted and amusing as his own, and here was a distinct step away from Victorian and early twentieth-century hypocrisy, where extramarital adventures by males were regarded as hearty and normal and by females as the ultimate in moral degradation. So Max Miller, in his tiny way, was a liberating spirit, anticipating a time when many more accepted that what was saucy for the goose was saucy for the gander. Whatever one's ethical view, it was, at least, a less cant-ridden approach. Thus:

A fellow came up to me the other day and said, 'Maxie, I don't want to cause any trouble between you and the wife; I know how you are; fifty-fifty in everything.' 'E's right. We never argue, the wife and I. And I'll tell you why. She does as she likes and I do what she tells me. And I tell my wife everything. Well, everything I'm thinking. The neighbours tell her what I'm doing. But he said, 'Max,' he said, 'watch her, now watch her,' he said, 'because I think . . . ' And when they start to think, well, it makes you think, doesn't it? So I thought, 'Well, he might be right; you don't know; so one night I went home, *one* night; I went in the back way through the kitchen, through the living-room, into the drawing-room. I got in the drawing-room – there they were. I'd caught 'em, sitting on the settee and he'd got his arms round her. So I looked at the wife and I said, 'You can turn that up. I'm not standing for that. I'll take a lot from you but not that.' So I look at 'im. I said, 'Who are you?' 'E said, 'I'm the coalman.' The coalman! I said 'Where's your horse and cart?' 'E said, 'I didn't bring it in' – 'e was clever. Well, I lost my temper; well, you would, wouldn't you? A thing like that and I've got a shocking temper. I went outside; I didn't half kick his horse – 'ere!

Max Miller ensured that generations of innocent coalmen, milkmen, window-cleaners and other domestic visitants would be the subject of unsavoury jokes.

This element had a slightly transatlantic flavour, and Max Miller's cosmopolitan attitudes seemed to convey this taste of worldliness. Indeed, to the northerner, there was a twang of American in his accent. It was in the fifties that the United States, having secured an enormous beach-head in the cinemas, invaded the whole of our entertainment industry, with notable victories in records and television. The American assaults on the theatre were on two fronts. There was the musical theatre, with *Oklahoma* in the late forties triumphantly in the van, and other hits, right through to *West Side Story,* in buoyant support. There was variety, with singers like Guy Mitchell and Johnny Ray and star entertainers like Danny Kaye and Judy Garland making highly successful landings on our shores. The Palladium, often the far from stately home of Max Miller, was the command post for this invasion, and it was here that Max Miller fought some of his liveliest and most defiant rearguard actions on behalf of dying variety.

It is interesting that, in style, he was not unlike the American entertainers at their fast-talking, wise-cracking best. Although his content had a more political element, Bob Hope at his peak sparkled verbally with the same dexterity as Max Miller. It could be said that Miller was perhaps the only British comedian who could rival the Americans at their own strategy of brash,

Max Miller was not unlike the American entertainers at their fast-talking, wise-cracking best, although Bob Hope's content had a rather stronger political element.

self-assured fire-power. His third and final royal command performance in 1950 made this point dramatically, when, in yet another show of cheery independence, he overran his allotted time by an appreciable amount, delighting the audience and doubtless sending his fellow artists near to hysteria; fellow artists who included several transatlantic stars like Jack Benny and Dinah Shore.

Overall the United States defeated the home team, just as Hungary crushed the vanity out of English football with their soul-searing victory at Wembley in 1953. As in politics, so in entertainment and sport, the new imperialism to West and East was growing dominant. In the entertainment industry what loosely had been called variety could not survive. Other comedians would survive and develop to meet the harsh modern demands of the television screen, the summer season and Christmas spectaculars, and, later, the exorbitant allure of the theatre clubs. But Max Miller's milieu, that twice-nightly parade

'the hilariously precise antics of Wilson, Keppel and Betty' – who had also to face the decline of music-hall variety at the same time as Max Miller.

of oddly assorted acts, was destroyed.

With that destruction went the demolition of a thousand theatres, and the subsequent concentration of live theatre in the biggest cities or boldest seaside resorts. From our evening papers passed those compact advertisements, alerting us to the prospect of witnessing score after score of soubrettes, cross-talk duos, ventriloquists, instrumentalists, conjurors and specialities.

Many will recall the hilariously precise antics of Wilson, Keppel and Betty in *Cleopatra's Nightmare,* a veritable symbol of variety and thought by good judges to be its finest manifestation. Jack Wilson, an English dancer, met an American dancer, Joe Keppel, and, with Betty Knox, they formed an eccentric sand-dancing act before the First World War which brought them international fame from the Palladium to Las Vegas. They enjoyed royal commands in 1933, 1945 and 1947, and they have been shown at least three times on television in the last year or so as a mark of all that was most immaculate and most satisfying about variety. Their impeccably timed cameo of work and play in the Arab bazaar rightly earned both the earlier adulation and the later tributes. But what of in between times? I was prepared to travel at some length to watch them, and eventually found myself in dilapidated halls, scheduled for closure, until, deep in the fifties, I last saw their names low on a bill posted on a wall for a third-rate revue in a declining Lancashire mill town. Their act was unchanging, one might say as eternal as the sand they sprinkled for their sandals to grate and rasp upon. But suddenly there was really no place for it, and a torn poster on the derelict wall of a now declining once humming textile centre told it all.

Max Miller, no mean soft-shoe dancer himself, did manage to sustain his counter-offensive to the end, and, of course, his highly accomplished skills and easygoing personality would have carried him to the comic fore in any age, whereas peculiarly 'variety' acts would have fallen along the way.

However, and in retrospect, his role was to be chief prospector in variety's gold-rush, and to ensure that, as interest and excitement dwindled, it was not all tawdriness and nastiness. Over thirty and more years he was a comic equivalent of those death-defying heroes of film and box in whom a staid public could see their more dangerous fantasies portrayed from the security of plush stalls or armchair. Like such brave warriors, he courted danger, as he appeared to court a formidable list of 'girls-who-will' and 'girls-who-won't', to say nothing of 'girls-who-might'. It had its fragment of titillation, but its comic context saved the watcher and listener from an undue embarrassment about such carnal preoccupations. On record and tape now, one can gauge just how shocked the laughter was.

Max Miller was as bright as he was lusty and he was cock of the midden.

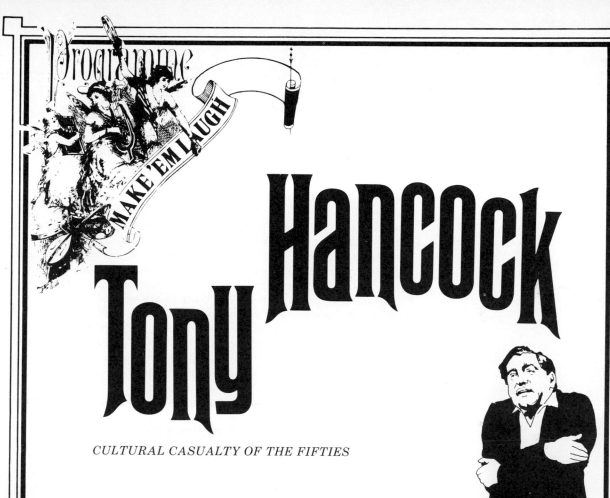

Programme

MAKE 'EM LAUGH

Tony Hancock

CULTURAL CASUALTY OF THE FIFTIES

'British. Undiluted for twelve generations. One hundred per cent Anglo-Saxon, with perhaps just a dash of Viking . . . I've always thought I was somehow different from the rest of the herd. Something apart . . . One of nature's aristocrats.'

If Max Miller had affinities with Archie Rice, Tony Hancock might, in part, be likened to Jimmy Porter. John Osborne's *Look Back in Anger* was first produced in 1956, and the shouts of protest, even the scuffles which occurred, confirmed that it made a radical theatrical statement. Perhaps Tony Hancock played a middle-aged, frustrated rather than an 'angry young' man, but there were similarities of approach. Both found themselves, apparently without means of support, in dingy residences, at 23 Railway Cuttings and a midlands top-floor flatlet. They were both declaimers, given to windy, verbose monologues about the triviality of their circumstances, with their companions listening quietly, maybe a little bored and occasionally a trifle irritated. They both swung from irascibility to forlorn resignation – anger is probably too incandescent a word for either of them. They tilted orally at the appurtenances of their condition (Jimmy Porter blasting the Church and royalty; Tony Hancock severely scolding the pettiness of minor officialdom) but they never attacked any root causes. Both were noisy and yet ineffectual.

Both were snobbish, yet scornful of snobbery, and much of the so-called 'angry' literature of the fifties was about class distinction of some kind. Jimmy Porter had two equally well-known literary confrères. They were Kingsley Amis's 'Lucky Jim' and John Braine's Joe Lampton, seeking and gaining room at the top. They were the symbolic trio of fifties culture, and interestingly each sought – respectively in the sexual, academic and commercial fields – to rise beyond his ascribed social station: indeed, all three married, as used to be said, 'above themselves'.

Tony Hancock constantly looked above himself. He had not, of course, Jimmy Porter's intellectual grasp, Jim Dixon's saving self-awareness or Joe Lampton's single-minded drive. But he shared with them, however romantically, that total dual distaste for one's origins and for one's destination, for what one was and for what one wants to become. The fifties were a time of unease. The 'silent revolution' of the late forties was over, the compactness and earnestness of the war and post-war era had become fragmented, and, despite the benefits, another kind of truth began to dawn. It was a truth about those whom the reformation had converted being faced by new problems set by the old establishment. Porter, Dixon and Lampton were the exceptions, the ones for whom the social revolution had brought alterations, like the working-class boy going to university or becoming company director. They were the children of the post-war social shake-up; they were the representatives of mobility. But, as it was not all change, indeed, as it was change for just a few, their upward mobility merely brought them into contact with the next immovable heights; hence the constant theme of working-class lad marrying upper-class girl. Tony Hancock would have recognised that deracination, and, in fact, felt himself to be a part of it. By way of contrast, the fifties also introduced the concept of the affluent worker, more self-seeking and cynical and less comradely and affable than the stock character of the thirties worker. The car, the continental holiday, even the private house and voting Tory might not be beyond him, in self-avowedly just reward for hours spent in the meaningless supervision of machinery producing inessential

goods. Arthur Seaton, of Alan Sillitoe's novel *Saturday Night and Sunday Morning,* made his appearance the same year as Jimmy Porter. If in Jimmy Porter one saw the *mobilisme* of some of the working class, in Arthur Seaton one observed the *embourgeoisement* of the rest. The former felt displaced and restricted; the latter acted selfishly and sceptically. Neither had loyalties: the one had lost them; the other had rejected them.

Consider pieces from these two famous passages. First the opening exchanges of a famed *Hancock's Half Hour* – 'A Sunday Afternoon at Home'. It is the one which exploited the longueurs

If Max Miller had affinities with Archie Rice, Tony Hancock might be likened to Jimmy Porter in John Osborne's Look Back in Anger *(1956). The photograph shows the original cast of Kenneth Haigh, Mary Ure, Alan Bates and Helena Hughes.*

Tony Hancock – 'the lad himself' – shared with Jimmy Porter, Jim Dixon and Joe Lampton – however romantically – that total distaste for what one was and for what one wants to become

of a tedious time so cleverly. I timed Hancock's opening statement on tape – it takes twenty-five seconds.

Tony Hancock:	Ahh, Oh dear. Mm, Oh dear, oh dear. Ahh, dear me. Ahhh. Stone me, what a life. What's the time?
Bill Kerr:	Two o'clock.
TH:	Is that all? Ahh, dear, oh dear. Ah, dear me. I dunno. Ah. Ohhh. Oh, I'm fed up.
Sid James:	Oi.
TH:	What?
SJ:	Why don't you shut up moaning and let me get on with the paper?
TH:	Well, I'm fed up.
SJ:	So you just said.
TH:	Well, so I am.
SJ:	Look, so am I fed up; and so is Bill fed up; we're all fed up; so shut up moaning and make the best of it.
TH:	Ahh.
Hattie Jaques:	Oh, look, it's started raining!
TH:	That's all we wanted. You watch, it'll go dark in a minute; we'll have to switch the lights on. I think I'll go to bed.
HJ:	You've only been up an hour.
TH:	That is by the way and nothing to do with it. I might just as well be in bed. There's nothing else to do. I wish I hadn't got up now. Your dinner wasn't worth getting up for, I'll tell you that for a start.
HJ:	Well, I don't know. I ate all mine.
TH:	That is neither here nor there. You also ate Bill's and Sid's and mine. I thought my mother was a bad cook, but at least her gravy used to move about. Yours, yours just sort of, sort of, just lies there and sets.
HJ:	That's the goodness in it.
TH:	That's the half a pound of flour you put in it. Oh, dear, what a life. Sunday. A rotten dinner. It's raining. And I've got nothing to do.
HJ:	There's plenty of odd jobs you can do around the house.
TH:	Oh, shut up. It's a day of rest. I'm not mending your bed again.

Compare this with a few lines from *Look Back in Anger,* another exposé of boredom on the Sabbath.

Jimmy Porter: God, how I hate Sundays! It's always so depressing, always the same. We never seem to get any further, do we? Always the same ritual. Reading the papers, drinking tea, ironing. A few more hours, and another week gone. Our youth is slipping away. Do you know that?

If literature and drama speak for and champion their age, then Tony Hancock was their veritable comic esquire of the fifties.

I was fourth time lucky in actually seeing Tony Hancock in the somewhat podgy flesh. Three times over the fifties I had journeyed to theatres to see him (twice starring with Jimmy Edwards at the Adelphi) only to find the 'indisposed' apologies mounted. Eventually it was into the next decade when I tracked him down on stage, this time, with Ronnie Hilton, at the Manchester Palace in 1963. He was experimenting in the provinces with a cabaret act and, truth to tell, it was not very compelling. He looked tired, even sickly and certainly cumbersome, and much of the material was a trifle jaded – the once famous pastiche of the Gaumont British News, the once famous Americanised crooner on the Johnny Ray model, the once famous reincarnations of Newton's Long John Silver and Laughton's Bligh and Quasimodo (ending 'Sanctuary! Sanctuary! Sanctuary much'). Five years later he was dead. Watching him then, one looked back in sympathy to his comical fitting of the fifties like a glove. He was not of the sixties, and did not survive them.

Still, it was good to have seen a great performer on stage, and to note the effective shifts of facial emphasis and to hear that unmistakable accent. How would Professor Higgins have evaluated it? Part repertory, part RAF-ish, part rakish, part ruffianly, perhaps of all the comedians described in this book Tony Hancock was the least imitable. George Formby, Max Miller, Ken Dodd, Frankie Howerd – they have all had their imitators; but who ever impersonated, with anything like success, that enigmatic figure from East Cheam and Earls Court?

His voice and face were his fortune. He had a face pummelled from dough, with chins and ears and cheeks and eye-pouches added like pieces to a fancy loaf. The nearest face to his might be that of Jimmy James or perhaps the French comedian Fernandel. All have papier-mâché physiognomies, with the pulp seemingly moulded into a hefty base and exaggerated lumps pasted on as features. The heavy-jowled countenance emphasised, for Tony Hancock, the brooding, introspective character of his comic persona. Occasionally there would be glaring flashes of smugness, those flares of conceit and complacency which would irradiate his whole face and especially his eyes. But one now remembers his face more in melancholy repose, eyebrows, cheek-lines and mouth all hanging downwards, upturned U-shapes, signifying that inner lack of tranquillity, like frozen pyjama trousers slung over a wintry clothes-line.

It was perhaps the concentration of attention on face and voice which made Tony Hancock a first-class radio comedian and the first, probably the finest, television comedian. It is worth observing the reverse. Apart from the rotund, rather ungainly, stooping posture, one remembers little of his bodily contribution to the characterisation. George Formby, with his duck-like gait and jutting throat, Max Miller, the adept skipping aligned with every laugh, Jimmy James, of the drunkard's precise promenade, Ken Dodd, striking his lunatic poses, Morecambe and Wise, with their elaborate round of jigs and hand motions, Frankie Howerd, crouched in obsequious defence – they were and are complete in their portrayal of funny human beings, of funny human bodies. Tony Hancock never achieved their distinction on the stage, as they have never attained his status in broadcasting. The radio brought his strange post-war argot and his belligerent, giddily ornate twang to the public for their undivided attention, while television caught his expression, sometimes vain, sometimes sorrowing, and thrust it into the living-rooms of the nation. In his last major television series, forsaking all company, he concentrated entirely on solo performance, and on one occasion he shaved and ruminated alone. The shaving mirror was the camera, and each television screen became his reflection, as millions thus looked into the mirror with him and shared his 'badger', his razor and his quietly spoken thoughts.

Tony Hancock appealed to each person in the singular, reaching across to each one of us, to buttonhole us individually, to invite our independent sympathy with his woes and complaints, with a view to provoking our private mirth. He attempted, with massive success, to establish an introspective and melancholy personality. This is not easy. Many drolls have been sad and have invited their audiences to chuckle at their miseries – Les Dawson does so today, just as Gus Elen ('I'm glad we've had a nice quiet day') and Jack Pleasants ('I'm shy, Mary Ellen, I'm shy') did long ago. But most of these confront you with their sadnesses and wear their bleeding hearts on their sleeves. Others have been introspective but reasonably cheerful: the commentator type of comedian – a Gillie Potter or a Jack Benny – is sometimes of this contemplative kind, musing but sane and balanced. Slightly outside the normal run of actual comedians, I would place Alan Bennett as premier in this class, with his byways of ironic and inner commentary built on a foundation of inward contentment and deliberate self-composure.

But Tony Hancock was both introspective *and* melancholy. He was perpetually soul-searching and as frequently soul-seared, yet his self-deception knew no bounds as he created flimsy, brash veneers of cocksureness. He did not thrust his sadness or his introversion at the audience. One had to perceive all this through the thin curtains of his hearty bravado. The only other comedian quite to achieve this was – although I never saw him and rely on my father's possibly biased testimony – George Formby senior. He was pathetic and woebegone, his all too real cough scorching his lungs, yet ever pretending that he was a gay and cavalier dog. His songs, such as 'I'm such a hit with the girls', managed to be both excruciatingly funny and excruciatingly painful. He was the most gauche of provincials, whistling in the dark of the metropolis. Tony Hancock transposed that guise to the fifties. He, too, was a provincial, feeling that it behove him to face the sophisticated metropolitan challenge, but that odd compound of self-delusion and insecurity shone frighteningly through all the time.

George Formby senior managed to convey this complex of emotions to a music-hall audience. Tony Hancock rarely managed this, but radio and, as if invented for him, television permitted him to identify on a one-to-one correspondence with a vast audience. Some might argue that there is a Falstaffian quality about that braggart posture, but this fails at the last – Falstaff ultimately had no illusions; Hancock maintained some shreds of vainglorious deception to the end; because he was self-deceitful, he was mystified by his fears. With voice alone or with close-up face to twos and threes in their armchairs, the magical correspondence was brilliantly possible. With the huge theatre audience it was much less possible. A theatre audience takes on its own character. It was never as cosy for Tony Hancock as for more relaxed comedians: he once remarked that audiences met secretly in Hyde Park to decide what character they would adopt for the evening. It reacts with composite emotion. Hence the outgoing comic, full of bonhomie, is so much more likely to woo and win that collective heart.

The diametric opposite – extrovert and merry – to Tony Hancock would be Ken Dodd, who, while admiring the other's skills, was disturbed by his excess of melancholia. Ken Dodd, exhorting a packed crowd to ever more extravagant heights of gaiety, takes on something of the evangelical revivalist. With merriment replacing religiosity, the corporate emotion is as infectious, consuming and, sometimes, unstoppable. Tony Hancock rather beckoned us to join him in the privacy of a humorous confessional. That lack of inner comprehension, hidden behind the Mitty-like imaginings of his vainglorious recitals, cut him out as a fifties figure. Sometimes an event does become the heart of a decade, and the critical nature of Suez had a strange show-business repercussion. For the only year,

Tony Hancock – 'his flimsy, brash veneer of cocksureness' – and perhaps his most effective partner Sid James – 'ever the Sancho Panza, continually trying to channel the wasteful tides of romanticism into lucrative pools'.

apart from war years, there was no command performance in 1956 because of the crisis, and the likes of Liberace returned home, candles unlit, smile still unzipped, keys unmolested. If ever there was an Hancockian adventure in stark political life, it was Suez. Its pretence, indeed its dishonesty, its bewilderment, its vanity, its fearful refusal to examine the psychology and the reality of the national condition – these were the grave defects of the Suez fiasco.

Imperialism ebbed swiftly. At junior school at the beginning of the war, there were quite grandiose affairs to celebrate Empire Day. Once I declaimed a verse in the part of and in self-eulogy of Cecil Rhodes, a white handkerchief tucked in the back of my cap to protect it from the merciless Mancunian sun. By the time I was teaching in the fifties that had almost gone, to be replaced by the rather wan and half-hearted (although, to be fair, equally politically motivated) United Nations Day. Yet the collapse of the Hungarian Revolution at exactly the time of Suez was the straw that broke the back of the leftist camel. The Russian brand of supposed Marxism no longer had a shred of credibility, and, for a generation, the doctrinaire left was bereft.

Jimmy Porter moaned that 'there were no good causes left', and Tony Hancock might well have agreed. Quixote-like, he searched for windmills at which to tilt. Many will remember his masterly role as a juryman in what, in my view, was his funniest TV programme, perhaps because it so accurately echoed the realities of that somewhat effete decade. After a brush with the judge for his theatrical response to the closing speeches (sneers for one counsel; a polite patter of applause and a patronising 'you will go far, young man' for the other) the jury retired. Another juryman was Sid James, ever the Sancho Panza, continually trying to channel the wasteful tides of romanticism into lucrative pools. Remember Sid James Mystery Tours on the occasion Tony Hancock was extolling the virtues of travel? A short tour of the Western Highlands was only seven pounds ten ... but 'meet at Aberdeen' lay in the small print. Many critics have in fact argued that when Sid James acted as his *alter ego,* as the foil, physically and philosophically offering the counterpoint, Tony Hancock was at his most entertaining.

In the jury room Sid James soon fastened on to the fact that the longer the session the heavier the expenses, and thus supported Tony Hancock as he swayed hither and thither. There was a sense in which Sid James was the tempter at the elbow, craftily mentioning a financial sideline to a Hancockian concept which brought a gleam to the master's eye and steeled his determination further. As a juryman, Tony Hancock was a suburban Henry Fonda in the tradition of *Twelve Angry Men.* But where Henry Fonda was convinced of the accused's innocence, Tony Hancock was convinced only of the role he felt obliged to play and was eminently indecisive about objectives.

First he persuaded the jury to vote one way, against their combined better judgements, and then, with the same rhetorical flourishes, moved them in the reverse direction. He espoused both causes, because neither was worthy nor dominant. On the grounds of civic liberty, he fought for guiltlessness; on the base of protecting society, he argued for guilt. Included in his florid oratory was a quintessence of Hancock, a line which summed up that half-digested and shallow intellectualism of which he was so cockily proud. Hammering the table as if at Hyde Park Corner, he cried 'What about freedom? What about liberty? What about Magna Carta? Did that poor Rumanian girl die for nothing?'

One of the two films he starred in (the other was *The Punch and Judy Man* made in 1962) was aptly called *The Rebel*, given that the title had ironic undertones, for his rebelliousness was always superficial, and ill directed. A more correct title for that 1960 film might have been the one chosen for the younger, agonising figure of James Dean in 1955, *Rebel without a Cause*. That was the problem. Tony Hancock had no stomach for the fight and no good fight to fight. So he sat among the newspapers and teacups of East Cheam, inventing self-adulatory pieces of nostalgia. The necessary snobbism of those imaginings was an essential aspect of the fifties. Perhaps the most popular of his television cameos (and it was later sold as a record) was *The Blood Donor*. Not only did this have present all the Hancock qualities, it exhibited them atavistically. There was the cause, the donation of blood, about which he huffed and puffed, while others gave it matter-of-factly, as if he was ready for slaughter on the ramparts of some idealistic revolution. There was the terror when, after shouting with anguish at the pinprick for the grouping test and which he presumed was the actual gift of blood, the doctor asked for a pint. 'A pint?' he said. 'A pint? That's nearly an armful.'

But it was the elitism which was most amusing. The discovery that his blood fell into a rare group confirmed all his most optimistic suspicions about himself. It was pure and English and aristocratic. It was blue blood. One can go no further in snobbery than the assumption that one's very life-blood is a special and noble fluid. 'British,' he explained, 'undiluted for twelve generations. One hundred per cent Anglo-Saxon, with perhaps just a dash of Viking.' And later, 'I've always thought I was somehow different from the rest of the herd. Something apart . . . One of nature's aristocrats.'

Harold Macmillan, who stage-managed the advent of affluence, was not guiltless in this matter. Himself married into the Devonshire family, a third of his Cabinet were related to him by marriage and a half were Old Etonians. It had an eighteenth-century ring although presiding over an era of extremely modern materialism. Tony Hancock, with a dab or two of his shaving brush, offered a passable impersonation of Harold Macmillan to his shaving mirror. It was a Cabinet he would have been delighted to join; instead he had to settle for – using a symbol taken from another Hancock piece – the plastic bandsman in the cornflake packet.

There was a little of Will Hay about this, for the pretension was cultural as well as social. Tony Hancock would thumb through the titles of classic books or reminisce about bravura stage performances or misquote with abandon: 'This is a far, far better thing I do now that I have ever done. Rembrandt!' But it was the telly which always caught his chief attention. He once spent an entire programme trying to find a spot to watch his favourite *Robin Hood* serial, when his own set was out of order. And he splendidly parodied that same mindlessness in his visit to the launderette, where he sat gazing entranced by the revolving washing and asking his neighbour 'Is there anything interesting on yours?'

Educating Archie with *Peter Brough and 'Archie Andrews'. Here Archie's tutor is Robert Moreton. A previous tutor was Tony Hancock. Ironically both men died tragically and early.*

In *The Bedsitter,* the programme he played entirely alone in 1961, he spent several minutes fiddling aimlessly with aerial, window and defective television set. Faced with a choice between a gangster series and Professor Bronowski, he rejected the latter, rationalising thus: 'He's all right on theories, but when it comes to adding up sums, he's right out of his depth.' Tony Hancock was especially happy with that kind of crushing ignorance. When he was standing for a parliamentary election, a questioner asked: 'What do you intend to do about England entering into the European Common Market, thus bringing about a more sound economic structure of Europe without endangering interest in Commonwealth trade and Imperial Preference?' Tony Hancock was very severe. 'Come now, sir,' he replied, 'this is no time for frivolous questions.'

But when one is done with all the political, social and cultural linkages between Tony Hancock and the fifties, one must turn to the technical connections. This is strictly the chief

On radio Hancock's Half Hour *followed in the tradition of* Bandwaggon *and* Much-Binding-in-the-Marsh *while the surrealist style of* ITMA *descended in the early 1950s to* The Goons – *originally four, from the left, Harry Secombe, Michael Bentine, Peter Sellers and Spike Milligan.*

distinction with Max Miller: If Max Miller was the last of the music-hall comedians, as variety declined in the fifties, then Tony Hancock was the first of the television comedians, as that medium expanded. Television licences numbered 200,000 in 1950 and nearly ten and a half million by 1960. Where Max Miller looked back over jostling years of crowded, cheerful theatres, Tony Hancock looked towards a future of home-oriented entertainment.

In 1954 the Independent Television Authority was created, alongside many other expansions of consumption and advertising. It is scarcely a coincidence that the bingo craze and betting shops were creatures of that age, and that the proletarian 'I'm alright, Jack' shared with the more bourgeois 'You've never had it so good' some claim to being the token phrase of the decade. In his book, *The Affluent Society,* published in 1958, J. K. Galbraith warned that 'to furnish a barren room is one thing. To continue to crowd in furniture until the foundations buckle is quite another.'

Tony Hancock played the cultural casualty of the affluent society, and, wryly enough, the brand new television sets – one to every five of the population, practically one in every home by the end of the fifties – enabled him to play it to a massive audience. But first he had to serve his apprenticeship on radio. A native of Small Heath, Birmingham, he lived much of his early life, when not at boarding school, in Bournemouth, where his father, a semi-pro entertainer, ran a hotel. Through him his son met a large number of showbusiness people. This kind of contact encouraged him to pursue a stage career, but, initially, it was most fitful – RAF concert parties, a Windmill booking, a few *Workers' Playtimes,* a summer in Bognor Regis, a flop on *Variety Bandbox,* and so on. Then, after a regular spell with Derek Roy in his *Happy Go Lucky* radio series, Tony Hancock became Archie Andrews's tutor in *Educating Archie.* That was in 1951, and, supported by his gruff catchphrase – 'Flippin' kids' – he became something of a star.

When one considers the broad range of comic invention for which he became famous it seems odd that a show like *Educating Archie,* written almost to a strict pro forma, could have been so influential on his career. I once summoned up the stamina, over three or four Sunday afternoons, to listen and note the thirty-minute programme. I reckoned there were fifty-two sayings, situations, characteristics and so forth which cropped up every week. The further eccentricity was that of a ventriloquist on radio, although I once asked a professional 'vent' of my acquaintance at that time what his personal opinion was. 'Peter Brough', he sniffed, 'isn't a ventriloquist. He's a child imitator, like Harry Hemsley.'

Nonetheless, it led to Tony Hancock's chief theatre bookings in the West End, and, in 1952, he found himself in the Royal

Variety Command Performance; a second followed in 1958. In 1954 *Hancock's Half Hour* commenced, with quality support in the guise of people like Bill Kerr, Hattie Jacques and Kenneth Williams. That weekly tryst with the hostile context which Tony Hancock faced with a strident, pompous and inaccurate buoyancy soon became extremely popular.

If one can retrace the lineage of radio shows to early origins, like referring philosophers back either to Aristotle or Plato, then where might *Hancock's Half Hour* be placed? To my mind, it follows the line of *Bandwaggon* and the service shows like *Much-Binding-in-the-Marsh,* with its development of funny but not grossly abnormal situations within a set and controlled environment. It was the other famous radio programme of the fifties – *The Goon Show* – which picked up the surrealist label from *ITMA*. Its immediate predecessor as the top comedy programme was *Take it from Here,* something of a hybrid, with the mock realism of the Glums and its pun-ridden extravaganzas on cinematic themes.

Tony Hancock, in fact, strode beyond the mere effect of realism: he took cliché after cliché and made his listeners identify with these, the clichés of their time, from the individual fruit pie to the fear of intruders. It is perhaps forgotten now that Tony Hancock, with the mixed coterie of Railway Cuttings, was the last of the great radio comedians. There has been enjoyable revue-type, rather university-like, radio comedy since, but no comedian since Tony Hancock and Al Read has commanded popular acclaim through radio broadcasting.

For, by the mid-fifties and with the inauguration of commercial television, the cathode tube replaced the wireless, especially in terms of star-making. *Hancock's Half Hour* transferred to television in 1956, and with it the script-writing duo of Ray Galton and Alan Simpson with whom, until 1961, Tony Hancock found the purest expression of his idiosyncratic line on the comedy of frustration and anxiety. Several of those half hours became regarded as classics, like the one in which he played a Walter Gabriel role in a mock Archers serial and the producers were keen to kill him off. His vocabulary enlivened the conversations of the time: 'stone me' and 'hooter' were practically his coinages, particularly when deployed in the context of one of his pseudo-intellectual ramblings.

In his 1958 command performances he superbly brought theatre and television together for perhaps the only time in his career. Few will forget his budgerigar act. He carried the impersonation well enough on stage, with a cage and its accoutrements in goodly proportion, while television adjusted the perspective to give a weirdly authentic effect. It was Hancock with a beak. He strutted and waxed superior; his petty whining was unabated; his genteel pretensions were rampant as he preened himself in the mirror; but he was resigned to the mournful truths of his existence. 'I suppose', he grumbled, 'I'll have to stick me head in the bell again before they'll give me some more millet.'

It was Tony Hancock's splendid utilisation of situation comedy on television which probably clinched what is now the dog-eared platitude of telly humour, namely that such comedy is preferable and that actors are likelier to handle it more successfully than comics. In the radio tradition of Robb Wilton, Richard Murdoch and Kenneth Horne, he was able to establish what in effect was the one-act play as the leading television comedy device. Nor should it be forgotten that Tony Hancock was one of the first to insist, when with a live audience, on producing the half hour in segments, rather than as a straight run through. This had an enormous effect on writing and presentation for the screen. The pressure, of course, was on the wealth of the material. Where a lengthy music-hall sketch might have carried someone like Harry Tate practically through their career, or the one-act play might run for months, the conjunction of both types on radio and television required a series of one-act plays, and, *Steptoe, Porridge, Dad's Army, Likely Lads* and *Till Death* apart, this has not been easy to sustain. On the other hand, the stand-up comic, doing a Max Miller act, has much more rarely succeeded on television.

This was a crucial difference between radio and television. Radio did manage to project comedians, from Arthur Askey and Sandy Powell onwards. Probably the only methodological common denominator of the dozen or so comedians discussed here is that they all, at some time, triumphed on radio. Some comedians, like Stainless Stephen and Al Read, scarcely needed to develop an extra-radio trade. There was the elitist pull of *Variety Bandbox,* the solid benefits of *Saturday Night Music Hall,* and the more mundane slot of *Workers' Playtime.* Comedian after comedian did his or her (Suzette Tarri, Hylda Baker) five-minute spot in a style television has never managed or perhaps wanted to manage.

Television is, naturally, about pictures, and sometimes this obsession becomes patently absurd, as David Frost once showed in his satire on the news bulletin, with every sentence being framed around yet another over-conscious still. Some variety acts prospered again as television expanded. Dancers, conjurors and illusionists and ventriloquists have all made a comeback, for, Peter Brough apart, there was no scope for them on the radio. There were a score of imitators on radio, like Afrique, Maudie Edwards, Florence Desmond and 'the Voice of them all', Peter Cavanagh, but, in turn, they lost out to the telly – one had to look as well as sound like the stars, and the screen became available eventually for Mike Yarwood. One or two comedians tried to find a compromise by using the techniques of television to create and exhibit a number of characterisations during the

136

same programme. Stanley Baxter, Benny Hill and Dick Emery are instances of this, although, apart from some inspired sketches from the first, they tend to suffer the perennial ailment of impersonators, namely frail material. Ronnie Barker is an interesting case of theatrical schizophrenia. He is the shrewd convict in *Porridge* and a gamut of characters in alliance with the less versatile Ronnie Corbett: is he comic actor or comedian?

Whichever it is, he has few peers. Since the fifties, singers and musicians have generally exerted a much greater thrall than hitherto, for they can be visually exciting. The transatlantic influx, which Tony Hancock cleverly parodied in his crooner take-off, began then, and now, compared with earlier times, it is the musical acts which top the television bills much more than comedians. The circus is another entertainment which is frequently seen on television, but on Saturday nights there has hardly been a comic in sight, apart from Bruce Forsyth and the genial pranks of *The Generation Game,* or Mike Yarwood.

Tony Hancock had the fortune to find his peak of performance at the conjunction of radio in retreat and television on the advance. He was the last of the great radio comedians; he was the first of the great television comedians. The question is: was he also the last of the great television comedians? Only Morecambe and Wise could, with any confidence, place themselves in the Hancockian televisual category, and, surely, much of their success is dependent on the transfer of their stage performance, carefully adapted, to television. By inventing for television the concept of the comedian-actor, Tony Hancock opened the door to comic actors rather than to comedians who might attempt to act. It is significant that Galton and Simpson turned immediately from writing for Tony Hancock to preparing equally fluent and funny scripts for two actors, Wilfred Brambell and Harry H. Corbett as Steptoe and Son. By the sixties there was scarcely television work for top-rate comedians. There would be some variety spectaculars with slots for comics and some feeble efforts to encompass comedians within the confines of domestic serials. But there has been little or no contribution by *comedians* to the progress and development of TV comedy since the end of the fifties.

Tony Hancock was so very rooted in the fifties that one is almost apologetic, looking for exceptions to the rule to avoid the accusation of contrivance. It was a coming together of content – the substance of his humour – and method – the arrival of television. But, as with George Formby, the private life also obtruded on the public relentlessly. Few would argue that Tony Hancock's professional quality was not, in the last years of his life, reduced by the instability of his relations with others and by his heavy drinking. It is a negative, but sadly accurate, point. Tony Hancock was not able to reproduce his fifties form in the sixties. If anything, and in a pother of insecurity, he relied even more on the ageing material of his earlier, happy days – the impersonations, the crooner, the news-reel, the cod-Shakespeare – and became unable to have confidence in new scripts.

It is shattering to read that *The Blood Donor,* so treasured a memory of every Hancock aficionado, was recorded with the almost total use of teleprompters and idiot boards. His growing difficulty in remembering lines had been accelerated by a minor motor accident, and Tony Hancock, at the point of production, could scarcely repeat one line of a script of forty pages. Sudden holidays abroad and sojourns in clinics and hospitals punctuated his later career; his memory was badly on the blink; and there were times when he let down colleagues and audiences outrageously. That unreliability which, I discover twenty years on, caused me to miss him on stage thrice, became ruinous and, conversely, it is a massive tribute to his genius and to the affection in which many held him that he was able to continue at all, as, one by one, he ruthlessly cut the supports that aided him. Agents, close friends and relatives, fellow actors – he treated them abysmally, perhaps anxious to prove that he was the only indispensable element. It must have been but cold comfort to them to perceive that he treated himself as brutally and unkindly and that, at the last, he was prepared as ruthlessly to cut out himself. He committed suicide one night in 1968 in an Australian basement flat, and his notes, scribbled on the back of a script he was trying to study, included the phrases: 'This is quite rational . . . but there was nothing left to do. Things seemed to go wrong too many times.'

Unluckily for Tony Hancock, these inconsistencies of character boded ill for one so heavily reliant on others for his material. He was not noted for his creative energy in that sense, and his reluctance to improvise was legendary and must have fed his anxiety about fresh scripts. Of course he contributed to those scripts, in much the same way as George Formby played a part in the composition of his songs or Morecambe and Wise, in conference, aid the development of their duologues. The likes of Will Hay, Robb Wilton and Jimmy James and, to a lesser but still marked degree, Ken Dodd and Les Dawson create their own substance, but, more than most, Tony Hancock had perforce to inhabit a world made for him by others. It was Ray Galton and Alan Simpson who most sympathetically and eloquently achieved this act of artistic construction. They wrote the memoirs of a petulant, childish, half-educated buffoon living first with his East Cheam ménage and then alone in his Earls Court flatlet. Tony Hancock played that character, and, although the character kept his name for itself, it should not be forgotten that that was the fashion of it. The relation between Galton and Simpson and Hancock was nearer that of novelist and character, than script writer and jokester. It was a world away from Bob Hope's scintillating displays of fast-talking humour, with a posse of writers loading the magazine of his deadly accurate light machine-gun.

It may be ostentatious to think of Henry Fielding or others in the tradition of the rollicking English comic novel. Interestingly, however, J. B. Priestley's character Len Braston in his novel *London End* was based on Tony Hancock, while the egoism and self-importance of Hancock is not unlike that of Widmerpool, that complex comic creation of Anthony Powell in his series of novels, *A Dance to the Music of Time*. But what one is arguing is that the script-writers of the audio-visual age need feel no embarrassment when classified with novelists and playwrights. Frank Muir and Denis Norden, particularly with some of their *Take it from Here* scripts, Ian le Frenais and Dick Francis, especially for some of the *Porridge* and *The Likely Lads* playlets, as well as Galton and Simpson, must be seen in this light.

This underlines the importance of Galton and Simpson for Tony Hancock. It is difficult to assess how much of his actual character, either in a professional or a personal sense, they assumed as a base for the Hancock of radio and television, and how much they invented from scratch. It is, in any event, immaterial. Dickens may have based Micawber on his father, but without *David Copperfield* Mr Dickens senior would be lost to us. Tony Hancock decided he could manage without the two co-authors. Their one hundred and fifty-odd film, radio and television scripts were abruptly forgotten; but no one was able quite to take their place, and, so to say, Mr Micawber reverted to Mr Dickens. It was 1961. The timing was exquisite: another decade was beginning, but Tony Hancock's career as a top-ranking and original comedian closed.

There is another uncanny analogy to be drawn in terms of Tony Hancock and the fifties. The nation struggled desperately to regain and earn some international status, and this was precisely what Tony Hancock attempted. Both failed in this, and, for both, the failure was crucial. Tony Hancock became extremely anxious to attain world-wide recognition, and he tried, without conspicuous reward, to find fame in the United States. He felt that true comic stature could only be found in emulating Charlie Chaplin or Laurel and Hardy, who seemed to him to have dispersed frontiers with their humour. Charlie Chaplin and Stan Laurel are the exceptions – highly Americanised if English-born clowns – to the general rule that English clowns do not travel easily and have rarely succeeded in the United States. The parochial nature of their stance and idiom tells against them.

The reverse process does operate, however. The American comedians have had remarkable successes in Britain, partly because their language and social system is so well known to us through a variety of media. Jack Benny, Bob Hope and George

Burns and Gracie Allen have been the firmest favourites, but one could reel off a roster of American comedians well known on this side of the Atlantic, beginning with Abbott and Costello, Jimmy Durante, Danny Kaye and W. C. Fields. Our actors, dancers and singers have carved out American reputations for themselves, but not our comedians, and Tony Hancock dissipated energy and shredded his fraying nerves on such inglorious ventures.

This illustrates his allegiance to the double-headed god of ambition. He was unrelentingly ambitious to drive his talent to ever fresh and distant frontiers, both geographic and artistic. It spurred him on, and that, for the public and as long as he succeeded, was fine; but each time he failed to deliver, it lashed him cruelly. Moreover, he refused, to his eternal glory, to tumble back on the comedian's creaking stand-by, pathos. That touch of piteous sentiment, upon which comedians in the Norman Wisdom or Charlie Drake mould rely, was alien to his comic nature: he never appealed to his audience for a shallow sympathy. He saw, and was able to project, the humour that lay in the frustration, the ennui, even the despair and humiliation of modern urban man. It is yet another trait from the art of the fifties. He was the comedy equivalent of the anti-heroes of that decade. Jimmy Porter, Joe Lampton, Arthur Seaton – their authors hoped we would like them a little in spite of their glaring nastiness.

Tony Hancock was accepted as lovable by millions who saw only too readily the faults to which he was heir. Poles apart as they were in generation, style and attitude, it was not unlike the adulation paid Max Miller: he never traded on pathos and he made no pretence that his sins were excusable. They were comic anti-heroes, ancient and modern. Max Miller will be long remembered as the golden boy of the old music hall. And, when the espresso bars, teddy boys, rock and roll and cha chas have been forgotten, Tony Hancock will be remembered as 'the lad himself' of the fifties.

Programme

MAKE 'EM LAUGH

Frankie Howerd

A GOSSIP FOR THE SIXTIES

'The circus, what, that's the life; if you live; I know,
I'm telling you this; listen; there's one phase of my life,
there's one phase; and I never forget a phase. Hah,
hah, hah, – every gag fresh from the quipperies.'

*'Now, er, ladees and gentle-men,
Hearken. Now, hearken ...'*

Now, er, ladees and gentle-men. Hearken. Now, hearken.
Listen, now. Harr-Ken. Now, Harr-Ken. Harr-ever so Ken.
Now, that's the life, the circus, what, that's the life; if you
live; I know; I'm telling you this, listen; there's one phase of
my life, there's one phase; and I never forget a phase. Hah,
hah, hah – every gag fresh from the quipperies. One day, you
see, there I was, I was cleaning my boots, and the ringmaster
came up, the ringmaster came up and he said, 'Listen;
Howerd, I've been watching you for some time,' he said. 'You
are ambitious, hardworking, courageous.' Oh, I, I didn't
know what to say, heh, heh; well, I felt such a fool really;
stood there in me nightie. He said, 'Here look', he said; 'put
this uniform on', he said, 'put this uniform on', he said.
'Have you put it on? Right.' I said, 'Look, you know this is a
bit of a cheek, after all I've done for you, asking me to sell
ice-cream.' He said, he said, 'Don't worry', he said, 'Have
you got your uniform on? Right. Stand by; cos you're on in a
minute.' I said, 'What's the rush?' I said, 'We've got plenty of
time.' I said, 'The interval's not yet, is it?' I said, 'They've
got this lion act to do first.' He said, 'Ah, ahh. Now that's it',
he said. 'Now', he said, 'follow me.' So we got to the ringside
and there was this cage, all the lions inside, snarling and
grorlling and daddling and jostling. 'Oh,' I said, 'I love them,
a nice bunch of pussies, aren't they?' I said. 'They're waiting
for something, aren't they?' He said, 'Yes, the lion-tamer. So
when you're ready.' I said, 'I beg your pardon.' He said,
'Yess', he said, 'you're it.' Yess, I walked straight up to the
cage; I didn't make a clink. All the lions ran toward me and
– I – just – stared at them. And they all slunk away. They
did! I said 'How's that.' He said, 'Oh, yes, that's very good,
but you should be inside the cage.' I said, *'INSIDE!'* I said,
'They'll tear me to pieces.' He said, 'Look', he said, 'I don't
know what you're making all this fuss about. I can assure
you', he said, 'I can assure you we'll be all stood round the
edge with guns. And if there's the slightest chance of you
being torn to pieces, we shall shoot you,' he said, 'so don't
worry.' And before I could argue. Cease. And before I could
argue. Cease. And before I could – oh, you make me mad.

Now pull yourselves together. Before I could argue, he opened the door and, you see, pushed me into the cage. And, ohh, they all came behind me and something ran up and down my spine. I was too frightened to scratch it. Oh, I was in a shocking state. And all these lions, all these lions, crouched up at the other end of the cage. Arrghh, arguing whether they should play with me or get it over with. The ringmaster, the ringmaster said, 'Well, go on', he said, 'go on, do something; you've only got six lions.' I said, 'Six', I said, 'you want to look again.' I said, 'I can make, I can make, I can make seven.' He said, 'Seven, oh, not tonight,' he said. 'No, oh, tonight of all nights, it's happened. Leo's got in by accident. Oh,' he said, 'he's terrible – oh, I shall give these keepers such a scolding.' He said, 'Leo only came from the jungle yesterday. He's still savage.' Eh? I didn't know what to do. He said, 'Look, take your tunic, take your tunic off quick.' I said, 'Why?' He said, 'Well, we don't want to get blood all over it.' He said, 'I'll tell you what.' He said, 'I'll tell you what.' He said, 'Let him taste you,' he said, 'that'll put him off.' I was *amazed!* Then, without warning, there was a dead silence, there was a dead silence; it was so quiet I could hear the light shining on me, and the drums, the drums, started to roll. Then one of the lions came slowwwly forward . . . and I went slowwwly backward. And I was right within an inch of the bars and I couldn't go any further. And it came forward, this lion, it still came forward. Then it stopped and it opened its mouth. The ringmaster said, 'Well, this is it. This is the big trick. Yes, this is the head in the mouth trick.' He said, 'No, you put your head in the lion's mouth.' He said, he said, 'Look', he said, 'look, I'll show you what to do,' he said; 'look follow me, watch me,' he said; 'I'll do it once.' So he came in the cage. He said, 'Look, watch me,' and he put his head in the lion's mouth, yes, in the lion's mouth, top hat and all. The crowd applauded. The band played. Everybody cheered. It was wonderful. And as I said to his widow at the funeral: 'Oh yes, if he'd only remembered to take his cigar out of his mouth', I said, 'he'd have been alright!'

Unmistakably the words of Frankie Howerd, this is an extract from a vintage *Variety Bandbox* broadcast back in the late forties, and it details, above all, his capacity to sustain a simple tale over what would otherwise be an excessive period. This is a five-hundred word joke. And that is not counting the vocal gulps and sighs and stutters with which the Howerd delivery is punctuated. Unless, like Billy Bennett or George Formby, they are working to set-piece lyrics, all the great comics have a plenitude of oral mannerisms which are difficult to convey in print – the Miller repetition, the Wilton foreshortened syllable, the Hancock laboured breath, and so forth. But Frankie Howerd, originally making his name as a radio performer, surpasses them all with the amazing gamut of his vocalisms.

Born in York in 1922, Frankie Howerd was the son of a regular soldier who died when his son was in his teens. He was thus brought up chiefly by his mother, living most of his formative years in the Eltham district of London and cherishing ambitions of a legitimate stage career. During his war service he became very much involved in concert-party work, and, on demobilisation, joined that seemingly innumerable group of would-be comedians. Almost immediately, his distinctive style – the half-complaining, half-assertive perambulations, accompanied by his strange choice of syllables to accentuate or polysyllabics to fragment – led to a success which, while it has had to endure unenviable pitfalls, betokens a genuine, three-dimensional comic talent.

Smallness is often associated with comedy, in literature and film *(Tom Thumb, The Seven Dwarfs)* as on the stage. From Little Tich and Charlie Chaplin to Arthur Askey, Ronnie Corbett and Don Estelle, as Lofty in the BBC's *It Ain't 'alf Hot, Mum,* this has been the case, but the small comedian does tend to trade on sentiment, and my preference has always been for the non-cloying comedian. Whatever the reason, in this book are assembled the corpulence of Billy Bennett and Les Dawson, the looming height of Robb Wilton and Eric Morecambe, the bulkiness of Tony Hancock and Jimmy James, the gawky size of Ken Dodd and George Formby, and the fuller figures of Will Hay and Max Miller.

Frankie Howerd sits well among such a well-proportioned crew. He certainly, and especially in these middle years of his career, gives an impression of brooding bulk, either leaning forward to grip a theatre audience within his confidence or crowding out the television screen. Like Jimmy James or Tony Hancock, he has podgy, rather hangdog features, with soulfully pleading saucers of eyes (ever ready abruptly to sparkle with a hint of lechery) and somewhat pouchy jowls. A slack, mobile mouth gives him optimal control over a gamut of expressions from the incredulous and the shocked to the gleeful and the indiscreet.

His voice matches his countenance for range of expression. From the lowly intoned, almost growled, aside to the old-maidish squeal of amazement, he sustains an unbeatable breadth of oral attack. Its extremes were amusingly illustrated by the duologues he once held with his long-suffering pianist, Madame Veropa or Madame Blanchie Moore. The falsetto screech, aimed at overcoming her obstinate deafness, alternated with the subdued whisper to the audience. Thus:

To the pianist (shouting): 'Good evening, good evening.'
To the audience (whispering): 'No; now, no, don't laugh, poor
          soul; it might be one of your own.'
*To the pianist, who is rubbing her hands and shivering
          (shouting):* 'Chilly; yes, it is chilly.'
To the audience (whispering): 'Chilly? I'm sweating like a pig.'

Indeed like all the great comedians, he sounded and looked the part; appearance and voice in impeccable concert.

It was about the time of his first *Variety Bandbox* fame, when it needed only the strained, garden-party civility of his opening 'Lay-dees and *gentle*-men' to set an audience giggling, that I first saw and enjoyed this physical and verbal unity of approach. It was the Palace Manchester, yet again. My father was fireman there for a spell, giving me a slightly tenuous link with show business, rather like an obscure claimant to some monarchy. He was fireman the year that, in *Cinderella,* Beryl Reid had her first starring role as an Ugly Sister.

So I managed, as a schoolboy, occasional free rides in the Palace balcony, and, one week, up turned Frankie Howerd. With the same generous enthusiasm of a Max Miller or a Ken Dodd in full cry, he rode on the hearty response of the audience beyond his allotted time – it must have been some twenty minutes over, a very lengthy time in twice-nightly variety. Behind him, behind the main curtain as he did his stand-up piece on the apron stage, was Jackie the Boy Balancer, perched upside down on his sets of bricks, waiting philosophically to do his acrobatics for our entertainment.

Apart from his normal act with his silently suffering pianist, he played the soldier, floppily attired and cowardly. The sergeant, he told us, had scared him by creeping up on him on guard duty unobserved. 'What would you have done', asked the sergeant, 'had I really been a German?' 'I've done it!' was Frankie Howerd's anguished, screeched reply. That yellow streak runs through his characterisation and material to the present day. He is ever lily-livered and unwilling to risk the gamble which all those in authority, from sergeants to ringmasters, are eager for him to take.

It is this endearing quality which places Frankie Howerd more suitably in the sixties. That was truly an age of surface flamboyance, with few, deep down, prepared to take up major challenges. Shallowness masquerading as outrage is as fitting an epitaph for the sixties as it is the text of Frankie Howerd's comic sermons. The sixties did appear vividly outrageous, but, basically, the changes were not too substantial. They were often in the superstructure of society, in the cultural fashions of some and the sexual *mores* of others. But the fundamentals – the economic and social determinants of society – were nettles that were not grasped, despite some brave words and vigorous gestures.

The fifties had posed questions for Britain at home and abroad, but the answers of the sixties were vivid rather than coherent. Permissiveness was the keyword of the era, and it began in 1960 itself with the *Lady Chatterley* trial: the failure of the prosecution to prove obscenity is often now regarded as the opening of the gates. In literature and film, and increasingly on the legitimate and musical stage, themes were explored with an expanding freedom of language and action. In 1968 stage censorship ended and few bounds were left. In the matter of sex, safer contraception, in particular the arrival of the pill, either helped precipitate a more libertarian view or ensured that the consequence of such a view was not too dislocatory.

The *jeunesse dorée* enjoyed much attention. From the boutiques of the King's Road, Chelsea, to student unrest on the university campuses, youth took a bow. The adjective 'swinging' managed to get itself irrevocably attached to the sixties. In politics the new mood was marked most dramatically with the Profumo affair in 1963, when the resignation of the Secretary of State for War led to trials and inquiries about vice and possible security breaches in high places. By the early sixties a thousand million pounds a year were being spent on alcohol, more on tobacco and almost as much on gambling.

Such were the sinks of affluence. In a huge phase of spending on consumer durables, practically the entire nation could boast an electric iron and a television set by the mid-sixties, while three-quarters had vacuum cleaners and close on a half, washing machines and refrigerators. But this meant that, to be added to the colossal expenditure on drink, tobacco and betting, there was a massively expanding debt. In the ten years up to 1964, the collective hire purchase debt trebled to close on a thousand million pounds. The country also had an overdraft of £4,500 million.

To the youth cult and the adoration of Mammon one must add the renaissance of the working class. Academically, this was stimulated by Richard Hoggart's *The Uses of Literacy,* published in 1957, and by the writings of scholars such as E. P. Thompson and Raymond Williams. When the vigour of youth mingled with the vigour of the popular culture, there was an eruption of talent, notably with the incandescent rise of the Beatles. Money

Frankie Howerd –
'outrageous and outraged'.

remained, of course, the cue to much of this. Long-playing records, transistor radios, scooters, clothes and cosmetics and the swiftly changing patterns of the 'pop' culture tempted the pounds from the pockets of a well paid young labour force. The Beatles were about youth, the working class *and* money. Alongside the mark of appreciation to their pert genius one must sadly note that, by the sixties, a third of indictable crimes were committed by persons under seventeen.

And the nation which was characterised by such mixtures of effervescence and nastiness had so shrunk in significance, with its Empire gone and with France reluctant to see it join the Common Market. The Aldermaston marches may have been gallant gestures, but, in the October of 1962, our place was that of fearful spectator as Russia and the United States tottered through their dreadful Cuban confrontation. A year later President Kennedy, seen by some as a kind of sun king for the youth cult, was assassinated, but Americanisation, in food, entertainment, advertising techniques and so forth, continued rapidly to extend, and there was precious little idealism left to temper the materialistic passions of the age. It was in the sixties that the anti-immigration movement which, however well-reasoned its case, always seemed a trifle tawdry, became effective.

Altogether, it was swinging but superficial. In the political and economic organisation of the country there was scarcely a change. Harold Macmillan retired, and, after the anonymity of Sir Alec Douglas-Home, there were six disappointing years of unrealised radicalism. Where the Labour ministries of the late forties had passed striking pieces of massive legislation, guaranteed to quicken the pulses of adherent and opponent alike, the late sixties could boast no more than fiddly and ineffectual bits of Acts of Parliament about prices and land-holdings. There were measures designed to protect and maintain individual liberties – divorce reform, changes in the law on homosexuality, the end of capital punishment – but there was no broad-based reform to fire the progressive or worry the reactionary. It was as if the Wilson governments were determined to prove that they were centralised, almost neutral, in political stance, in the hope of winning the 1970 general election. Maybe they lost it because of their apparent chicken-heartedness.

Economically, there was, for instance, no substantial redistribution of wealth. Five per cent of the population owned three-quarters of personal wealth in the sixties, much the same as in the immediate pre-war years. One per cent received well over half the investment income, and property was still largely concentrated in a few hands. Nor was social mobility much of a saviour for those who wished to see society more egalitarian. Professor Brian Simon calculated, during the sixties, that the relative chances of higher education for the daughter of a West Ham docker and the son of a Carmarthenshire solicitor were respectively one hundred and eighty to one! Sexual, class and regional differences were still very pronounced. Middlesbrough, with just about the highest number of children per thousand of the population, had the fewest general practitioners. Through education and health and then into housing, environmental amenities, job opportunities and the remainder of these factors which together form the frame for each person's life chance, the story was much the same.

This is not to press the case for an egalitarian society; nor, conversely, is it to scorn the liberal attitudes struck in the sixties. The argument is that the so-called spectacular alteration was little more than top-show. Britain might swing all the way from the Cavern to Carnaby Street, but no one could combine the courage, far-sightedness and power to grasp by the throat the economic and social problems of the nation, which, by the seventies, were to become chronic. There might be talk of 'the white-hot technological revolution' from the Labour Party or of the 'property-owning democracy' from the Conservatives, but there was not even the revisionism of the forties which at least produced a National Health Service and the Beveridge Report.

The most typical mode for humour in the sixties was satire. A permissive age but one not properly prepared to adopt serious reconstruction is ideal soil for the satiric plant. There were targets in plenty, and the barriers of censorship, legal and social, had been breached. But it remained a game of hitting targets, like some form of verbal archery. It was destructive enough in the sense that the targets were palpably hit, but alternative philosophies were rare indeed. There were times in England in the eighteenth century or in ancient Rome when, with society corrupt yet quiescent, satirists – Swift or Horace – could wax savagely ironic without, in the short term, constituting a genuine threat. There was no Voltaire in the sixties.

The trend began towards the end of the fifties with the revue *Beyond the Fringe,* arguably the finest piece of satirical commentary since the war. One of the disappointments of the sixties was that it was never bettered, but, to be fair, it set an immaculate standard. Alan Bennett, Jonathan Miller, Peter Cook and Dudley Moore chose self-evident Aunt Sallies and scored every time. With the sparse elegance of Gregorian plainchant, the foibles of the Church, the royal family, the war myth, pseudo-Elizabethan historical drama, civil defence, politics, race, class, musical pretensions and a dozen other institutions and attitudes were exposed. It was a cleansing experience, but it was also very, very funny. For instance, in what bid fair to be the best ever written and presented revue item, Alan Bennett, with the bland, unthinking *non sequiturs* of his Anglican sermon, sent gales of laughter howling through the theatre.

Broadcasting picked up the atmospherics of the satirical movement, and in the early sixties the first of several series of late Saturday night shows became vogue viewing. *That Was the Week that Was* was, whatever else, a dramatic change of approach for BBC comedy. It was, of course, sanitised by its rather separist location at the witching hour each weekend, but the freedom it skilfully exploited in hunting down and slaughtering sacred cows cannot be denied. Unluckily for those of us who had admired the ascetic quality of *Beyond the Fringe*, there was an air of gluttony about *TW3*. It was overlengthy and self-indulgent and made something of a fetish of amateurism. One had to wait (although never in vain) for the tiny nuggets among the dross.

The same trait of attacking without offering replacement was

Beyond the Fringe – *Alan Bennett, Peter Cook, Dudley Moore, Jonathan Miller at The Establishment, described by Frankie Howerd as 'an upper-class canteen'. Compared to the ascetic quality of* Beyond the Fringe *there was an air of gluttony about TW3.*

That Was the Week that Was *(inset) marked a dramatic change of approach for BBC comedy.*

also present. It meant, as with much similar satire, that it tended to peter out a little or to seem to be a trifle too open to commercial blandishments. David Frost's name was invariably associated with *TW3* and two small benchmarks of his career illustrate the point. In a famous sketch he was the Dimbleby-type commentator describing the accidental sinking of the royal yacht, with the queen 'smiling radiantly' as she was submerged. Come the royal command performance some years later, it was David Frost who led three rousing cheers for her majesty. That may sound a picqued, even snide, comment; but such is not intended. It is hoped that it will demonstrate the normality of the sixties satirists. Like practically everyone else, they could both poke cheeky fun at an institution and be flattered by its attention. It also suggests that, again like practically everyone else, they were better at deposing than composing. There is no reason why they should not have been. If criticism is – as it assuredly was in the sixties – justified, then it must be publicised.

In terms of the comic muse, however, it meant that, eventually, the university satirists did much the same job as the older comedians, men like Robb Wilton or Will Hay who guyed venerable institutions and that was that. As was earlier argued of Robb Wilton, the lampooned bodies emerged, if anything, stronger for withstanding the attacks with such cheerful good nature. In the longer run, therefore, the main distinction was in the widening of aim, so that subjects once taboo were included in the comic reckoning. Homosexuality and the monarchy (ill-assorted pair though they make) were chief among them, although Max Miller had hinted at the first and the old-time music hall had not been averse to being cheeky about the second.

The Frankie Howerd story picks up its threads neatly from within that pattern of culture in the sixties. Following his swift rise to fame after the war (with the royal accolade as early as 1950 and the 'legitimate' imprimatur of playing Bottom in an Old Vic production of *A Midsummer Night's Dream* in 1957), he as abruptly found himself struggling for worthwhile employment in the later fifties and into the sixties. It was partway through a *TW3* series in 1963 that he was given the opportunity to address a presumably large and discerning audience. Among the longueurs and scrappiness of that programme, his sheer presentational skill, allied to shrewdly selected material, re-created a star. This was consolidated by appearances at the satirical night club of that era, the Establishment – 'an upper class canteen', as Frankie Howerd described it – and then back on the West End stage as Pseudolus in *A Funny Thing Happened on the Way to the Forum,* and later on television as Lurcio in *Up Pompeii.* As the scheming and lecherous Roman slave, he realised that earlier promise that, inexplicably, had

been temporarily blighted.

However, if it is difficult to calculate why his popularity fell so dismally in the late fifties it is simple enough to decide why he rated so highly in the late sixties. His successful appearance in *TW3* was a token of his being the most satirically funny of English music-hall comedians, certainly since the Second World War and perhaps of all time. It is a pleasing conceit that, as Pseudolus and Lurcio, he adopted a Roman guise to attain this status, given that classical Rome coined the genre of satire. Frankie Howerd became variety's Juvenal. The prevalent vices and follies of the sixties were apt choices for the astute sarcasm, even the hint of veiled malice, of his remarks. There was a sufficient feeling of dismay, sometimes disgust, with the foibles under review to make the satiric label stick. It was partly the political nature of the attack, but telling 'political' jokes and being satirical are not necessarily synonymous. Plenty of comedians push gags about politicians and urge us to laugh at their more obvious cupidities. This is the sort of joke which audiences, in theatre or studio, clap rather than laugh at, their applause being a dual symbol of the joke being 'clever' rather than funny and their self-adulation in recognising it as such.

Frankie Howerd has journeyed beyond that point. Like a latterday and vulgarised Pope, he reserves his most cutting and sardonic *mots* for the social *mores* of the age and their most florid exponents. Tony Hancock developed a character who represented much of the emptiness and tediousness of the post-war years, but Frankie Howerd rather deployed the character he created to observe the passing social and cultural scene. He became, as he matured, a kind of diarist, remarking the manners of his society and pointing up their silliness or nastiness in an essentially private style.

It is not easy, more particularly with comedians, to distinguish the satire from the rest. Presumably some serious purpose is required for it to attain that lofty label. Frankie Howerd's autobiography, *On the Way I Lost It,* certainly suggests a seriousness of approach, not by way of characterisation as in Tony Hancock's case but in the sense of a message. Sometimes he does appear to be mocking institutions because they are inept or unjust, and not merely poking fun at them. Having known dreadful as well as happy days in show business, it is interesting to observe how often he will jeer at the pretensions of entertainment itself. It is more than the gratuitious crack about the salary or the producer, which is par for many a second-rate comic's script. Frankie Howerd can weave an entire act around the iniquities and tribulations of the life and times of the theatre.

From another angle his entire spinsterish methodology takes a rise out of stage comedy. It is a piece of sustained opaqueness. Frankie Howerd has created his art out of the inarticulate,

'Shallowness masquerading as outrage is as fitting an epitaph for the 1960s as it is the text of Frankie Howerd's comic sermons.'

where many of the pundits would argue for a punchy, sharp, highly comprehensible attack. He stammers and gasps his halting and distracted way through a labyrinth of digressions among which the main line of the story is but feebly apparent. The sort of stand-up comic, who conventionally begins 'A funny thing happened to me on the way to the theatre . . . ', has been overwhelmed by Frankie Howerd. His act sometimes consists wholly of his difficulties in obtaining the booking in the first place, let alone the grave problems encountered in reaching the theatre.

The tribulations of his career, its often draining effect on his life and health, and his astute mockery of showbiz mythology underline a growing problem which comedians increasingly have to face. It is a truism of the recent history of entertainment that, as the mass usage of the media intensifies, the pressure on comic material becomes intolerable. Harry Tate is often quoted as an illustration. He hawked his motor-car sketch from theatre to theatre, often to several in the same city, with just a few hundreds watching, without having to revisit one in a twelvemonth. Thus he was able to hone and smooth one act and construct a lifetime's career around it. Films and records affected this only marginally. George Formby was the chief cinematic and gramophonic protagonist of the music hall, and his career was admirably served by both media. It publicised him, and, in any event, the cinema has the same public character as the theatre – a Formby movie would run a week at the local Regal or Gaumont for audiences of some hundreds, while George Formby himself might have been topping the bill at a nearby Hippodrome.

It was the private projection of the media which caused the fiercest exposure. Radio, first of all, had a voracious maw for verbal material. It is mournful to recall comedians who made an initial impact just after the war and then faded. Like the leaves in the hymn, they blossomed and flourished, then withered and perished. Some of them, like Frankie Howerd in 1947, were *Variety Bandbox* discoveries. The Australian Bill Kerr ('I've ownly got fower minutes'), who later did some comedy acting, and Derek Roy, genial and gaily wisecracking, were two of these. Arthur English and Robert Moreton (Moreton, like Tony Hancock, died tragically in Australia) were two more who never quite sustained the star billing radio originally offered them. Unless they were able to develop a profounder sense of character or find some formula the familiarity of which would in itself appeal, public taste for them quickly palled.

Television was an even hungrier master, and, in grasping also the visual as well as the oral, it robbed the stage of its one commanding advantage over radio. It is not just a question of some comedians failing to make the transfer adequately. One thinks rather of those who won instant fame on television, but could not sustain it. Jimmy Tarbuck was an overnight success on *Sunday Night at the London Palladium* and, exceptionally, made an immediate return the following week. Norman Vaughan and Bob Monkhouse were two others who created something of the same kind of stir. Few would now place them, likeable and competent as many find them, in the comic grade their earlier television shows promised.

A striking example of this tendency might be Granada's *The Comedians,* a spirited attempt to retain on television the simple virtues of stand-up patter comedy. Some of the comedians looked and sounded funny. Bernard Manning, portly and genial, had a nice line in idiom: 'There was this Jewish tailor, yahmulka on his head, chalk on his waistcoat, and a teardrop in his eye'; or, quoting Ted Heath explaining to Kruschev about the premature end of the working day at Trafford Park, 'They're pumping their bikes up at twenty past three at Metro Vicks.' Ken Goodwin was the innocent abroad, giggling over his childlike jokes and offering a credible Formby imitation. 'Settle down now,' he pleaded, as, seemingly pleased with what he believed to be his cavalier approach, he ventured another naïve tale with the air of one taking untold risks. There was Charlie Williams, the coloured comedian with the thick Yorkshire accent, and cigarette-smoking Colin Crompton with his unending slights on Morecambe: 'They don't bury the dead in Morecambe; they stand them up in bus shelters with bingo tickets in their hands.' There were others, south-westerners, cockneys, Liverpudlians and Irishmen, a polyglot collation attempting to satisfy every ethnic and subcultural palate. For a time it did, and in 1972 there was a royal command performance for six of the comedians. But the usage of material was profligate. It was little short of alarming to watch seven or eight comedians burn up valued gags by the score for millions of viewers. It was nothing short of a prairie fire sweeping through the corn, and then all those jokes, like Clementine, were lost and gone for ever.

To a large extent, the poor gagsters came with the gags, and, as suddenly as they had arrived on the scene, they were removed. Bob Hope said ruefully of television that 'it was the box they buried entertainment in', and this is true on two counts. First, material is wasted or, at best, shrewd performers only use their second-best scripts, saving their Sunday-best for the theatre. Second, by closing down variety – or, in Bob Hope's context, vaudeville – the proving ground for comedians was destroyed. Northern clubland has, over the last few years, replaced this to some extent, but by and large the apprenticeship served by a Max Miller or a Jimmy James has vanished. We are frequently left with comedians who, after Raffles, are little more than amateur cracksmen, and the substance of their acts cannot maintain them. Radio and television, then, combine to make and break comedians speedily, so that we see and hear chiefly two-

dimensional comedians with mediocre patter. They have neither the time nor the chance to mature into full-blooded comic characters, with independence of style and content.

Frankie Howerd survived the slaughter of the sixties. Forged equally in the heat of success and the fires of distress, his talent was well hardened. It is not unfair to add that his talent has been over-pressurised in the entertainment broiler of the last twenty-five years. A little more leisure and a little more security, and Frankie Howerd might have been even more accomplished. Often he has had to handle material spread too thinly or situations constructed too clumsily. There are times when some might complain that the crudities are no more than that – lewd items included to startle people into laughter, neither helping

'That arch penchant for gossip, with eyebrows vaulting and mouth pouting in simulated dismay, places Frankie Howerd very near the long line of female impersonators who have starred on the English stage – Dan Leno, Wilkie Bard, G. S. Melvin and Danny La Rue'.

character nor making comment.

Nonetheless, he has created a kind of minor John Aubrey figure for the mid-twentieth century, chattering away in a compound of social irrelevancies and malicious comments. He became something of a Robb Wilton of the sixties, less masculine and lugubrious but displaying a modicum of high camp and a womanish gossipiness which struck a definite sixties note. One thinks how, in their separate ways, long-serving performers like Kenneth Williams, Danny la Rue and Larry Grayson came into their own with this camped-up tradition in favour.

That arch penchant for gossip, with eyebrows vaulting and mouth pouting in simulated dismay, places Frankie Howerd very near the long line of female impersonators who have starred on the English stage. It has been, of course, associated with the well tried institution of the English panto dame. The grand protagonists of this strange art have been numerous. Dan Leno is normally regarded as the finest of all dames, returning to the Drury Lane pantomime every Christmas from 1888 to 1903. Wilkie Bard next established himself as the leading panto dame, and George Robey, too, was noted for his dame characterisations. In the 'middle' generation it was G. S. Melvin who caught the eye, especially with his famous songs for the thirties, 'I Like to Jump upon a Bike' and 'I'm Happy when I'm Hiking'. Perhaps better remembered today would be Clarkson Rose, Old Mother Riley and Norman Evans, who died in 1962. Many will remember his 'Over the Garden Wall' sketch, when, as Fanny Fairbottom, he struggled with the bricks that threatened his voluminous bosom and the indiscretions he apparently heard from an unseen neighbour. 'I could taste that tom-cat in the rice pudding a-Sunday,' he would complain. Today the flamboyant Danny La Rue has inherited the mantle. Frankie Howerd has, in a sense, never gone quite so far in costume and properties as any of these in creating a female role. Nonetheless, he lacks none of their old womanly appetite for prying into the secrets and foibles of neighbours and colleagues.

In all this, he has mastered all the arenas on offer to the present-day clown. His many fans could fairly state that he is more effective on television than Ken Dodd, more effective on radio than Morecambe and Wise, and more effective on stage than Tony Hancock. Frankie Howerd is the premier sixties comedian, therefore, for three reasons. He came nearest to being a satirical comedian. He took ebullient advantage of the expansive scope of the permissive era, so that some of his more explicit material (in *Up Pompeii,* for instance) has made Max Miller look positively episcopal. He has, like the sixties, adopted the character of external belligerence and extravagance, disguising the internal normality of fear of hazards and affection for stability. He was, and remains, both outrageous and outraged.

MAKE 'EM LAUGH

Morecambe & Wise

TWINS OF MIRTH

Ernie: My mother has a Whistler.
Eric: Now there's a novelty.

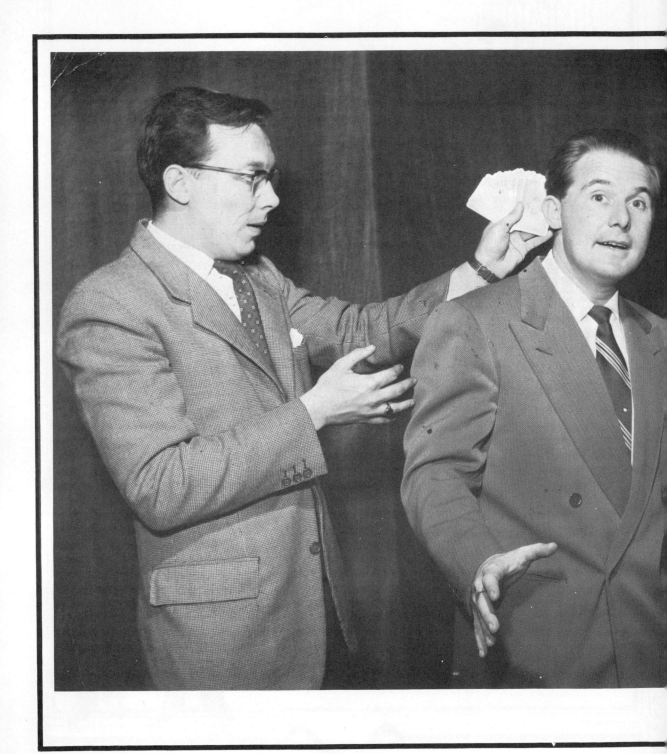

Morecambe and Wise – Music Hall revisited. Fundamentally a cross-talk duo from the 1940s.

If the sixties glittered to deceive, and the glistening dazzle of the decade was far from the pure gold of actual reformation, then much the same was true of comedy. *That Was the Week that Was* might compete with the Beatles and Mary Quant as the chief seminal influence of the sixties, but for many the underlying themes of comedy as well as music and fashion remained firm. *Plus ça change* . . . There were many who rejected, even resented, the new morality and the miniskirt, the mods and rockers and their musical accompaniment, and the arrival of mobile nudity in shows like *Hair*. There were many more who tolerated the bravura of the sixties but who felt more comfortable with older traditions.

Not that Frankie Howerd represented only that which was novel in the sixties – witness his placement in the dame lineage of British non-legitimate comedy. But he did speak with the modish voice of the new era: even in the dame tradition, he pulled the double-bluff of playing the woman in male clothing at a time when drag was becoming the vogue. That virtuoso trick – the female-like gossip in the crumpled, baggy male suit, camp but not butch – was characteristic of the sexual blurrings of the age.

For those who looked for a quieter, more obvious, less bizarre life-style, the sixties still had much to offer. The fortnight package tour to Lloret de Mar might have replaced Wakes Week in Scarborough, but the transference of values could plainly be seen and the similarities were, indeed, sniffed at by the *avant-garde* traveller. Television inherited many of radio's attributes and formulae. Raquel Welch replaced Betty Grable, just as she had replaced Mary Pickford. More houses had refrigerators and washing machines, but they were still houses, and the family remained the norm for society's social pattern.

During the sixties Morecambe and Wise became our most celebrated double act since Flanagan and Allen, and few would rate them less humorous. Quite simply, they are an old-fashioned variety act. It is likely they are the greatest ever cross-talk act, but, at base, they are, as they never cease to remind their audiences both explicitly and indirectly, a music-hall double act. Just as Frankie Howerd, in his sixties posture, retained elements of the old school, for their part Morecambe and Wise have added novel bits and pieces to their performance. Nonetheless, they remain fundamentally a cross-talk duo from the forties, and their appeal lies in the nostalgia and comfort that that brings to the many millions who suspect flashy change and brash insecurity. Their individual talents are such that younger generations also accept and applaud them – no easy task in an age when, in practice, the double act has generally been rejected. They are therefore able to transmit a tradition of lengthy standing, and long may it reign – that combination of long, thin one and short fat one.

Their material is familiar, but let us refresh our memories with some excerpts from their television shows of 1971. The doctor has suggested Ernie has flu, and Eric sympathises: 'Take no notice of him, he'll say anything for a laugh. I went to see him last week. He said "I haven't seen you in years." I said "No, I've been ill." Fell about he did. Fell off the chair. Got his foot caught in the stethoscope; pulled an ear off.'

Ernie sneezes, and Eric is fascinated.

'When you sneeze like that, your wig lifts about half an inch; I see daylight.'

Eric is encouraging – 'You can die from flu' – but feels secure in his injection.

'You can still get it,' warns Ernie.

'But my arm won't,' confides Eric.

Ernie is so ill he hasn't 'written a play for twenty minutes'. But tomorrow he'll write six. 'Only six?' 'I'm going out in the afternoon.' Ernie realises Eric is dosing him with dog powders.

Ernie (angry):	Bob Martins!
Eric:	That's his name.
Ernie (angrier):	Bob Martins!
Eric:	Do you know him?
Ernie (angrier still):	Bob Martins!
Eric:	Do you know him that well?
Ernie:	You've been giving me dog powders!
Eric:	Sit. Sit. Sit. Sit, or I'll hide your lead . . .
Ernie:	Could I have a cushion please?
Eric:	You haven't eaten that one yet.

Ernie asks Eric to look out for the doctor's arrival. Eric peers through the window.

Eric:	Ada Bailey's hanging her knickers out again if you're interested.

With Ann Hamilton as the girl friend, Eric is buying a diamond ring from Ernie, as the jeweller.

Ernie:	Would you like me to take it out so you can have a good look at it?
Eric:	Well, there's not many people in the shop; how do you feel about that?

As he goes for the ring, Eric tells his fiancée Ernie's a QC: 'Queer as a Coot; he can't help it.'

The ring is too small.

Ernie:	We can always have it made larger.

Eric:	Can I ask you something?
Ernie:	Yes?
Eric:	How can you make her finger larger?
Ernie:	We make the ring larger.
Eric:	Oh, 'cos if you can make fingers larger, there's a little job I wouldn't mind you doing.

The cost is £3,500. Eric offers a cheque.

| Ernie: | Certainly sir. |
| Eric: | Vladimir! Here's a Czech all the way from Prague, he's all yours. |

On the occasion of Ernie's retirement, Eric runs through his biography.

Ernie:	My obligations are fulfilled.
Eric:	They were a hell of a size, I must admit.
Ernie:	Keep it short.
Eric:	That's what the doctor said.

Then came war.

| Eric: | When your country sent out a plea for all able bodied men to take up arms, you didn't hesitate: you put on your mother's frock and pleaded insanity. |

On to the theatre.

| Ernie: | I finished my act by leaping from the balcony into the stalls and doing the splits. |
| Eric: | And two months and thirty yards of sticky tape later . . . |

And the retirement present, for which many had chipped in.

Eric:	The rich; the famous; the talented; and Jimmy Tarbuck . . .
Ernie:	I always said there were no people like show people.
Eric:	Ask any prison warder.

And finally, the magnificent gift: a quarter-pound of pear drops, with 'Lest we forget Ern' scratched on one with a nail.

In style and in material they invite us to roll the years away and wallow in the luxury of the music-hall stage revisited. That, of course, is where they served their apprenticeship. Both were

Morecambe and Wise – Lords of Misrule.

Morecambe and Wise – which one is the comedian?

born in 1926, Eric Bartholomew in Morecambe and Ernest Wiseman in Leeds – in every appearance since they have fought a miniature War of the Roses. Both did stage and radio work as boys and both were among Bryan Michie's discoveries – he was a forerunner of Carroll Levis and Hughie Green. They were only fifteen when the double act was first established, but the war removed Ernie Wise to sea and Eric Morecambe down the pits, and it was 1947 before they properly re-established the act. It was, however, in 1941, at the Liverpool Empire that they made their first appearance as a double act, and began their incredible 36-year partnership.

I first saw them in the early fifties, lost among the wines and spirits, billed as 'fools rush in', opening each half with a compound of cross-talk and song and dance. And very amusing they were too. It was the Manchester Hippodrome's golden jubilee, and G. H. Elliott was top of the bill. A year or so later I saw them in Blackpool, sharing the Central Pier bill with Jimmy James. They had matured considerably, and were benefiting from the arduous combat training of weekly variety and radio shows like *Workers' Playtime*. Since then I have watched them with growing admiration, not least in pantomime, as when, at the Manchester Palace, at the Christmas of 1964, they starred in *Sleeping Beauty*.

Like other entertainers, they have had their ups and downs, but one major disaster befell them. The unutterable débâcle of their 1954 television series *Running Wild* led them to abjure telly, or be abjured, until the sixties, when first on the independent channel and latterly with the BBC they triumphed again and again. They remain, as ever, splendid stage performers, although their radio work has perhaps been by their own standards no more than competent, and on film they followed a growing list of English comedians who have failed. Their ability to conquer television has been remarkable. Remembering how near Tony Hancock was to becoming a comic actor rather than a comedian, it might be argued that Morecambe and Wise are the only unalloyed high-ranking comedians who have made the television grade. It has constantly been pressed that actors, not comics, have brought humour to the small screen. Not only are Morecambe and Wise the exception, they have accomplished this by retaining almost wholesale their original position.

Their television shows are as near theatre as the newer medium can tolerate. They work from a stage and use, most overtly, the plush drapes borrowed from the old halls. The difficulty in finding the split in the curtains, the belated appearance, the eavesdropping, the mime of the mad throttler – each of these makes the viewer comprehend the curtains. They salute and insult their audience good-naturedly; they end with a song and take a curtain call. They swap straight duologues with costume sketches, and normally demonstrate their dancing prowess. They are the 'Lords of Misrule', and it has become almost another kind of award for the great ladies and gentlemen of the theatre and the arts, like Glenda Jackson as Ginger Rogers, to have found themselves in a musical burlesque or in one of Ernie Wise's smug little plays.

Of course they use television techniques, like Eric Morecambe's increasingly fixed fascination as he beams into the camera, but, all in all, they remain a middle-aged stage act, and, whatever the explanation, it is a rare phenomenon. One could talk of the sixties as a time of vacillation, as those equivocal years when we were undecided on economic matters, such as nationalising more or de-nationalising what we had; on social matters such as trying to look both ways on immigration, and how to re-organise local government and a dozen other institutions. They could be seen as years of quavering doubt about whether to join the common market or not. It could be urged that years of argument, of tossing ideas from one to the other, is reminiscent of a kind of intellectual battledore and shuttlecock, and that the verbal and physical ping-pong of a highly effective cross-talk act is only too characteristic. The sixties were assuredly an era of to-ing and fro-ing of this nature, with wide tracks of indecisive debate and wrangling, and for that reason a top-class duo is an appropriate symbol of that age. Nonetheless, the public appraisal of Morecambe and Wise is scarcely connected with this; it is surely much more to do with the safety of their known and familiar method. This applies to their material as well as method. Denis Potter has written that their genius 'consists precisely in knowing how to salvage material from a yellowing stock of back numbers of *Dandy* and *Beano*: they do not so much deliver their lines as resuscitate them'. He quotes as an illustration Eric Morecambe's reply to the festive question: 'What would you say to a little drink?' The answer, inevitably, was 'Hello, little drink.' There is no pretence at novelty: they signpost and neon-light the more antiquated gags, all the while appealing through our memories to their dim past of theatrical landladies and performing seals; then back beyond that to Ada Bailey's knickers and the travails of Milverton Street infant school, with Ernie, even then smarter and richer. Were it to amuse and cosset us, they would take us back into the womb.

Ernie's plays are usually historical, relating to popular figures of our island heritage or its well-thumbed literature – the Dick Turpins, Beau Gestes and Long John Silvers. They offer cinematic spoofs, especially musical ones, recalling Fred Astaire or Gene Kelly. They refurbish, like Sandy Powell, old variety turns, such as the ventriloquist (remember the twenty-foot doll?) or the conjuror. Probably the funniest trio of items that have been set before the king or queen since the war at royal command performances have been Jimmy James's 'the permanent wink', Tony Hancock's 'budgerigar', and Morecambe and Wise in 1966, as 'Marvo and Dolores'. With an enormously bulky tailcoat, apparently densely packed with bird life, Eric Morecambe, with Ernie as his charming lady assistant, went through all the staccato drills of the conjuror, fluff and feathers suspiciously scattering in all directions. 'Send the budgie up,' Eric Morecambe would urgently whisper down his sleeve.

It may be unwise to analyse *The Morecambe and Wise Show* too closely, but not since *ITMA* has a programme contained so many items which are both familiar and consistently funny. Often that kind of formula palls: *Educating Archie* suffered from that; but Morecambe and Wise produce and re-produce an inexhaustible series of gags, gestures, catch-phrases and meaningful glances. 'Short fat hairy legs', 'there's no answer to that', 'good evening, young sir' (always to the beautiful girl), the high pitched squeal of glee or in shock; 'let's be honest', 'what do you think of it so far?' – 'rubbish', 'this play what I have wrote', 'pardon?', 'now there's a novelty' – these are a few of the lines frequently repeated. Then there are the confidential exchanges with the audience – 'this man's a fool' – or the by-play with the spectacles, frisking them rapidly up and down or transforming them into mock binoculars. There is the invisible stone in the paper bag; there is the ceaseless reference to Ernie Wise's purported toupee and its overt join; there is the glaring confusion with the names of famous guests and the stinginess over their fees; there is the gawky exit dance; there is the bickering over gifts and parts in the plays.

The scripts are stuffed with double entendres, almost all of them of a sexual or biological connotation. Here again there is a retrospective quality, harking back to the thirties. It is rarely the direct punchy naughtiness of Max Miller; it is rather the impudent misunderstandings of George Formby and the seaside postcard. Whatever roles are adopted – flowers, animals, bullfighters, Mexican dancers, football machine players – there are always words and phrases to be misinterpreted as sexual euphemisms. 'He had his convictions squashed – and appeared throughout on a stick'; (of an uncovered affair) 'it would have come out sooner or later – that would have been worth waiting for'; (of last Christmas) 'it doesn't seem a year since last time' – 'don't bring your personal problems to me, Ern'. They spot an item in *The Stage* – 'Herbert and Sylvia Hargreaves still at it on the grand piano' – and Eric wants to know if Ernie's mother knows he's reading such stuff. Talking of art, Ernie claims: 'My mother has a Whistler.' 'Now there's a novelty,' admires Eric. It really is a boundless vein: one would grow wary of uttering any word or saying lest it be subjected to their Freudian slipperiness.

This apart, they joke about fellow artists, which, like the use of André Previn or Angela Rippon in unaccustomed roles, is an age-old convention. It stretches back to courtly masquerades and all those fairy-tale exchanges of role, like Prince Charming and Dandini. It is, of course, rather more homely than that, and also somewhat more pertinent. The main butts among their confrères are Des O'Connor and Max Bygraves, and many might feel that true words mingle with the jests. 'Is there life on Max Bygraves?' – 'Terrible news, Des O'Connor has made an unbreakable LP' – 'In our lifetime will a man land on Julie Andrews?'

So piece by piece, the performance is formulated from these we have loved, a comforting drawerful of souvenirs. And the very act which brings it all back to us, is itself as old as the hills. Double acts have as long a tradition as any in the world of entertainment. Some commentators talk of Andrew Aguecheek and Toby Belch as the original Abbott and Costello, the original tall thin one and small fat one. But one might delve way back into the folk memory.

Perhaps the best known cross-talk act of Western society is Punch and Judy, a duet which evolved from the Italian *commedia dell'arte,* which, in turn, may well have had links with the Atellan tradition of farce in ancient Rome. Pulcinella was certainly around by the beginning of the seventeenth century and soon moved to Britain, and by the 1790s Punch and Judy were well established. Their violent interaction has long been a staple of the double act, and it has been, like theirs, physical as well as vocal. The hand under Ernie's chin ('Get out of that'), the aggressive clutch at the other's lapels, the flimsy show of martial arts, and, most of all, the shoulder hug and face slap – these are Morecambe and Wise's token equivalents of Punch and his murderous truncheon.

Morecambe and Wise are the one double act proper in this comical collation. Billy Bennett had begun life in the knockabout team of Bennett and Martell. On radio, he joined with Albert Whelan as Alexander and Mose, just as, for broadcasting purposes, Tommy Handley and Ronald Frankau combined in the extremely slick and verbally inventive Murgatroyd and Winterbottom. George Formby and Robb Wilton both used their wives paradoxically as straight men, while Will Hay in general and Jimmy James in particular used supporting comics. At times Frankie Howerd, with his lady pianist, and Tony Hancock, with – among others – Sidney James, and Les Dawson, especially with Roy Barraclough, have not worked alone. Ken Dodd, at least on television, has the use of stooges. Of this group Max Miller is the nearest to comedy's lone ranger, but all of them were or are, of course, stars in their own right. Only Morecambe and Wise stand apart as an inseparable duo, and thus they sustain a splendid tradition.

Strangely enough, in the modern, that is music-hall/variety,

genre of double acts, the ladies led the field. In the closing years
of the last century, it was the Sisters Levey, the Sisters Cuthbert
(tilting at the Salvation Army), and the Richmond Sisters with
their plaintive melody, 'Pretty as a Butterfly'. A later generation
will recall 'the long and the short of it', those cockney kids
Revnell and West, and the East End housewife team of Elsie and
Doris Waters, Gert and Daisy. Scotland weighed in with Billie
and Renee Houston. There were others with just one female,
such as Bella and Bijou, as the lawyer and client, Billy Caryll
and Hilda Mundy, Lucan and McShane, Claude Dampier with
Billie Carlyle, and the inarticulate Nat Mills and Bobbie. But
the old days did know male double acts, such as The Two Mikes,
with their highly modern-sounding song 'I lent ten pound to
Callaghan', the Two McNaughtons, and the Poluskis, a popular
knockabout act. Tennyson and O'Gorman, with their number
'The Wild Man of Poplar', were perhaps the most famous, and
the latter's sons, Joe and Dave, later took over as the O'Gorman
Brothers.

By the thirties and forties there were droves of double acts.
Like Morecambe and Wise at the Manchester Hippodrome's
golden jubilee, they often opened or took second spot in each
half of a variety show. 'Monsewer' Eddie Gray apart, the Crazy
Gang was composed of three such: Naughton and Gold, Nervo
and Knox and Flanagan and Allen. *Music Hall,* the regular
Saturday evening radio high spot of that time, always started
with a double act. It might have been Bennett and Williams,
with their wisecracking above the sawing note of their
phonofiddles; or Clapham and Dwyer, who made a star of 'Cissie.
the Cow' on the wireless; or Morris and Cowley, or Scott and
Whaley from the Kentucky Minstrels. Syd and Max Harrison
were another couple whose sons Mike Hope and Alfie Keen were
to team up as a double act in the present era.

Army life provided another setting for them. There was
Collinson and Breen – the tall, jeering sergeant and the little,
awkward private who cried 'someone's pinched me pudding' and
explained that the command had been issued 'all put your
puddings out for treacle' and, when he had, his had been stolen.
There were the Two Pirates. A niche was found for all of them
in pantomime. There was ever a set of broker's men for
Cinderella and Chinese policemen for Aladdin. For many years
after they joined forces in 1934, Jewel and Warriss were
particular favourites. Year after year they played the Robbers in
Babes in the Wood, invariably featuring their 'haunted house'
effects. Rather tamely, in my opinion, Mike and Bernie Winters
have endeavoured to maintain a presence for cross-talk
comedians today, while some predict a splendid future for Little
and Large.

But probably the classic double act was Murray and Mooney.
They became, in the thirties and forties, what Edward Lear had

*The classic double act is that of
Murray and Mooney who, in the
1930s and 1940s, became the
guardians of a restricted and tight
format.*

been to the limerick – the guardians, if not the creators, of a restricted and tight format. On every seaside pier and variety stage permutations on their theme were daily and nightly heard. There was the pompous, serious one (in this case Murray) offering his little monologue, 'a little monologue entitled "Jack"', to the ladies and gentlemen. 'Jack was a coward, a great big coward with a turned up nose,' he might begin. Another favourite was 'It's a funny old world we live in, but the world's not entirely to blame' while another stand-by was 'There's a little yellow idol to the north of Katmandu'. The Harry Mooney figure, irresponsible and iconoclastic, would interrupt almost immediately; one often wondered whether the straight man actually knew more than the first line of the monologue he was so anxious to present. 'I say, I say, I say' ran the classic interpolation, followed by a question such as 'Why don't elephants like penguins?' It was part of the convention that the question must be repeated. 'I don't know,' flustered and irate, the Murray figure would reply, 'why don't elephants like penguins?' 'Because', came the triumphant clincher, 'they can't

A drove of double acts (clockwise) – Jewel and Warriss; Revnell and West; Scott and Whaley; Burns and Allen.

get the silver paper off!' Murray used to produce an audible throat-swallowing before countering with the classical dismissal: 'I don't wish to know that. Kindly leave the stage.' An abject apology to the audience for the unseemly interruption, back to the 'little monologue', thus through the chain of versicles and responses like a pagan incantation, even unto the final hymn of always ending with a cheery song.

Suddenly they all vanished. Presumably they ended with the death of variety. Radio offers fewer 'showcase' programmes to comedians than it did, and both broadcasting media depend heavily on 'sit-coms' for their humour. The club circuit seems to prefer the harder-hitting, less ceremonial quick-fire stand-up comedian, and there are now no more than three or four double acts which the ordinary citizen could name, as opposed to a dozen or twenty back in the forties.

We turn to Morecambe and Wise for succour in such a dearth of double acts, and we are seldom disappointed. But why Morecambe and Wise? The answer is possibly a circular one. Morecambe and Wise are talented enough to have survived in any period; but they would probably have found it easier in the thirties and forties when double acts were at the peak of their popularity. Perhaps they are that much more effective for having had to make their way when the obstacles to their kind of act have been at their harshest. They have had to conquer through developing what the evolutionists call 'acquired characteristics'. While relying heavily on the time-honoured accoutrements and badges of their craft, they have to seek others. It has been a case of double-act Darwinism; the survival of the fittest. We now have, therefore, but one double act, but it is the 'fittest' ever in the story of British entertainment.

The secret ingredient is perhaps a transatlantic one. Morecambe and Wise have no compunction in confessing how they stole their early material from other performers and in particular from the Hollywood films of Abbott and Costello. Bud Abbott was hatchet-faced and bullying, dominating the exceedingly tubby Lou Costello, whose nervous stutter and twitching forefinger constantly revealed his despairs and fears. They did a straightforward enough wordplay and punning brand of dialogue, of the 'Who's at first base' variety, and, as a boy, it seemed to me that one of their films turned up at the local Savoy every month or so. Mars, the navy, the Foreign Legion, piracy, the Keystone Cops, an Egyptian tomb, Frankenstein, the invisible man – these provided just some of the backgrounds for their moderate custard-pie routines and silly double-talk.

Certainly Morecambe and Wise lived off this inheritance. Ernie Wise is the know-all, the one who attempts to galvanise his partner into serious thought and action, while Eric Morecambe appears to react more slowly and stupidly, until it really counts, when, like Lou Costello before him, he makes the kill. Dean Martin and Jerry Lewis, when in partnership, came much nearer to Abbott and Costello, with the former showing no affection other than a laconic and supercilious view of the latter's sqawking lunacies. Wise has been warmer, if vainer, than Abbott and Martin; Morecambe less cretinous and panic-stricken than Costello and Lewis.

As Morecambe and Wise draw ahead of their British and American counterparts, this last point hints at a clue. Where most double acts have been two-dimensional, Morecambe and Wise have become three-dimensional. Others have been no more than cardboard cut-outs, with nothing more than an accessory, like a phonofiddle, a blackened face, a cockney accent, to distinguish one from the other. There was always the grave, abrasive, dignified one and the seemingly subordinate but actually sly wag. What Morecambe and Wise have done is to create characters from the unpromising profiles of the funny man and the straight man. It is as if a thoughtful dramatist had decided to take the good and evil angels from a medieval morality play and think them through as rounded persons.

Nature offered them a goodish start. They reverse the convention. The straight man is the shorter and fatter and the funny man the thinner and taller, and he is also bespectacled, often a theatrical cue to sombreness. There, then, is an ultimate transposition, the final confusion of misrule, when even the comedians disobey their own traditions. Ernie Wise remains the serious one, but his *gravitas* has its own style and it is a style which attracts mirthful attention. His pseudo-intellectualism, his prolific authorship, his unsinkable conceit, his chirpy enthusiasm – all have evolved from the straightness of the straight man. He is a much more gifted character actor and song and dance man than straight men of yore, and, all in all, he is in no way a cipher.

Eric Morecambe, by the sixties, had matured into a well-balanced clown, deserving of such an admirable foil. With exquisite timing, a harmonious co-ordination of facial and bodily movement, a telling intonation with every syllable, he has been able, over and over, to make the excellent scripts of Sid Green and Dick Hills and later Eddie Braben seem little less than superb. He moves easily from the fashionable suiting and evening dress of some sketches to the hilarious wardrobe of others, normally making capital use of his spindly legs in the process. He is a droll figure, but much more in command than is usual for the clown. Other buffoons in double acts have by the intervention of providence succeeded in the end, like comic virtue rewarded after a series of buffetings. Not so with Eric Morecambe. He is cunning and aware at all times. However Ernie Wise may bustle and manage complacently, his partner has, in reality, assumed the authority, searching for chances to manipulate or undermine his friend's energetic resolve. There is

More nearly than any other duo, Morecambe and Wise approach Laurel and Hardy. Which of them, too, was the comedian?

an objectivity about Eric Morecambe's stance. There is almost the dispassionate element of the observer about him, as if he is standing back to watch the optimistic and blinkered Ernie Wise fall headlong into every one of life's snares and traps.

It is interesting that when Eric Morecambe was reunited with his boyhood pal after the war, he was designated the feed. Eventually, as their stage personalities have developed, the question must be raised as to which one is the comedian? Like well oiled dual pistons operating fluently, their interaction is impeccable. The psychoanalysts and political scientists could have a scholastic field day with a double act like Morecambe and Wise. Perhaps Eric's unending sexual misinterpretation of Ernie's innocent phraseology may be seen as the personification of the unconscious thwarting the sentry at the threshold of the conscious mind. As for the neo-Marxist, the proletarian rudely disturbing the bourgeois's cultural pretensions is well advertised by Morecambe and Wise, and that servant–master conflict, or its equivalent, was the stuff that plays were made of centuries before Marx.

Of course, in the last analysis, Eric Morecambe *is* the clown and Ernie Wise *is* the stooge. But, like Lear and his fool, the zone between the conscious expression and the probing conscience or between the king and the jester sometimes narrows to a fraction. This full-blooded filling out of character is more American than British. The Marx Brothers created highly idiosyncratic traits, and what of George Burns and Gracie Allen? The twittering, inconsequential Gracie; the laconic, resigned George, philosophic behind his huge cigar – which was the comedian? Abbott and Costello may have given some early leads for scripts, but it was the profounder American teams which have given Morecambe and Wise, as they themselves have testified, the key to their maturer success.

Laurel and Hardy are possibly the finest as well as the best known double act in the English-speaking world, notably through their cinematic adventures. It is perhaps the pleasantest tribute one can pay Morecambe and Wise to say that they more nearly approach Ollie and Stan than any other duo. Where Morecambe and Wise straddle the pennines, Laurel and Hardy, happily, straddled the Atlantic, the portly irascible yet fastidiously gentle Olly from Georgia, and, more mundanely, the mournfully put-upon Stan from Ulverston in the Lake District. Stan Laurel was the more dedicated artist, spending hours monitoring rushes, visiting out-of-town cinemas to measure the laughs and change the films before general release. Oliver Hardy, gentlemanly and relaxed, was not so committed, but both of them contributed to the humour inherent in their slow-motion struggle with the vicissitudes of American life. It is impossible to give a satisfactory answer to the question: which is the comedian? That is their most compelling epitaph.

Morecambe and Wise are akin to them in several ways, although the comparisons are not on a one-to-one correspondence. Ernie Wise appears, like Stan Laurel, to be the more serious from a business viewpoint, yet in character he represents the same pomposities as Olly Hardy. Eric Morecambe is scarcely as tearful as Stan Laurel, but they share similar gifts of puncturing such pomposities with their humdrum and commonplace habits. Morecambe and Wise follow Laurel and Hardy in their allegiance to a familiar compilation of gestures and sayings. The nervy tie-twitching of Oliver and the neurotic hair-tugging of Stanley; Oliver's daintily spread fingers, especially when impressing a lady; Stanley's squeaky weepiness when matters go astray; tag-lines like 'that's a fine mess you've gotten us into, Stanley' – as with the modern duo, it is possible to record a long catalogue of such examples. There are also the song-and-dance routines, with Oliver Hardy as buoyant a dancer as Stan Laurel is waif-like. Their 'Blue-rock Mountains of Virginia' was quite a hit when revived in the early seventies.

The two couples are nearest in style when Morecambe and Wise are exchanging notes in their flat. Their arguments are highly reminiscent of Laurel and Hardy chewing over problems in their stateside apartment. The bedroom scene, Ernie writing his plays with Eric alongside him, quietly disconcerting as always, is a particularly sharp illustration of this, for there were several occasions when Laurel and Hardy were to be found in bed together with problems of one kind or another. Then they also forsook their domestic setting, and like Morecambe and Wise worked through the same sort of comic drills in other climes and dress – as motorists, foreign legionaires, convicts, soldiers, and so on.

Through the thirties and forties, under the capable direction of Hal Roach, Laurel and Hardy produced humour with a consistency which made the jerky strains of their fluting signature tune act in Pavlovian manner on what Ken Dodd calls the 'chuckle-muscle'. During the sixties and into the seventies Morecambe and Wise, as a consequence of a long and conscientious apprenticeship, have attained something of the same levels of consistency. As the band strikes up the breezy melody of 'Bring me Sunshine', we settle back in our theatre seats or sitting-room easy chairs, prepared to be amused. We are rarely disappointed, for Morecambe and Wise have given stability to the shifting sands of entertainment in the fickleness of the sixties. This they have done by matching an important secret with an important quality. The secret is that the public relish the predictable and yearn for the familiar, and Morecambe and Wise quite explicitly build on that human need. The quality lies in their development – for the more effective meeting of that need – of two matching characters with conversation as closely observed as only very few playwrights manage.

Les Dawson

THE DOOM-LADEN DUMPLING

'There was a knock on the door. It was the wife's mother. I knew it was her because the mice started throwing themselves on the traps.'

About the dawn of the seventies I switched on the television set and saw Les Dawson, gloomy and podgy, for the first time. Talking of life in a Manchester overspill estate, he was explaining: 'I'm not saying our council house is far from the city centre, but our rent man's a Norwegian.' In 1975, in an August whose aridity was a portent for the drought of 1976, I took my two sons to see him at Southport. It was midweek, and sweltering; we went to the first house, and, in any event, Southport is not your Blackpool, nor even your Great Yarmouth, when it comes to seaside entertainment. So the Southport Theatre was by no means full. The curtains opened, and, following the sound effect of a flushing lavatory, on marched Les Dawson. He gazed around morosely at his slender flock. 'Bloody hell,' he said, 'I've seen more in Moscow Conservative Club.' With such doleful laments does Les Dawson place his dismal seal on the unhappy years of the seventies.

He is effectively one of the first atomic age comedians, still a child at the end of the Second World War and very much a creature of the late twentieth century. At the same time he maintains comic traditions, and historical and geographical strands as well, of some lengthier standing. He was born in Collyhurst, Manchester, not far from the Queen's Park Hippodrome, in 1935, a bricklayer's son, born into a district which he has described as peopled by 'bent women trudging to the off-licence with chipped jugs; the hard-lipped knots of unemployed men on street corners sharing their last smoke as their pride struggled for survival'. The parcels department of the co-op at fourteen and some training in electrics at the local tech. formed his adolescent days, by which time it was the fifties. So, while missing the sort of war service which influenced Frankie Howerd or Jimmy Edwards, he enjoyed a distinctly pre-war kind of upbringing. Bred among the 'doorstep doyens in bright aprons, arms akimbo as they pass judgement on the neighbourhood morality', his pedigree is Coronation Street out of *Hindle Wakes*. It is a reminder that the character of the thirties we associated with George Formby pushed hard for many into the forties.

He therefore springs from the people he now entertains, and they, in turn, are the first descendants of those who crowded into Blackpool, attracted by the insistent jangle of George Formby's ukelele or the soaring top notes of Gracie Fields. They would have warmed to Jimmy James as he fascinated them on the Central Pier, or tuned in eagerly to Robb Wilton as he recalled Rita's latest barbed comments. They are the people who, on television and into the theatre, avidly follow Morecambe and Wise and Ken Dodd. They would approve of Les Dawson's decision to settle, with his wife and three youngsters, in the affluent comfort of Lytham St Annes, just to the south of Blackpool. It reflects something of their own aspirations,

Les Dawson – 'A dumpling head surmounting a dumpling body'.

possibly to retire to a bungalow in Bispham or Cleveleys. It is not the swanky opulence of George Formby's Beryldene, to say nothing of our Gracie emigrated to Capri. It has not the swish quality of a metropolitan apartment. It is posh, but not pretentious, nor undignified; it maintains the link, culturally with Collyhurst.

Like the finest of funny men, he is, physically, all of a piece, with a dumpling head surmounting a dumpling body. In making a snowman, one rolls two snowballs, then rams the smaller one on to the larger. Les Dawson could have been so created, and his whole appearance, heavily bearing down and rounded, adds disconsolate weight to the glum tidings he brings us. It is interesting that the circular shape can betoken joy or misery. Les Dawson is the converse of the guffawing clown, clutching his well-filled paunch with gasping merriment. The hunched shoulders; the careworn eyes, screwed tight under the wrinkled, frowning brow; the sagging tummy; the pathetically stubby legs; most of all, the sad mouth which droops into a wellnigh perfect semicircle of depression – there has rarely been so complete a caricature of dejection on the English stage.

It is sometimes said that hard times breed a ghoulish humour, just as they are supposed to rear champion boxers. Les Dawson looks back to that past: 'I'm not saying we were poor, but my father used to tell us ghost stories so that we'd cling together to keep warm.' Now, after the money-spilling fifties and the sixties, the seventies wreak an unpleasant vengeance, demanding their toll in another phase of sullen recession. This time unemployment and means-tested benefits spread their dulling ache among the corporation estates and high-rise blocks, rather than among the terraced rows that these have substantially replaced.

Much of this is relative. The 'shawlies' of the thirties would cackle at the moans of their granddaughters about the difficulties of maintaining HP payments or the price of frozen fish-fingers. But people compare contemporaneously, not retrospectively, and, if poverty may be defined in terms of reasonable access denied to the current norms of social existence, then many are impoverished. The monetary crisis has since the war returned almost with the annual predictability of the swallow; indeed, the cycle began at – even before – the turn of the century. But, for perhaps the first time since the Second World War, the standard of living of millions has been arrested and often lowered. Les Dawson reflects this new poverty: 'My father was so poor he used to throw IOU's in the wishing well for luck.'

There is an unease about the problems of the seventies. A modern population cannot live from day to day even if it wishes, for its resources are tied up in hire-purchase debts and mortgages. But the disquiet bites deeper. Many of the public services – transport, health – seem to be teetering on the brink of disintegration, while the ramifications of too many world-wide issues have their stern daily effect. The seventies have abounded with forebodings of a dozen Armageddons. Once it was merely the risk of the nuclear holocaust of which we must be aware; now the hazards multiply. The energy crisis, the ecological crisis, the food and population crisis, the racial crisis, at home and overseas – every one of life's aspects suddenly carries, like the opening scene of a Greek tragedy, the cue to eventual doom. Here in Britain, the Tories' rasping confrontation with the miners, the staggering price of oil, a million and a half unemployed and a diving pound were just a few of the elements which hinted at possible disintegration.

People flee from the prospect of annihilation in their separate ways. There is the taunting incredulity of some; there is the retreat into self-help and do-it-yourself schemes of others – allotments, many of which lay idle in the fifties and sixties, have waiting lists galore now. Some become activists in the conservationist cause; others turn to the fictional solutions of non-reality, and television, for instance, has recently had its goodly share of mid-term futurism with programmes like *The Survivors,* as well as plenty of sci-fi in the persons of Dr Who or Captain Kirk of *Star Trek.*

There is little need to retail a painful itinerary of the ills of the seventies, all too close as it is to all of us. But, in a review of popular entertainment, it is worth emphasising the tedious and complex nature of today's problems. The fiscal system, the industrial process, devolution – what fiendish nightmares of unexciting complication? Most salutary of all is the Common Market. Entered with synthetic hails of euphoric jubilation, it has proved, in the outcome, to be a happening sunk in ennui. The EEC has successfully lowered its own temperature and cultivated an insidiously restrictive tangle of incomprehensible regulations. It is the bureaucrats' chief weapon: bore the pants off the populace, then kick them in the backside when they're not looking.

Whatever the disastrous effects of the techno-bureaucracy, British and European, on our everyday life, its influence on our light comedy has been negligible, neutral and thereby damaging. In brief, one seldom hears jokes about such matters. If one does, they are often of that feeble variety which rely on topicality rather than humour. They are of that category of political gags which, on TV spectaculars, the comedian will recount who wants to be thought clever, and which the studio audience, keen to please but unable to raise a laugh, damn with the faint praise of a round of applause. It is not just the basic unfunniness of the situation – humorists have often found their merriest inspiration in such tragedies as death, war or accident. It is the fact that they offer so few comic opportunities, and comedians can

Les Dawson as 'the short-sighted grimacing literary expert who finds extremely lubricious matter in the most innocent nursery rhyme'.

squeeze little blood and laughter from such tiresome stones. As was said of the philosopher William Godwin, they are 'either asleep or the cause of sleep in others'.

Like most of the nation under stress, Les Dawson resorts to a resigned plaintiveness for his humour. He has the advantage that, along with his down-in-the-dumps body, he has a melancholy voice. It is a low, gruff, slightly catarrhal growl, the flattened north Mancunian vowels underlining his dirge of despair. Others have turned to the comic equivalent of science fiction, enjoying the surreal ventures of *Monty Python,* Marty Feldman or the Goodies. Nostalgia has played its part, with the continuing success of series like *Dad's Army, It Aint 'alf Hot, Mum* and *Get Some In* on television being but one component of a great industry of documentary and fictional products from the twenties through to the fifties.

But as a complement to his authentic voice of the age-old notes of proletarian cheerlessness, Les Dawson has his modernistic side. He is essentially a wordsmith. He has a visual side, especially his countenance, which he moulds like molten rubber into the most despondent figurations. In a direct duplication of Norman Evans, his midde-aged housewife noiselessly whispers through the most elastic of gums about the most horrendous of operations. We lip-read delicacies like 'she's had it all taken away'. Another of his characters, the short-sighted grimacing literary expert who finds extremely lubricious matter in the most innocent nursery rhyme and stimulates himself into orgiastic frenzies, is also chiefly reliant on the visual. Nonetheless, he is, in the modern manner, intrigued by linguistics. Like Jimmy James before him, he savours the language of comedy, and, in his mainstay solos, he luxuriates in the ornate sentence, recollecting, for instance, 'a pock-marked Lascar in the arms of a frump in a Huddersfield bordello'. It paints a searing picture of alarming mediocrity. It recalls the pomposity of Tony Hancock's oblique flights of imagination. Both the melancholia and the overstrained semantics of the self-educated East Cheam hustler may be noted in Les Dawson's work: he is the plebeian Hancock of the north-west passage.

Alone among the twelve comedians celebrated in these pages, Les Dawson – a self-confessed essayist *manqué* – has written novels. Others have, like Frankie Howerd, turned to autobiography, or, like Morecambe and Wise, told their story for public perusal. Will Hay wrote on serious astronomical matters, and almost all of them have written comic material, much of it of the highest class. But Les Dawson has written a couple of novels which, while scarcely challenging Tolstoy or Dickens, are still novels, and, as J. B. Priestley sagely remarked, it takes a clever man to write even a bad novel. These are nowhere near bad: they are broad comic tales, one, *A Card for the Clubs,* written in 1975, and the other, published in 1976, a spy-spoof, also with a 'club' background, called *The Spy Who Came* . . . They strike a jaunty, Rabelaisian note, and, although they fade and tire a little after colourful beginnings, they are amusing *tours de force*.

Their more vivid pieces read like Les Dawson's plum monologues, when, alone on the stage or before the camera, he crowds metaphor after simile and adverb after adjective in flowery extracts from his eventful life story. Sometimes he cleverly plays the piano off-key, as an accompaniment to sentimental reminiscence, in parody of those awful acts where the piano was played but passably, the singing was unmelodic and the inter-song chat excruciating. Indeed, after a brief spell with a jazz band, Les Dawson began show business as a pianist-singer, until, the story goes, needled by the inattention of the robust trawlermen in a Hull club, he riddled them with a volley of agonised insults – and they rebooked him for the following week.

He especially enjoys the rather roughened metaphoric phrase: of his sleeping wife 'snoring gently with all the refinement of a bronchial wart-hog', he said the noise was closest in sound 'to the death-rattle of a moose with piles' and that, with mouth agape, it was 'like peering down the open end of a damp euphonium'; at his wedding reception the pickles 'were so tooth-defying that the pickle fork had to be crowned and capped'; the atmosphere in the family home was 'as cosy as a suicide attempt in Lenin's tomb'; as an accident-prone plumber's mate who scorched his superior with a blow-lamp, he claimed that 'to my dying day, I will see again that tortured craftsman pouring tea dregs on his singed crutch'; of his in-laws' television screen, it was 'so small that when they showed *Snow White* we only saw Grumpy and the castle damp-course'; of a fellow artist's loose dentures, 'they dropped over her bottom lip to resemble a porcelain portcullis'; of his wife's gooseberry flan, surreptitiously fed to the dog which, after sampling it, 'spent the rest of the night in a corner with its paw down its throat'; to a silent audience, 'let's hold hands and contact the living'.

His favourite device is the line beginning, 'I'm not saying . . . but . . .' Talking of his Bootle digs, for instance, while playing Southport (or, as he termed it, 'Blackpool with O levels') he commented: 'I'm not saying it's rough, but last night I got mugged by a nun.' Some might argue that he bruises language, but then, as the forties hit mourned, you always hurt the one you love. He may not caress words with the avuncular tenderness of comedians like Robb Wilton or Jimmy James, but his affection for them is as unabashed. He seeks out the unlikeliest comparisons, and the bluntness is frequently refreshing rather than shocking. Released by the permissive sweep of the fifties and sixties, the comedian of the seventies must perforce be more explicit. The opaque references of George

Formby and even the double entendres of Max Miller seem a little outmoded, some would feel perhaps a trifle hypocritical, for the open culture of today.

The patois of the barrack-room or the workplace has become the argot of stage and television. In a sense, art and nature are, at this conjunction, more integrated than of old. There is a link here with another major theme of social life over the present decade, namely the equalisation or liberation of womankind. This highly significant change has affected comedy considerably. The age-old distinction between the jokes of the shop-floor, the NAAFI queue, the rugby club booze-up and the stag concert and those of the music hall narrows. It has not altogether disappeared, but in the clubs and on television, equal treatment is expected, sought and obtained.

The finer susceptibilities are mortally offended, but that is the truth of it. Max Miller's appeal, through the female, to the male, would be more difficult now, although his essential bravado would doubtless have helped him conquer the difficulty in triumph. Men and women are prepared to listen, watch and laugh in parity. This means, for good or ill, a coarser edge to the humour. George Formby offered a hundred cheerful euphemisms for the rectum and its associated troubles, but he could never have brought himself or have been permitted to speak forthrightly, as Les Dawson can, of piles.

This is partly another result of the cultural equality of men and women, and the downward spread of this equality to children, who are less afflicted by linguistic separatism than in days gone by. The carefulness about what is said in front of the children has, with the ubiquitous insistence of television, largely been modified. The woman swearing in semi-public is a case in point.

In terms of light comedy, there has been the advent of the writer-performer. This has been made manifest at various levels – Alan Bennett, John Cleese, Marty Feldman, and so on are representatives of the university-style revue writers and performers who have come to the fore since the fifties and earn their keep on radio and television as well as in the West End.

A pluralistic and more open society has made for less inhibited private languages among peer groups and, to some extent, classes. However unhelpful for comedy may be the enervating politics and economics of the decade, comedians are at least allowed, possibly obliged, to explore a much wider, franker gamut of social life. As public and private thoughts and norms coalesce, public and private language likewise combine. While sustaining the traditional variety image, Les Dawson has exhibited this more *avant-garde* trait among the ranks of the comedians.

He has had to make his mark and demonstrate these proclivities in the cold world of the northern clubs. Just as

Frankie Howerd reserves some of his more acrid comments for the backstage grimness of the theatre, so does Les Dawson save his bitterest phrases for the iniquities and the inhospitalities of clubland. 'If they like you,' he cryptically says, 'they let you live.' Comedians of his generation are the first to have had to succeed initially on that club circuit, around which thousands of peripatetic artists endlessly orbit. Ken Dodd, Bob Monkhouse and others find prosperous bookings in the clubs, but they were already recognised. Les Dawson and his colleagues had to start like privates in the trenches, and win their commissions in the field. The older comedians are staff officers visiting the quieter parts of the front line.

A military analogy is not out of place. It is sometimes remarked that light theatre, born in the taverns of Victorian England, has, with the clubs, come full circle. People eat and, more prevalently, drink; they talk, roister, dance and frequently play bingo. A Saturday night second-house audience in the days of variety was often rowdy and none too sober, but the format was static and structured. Clubs have a restless, mobile character, full of distractions away from the stage. Their members have other reasons for their presence, whereas in music hall and variety most of those in attendance accepted that their priority was the professional entertainment. Les Dawson typifies the seventies for he is basically a club comic, and it was in this decade that the clubs consolidated their massive advances of the sixties, when variety petered out completely. The 'turns' – sometimes ushered by a figure not unlike the old-time chairman – must struggle for a hearing, and these industrialised equivalents of the suave night-club can be just as cool and ten times as noisy. They range from obscure and cramped working men's clubs to the huge theatre clubs of South Lancashire and West Yorkshire, with thousands milling, swilling and keen to participate. Like the football crowd, they are as jubilantly appreciative in gratitude as they are trenchantly candid in criticism: not for them the quiet disdain of suburban disapproval.

Trevor Griffiths's play, *Comedians,* which after opening in Nottingham to critical plaudits moved to London with enormous success in 1975 and 1976, describes some of this social history. Like Osborne's *The Entertainer* in the fifties, Trevor Griffiths chose a current entertainment medium for his own political metaphor, and it was club night. The opening and closing acts are set in a Manchester night school class for comedians, the preface to and the adjudication of the central act where the class members try their luck in a local club, the theatre audience becoming the club clientele. The ex-comedian turned tutor represents integrity – his charges must keep scrupulous good faith with humour and themselves – and his old rival turned London agent represents turpitude – however shabby and

Like John Osborne's The Entertainer *Trevor Griffiths's* Comedians *describes some of the social history of the profession through a northern club on 'club night'. Jimmy Jewel (right) as Eddie Waters, and Ralph Nossek as Challenor in the original Nottingham Playhouse production.*

false, the comedian must serve up what the customer appears to like.

Of course, the metaphor has a range of interpretations, from the simple, almost medieval, good angel versus evil angel, to a compelling statement about the mechanisms of society in the seventies. Its probing indictment of infidelity to principle makes it one of the most important plays of the decade. But, from the present standpoint, what is interesting is that West End audiences understood and accepted the metaphor with the same enthusiasm as they had the parable of Archie Rice twenty years before. The club secretary (aptly doubling as the school caretaker) is apologetic – it won't take long to put these young hopefuls through their paces, and then back to the bingo. There is an Irish joker, after the breezy style of Frank Carson, a tubby Jewish story-teller who scrapes the barrel somewhat, a quieter, pensive raconteur with some of the contrived and mannered deportment of Dave Allen, a confused clowning duo who collapses ineffectually, and (the touchstone of the drama) a performer of the most aggressive probity, as nakedly steel-hard as Dan Leno is said sometimes to have been. Naturally, the agent books the first two, although the second needs, he thinks, considerable buffing.

It is precisely on the club circuit, with few if any inhibitions remaining of language, value or approach, that the struggle for integrity in comedy is truly possible. The conventions are stripped aside, and the choice is independent save only for the not insubstantial point about whether one can make it pay or not. The question of whether to pander to a shallow demand or to have the courage to aim for self-realisation is boldly posed in the clubs. As with all art-forms, there are the journeymen and the masters, the magazine illustrators and the Royal Academicians, each of them, after their fashion, capable both of punctilious and of disingenuous work. There are comedy acts well known and fêted in clubland which, solidly and conscientiously, are built just for that milieu, and which would be useless for stage, radio or television. Miming to specially created tapes is one such speciality which, away from the intimate, intense atmosphere of the club, would seem odd and vacuous.

The Darwinian interpretation of show business now demands that, as we noted with Frankie Howerd, the fittest are those who can embrace all the media, and not merely one, proficient and worthy although they might prove to be there. Les Dawson has accomplished this. The novel showcases for television talent are provided by programmes like *Opportunity Knocks* and *New Faces*. Like Freddy 'parrot-face' Davies, Les Dawson was introduced to the screen through the former, and has proved to be its most enduring protégé. Quickly, he has grown into his own television shows, like *Sez Les* and *Dawson's Weekly*. Assisted by workmanlike actors such as Julian Orchard or Roy

Barraclough, he has developed a diverting formula. But, as with other comedians on television – Frankie Howerd or Ken Dodd, for instance – he remains at his best when performing solo, unencumbered by the restraints of the structured sketch.

His abrupt, funereal humour has won him the acclaim of high-class summer shows and other attractive stage work, while, unlike most of the seventies comedians, he has proved to be a godsend to radio. It is on radio that, with words to the fore, his affection for language can be indulged and he is able to embark on his florid prose poems at leisure. Some of his endeavours would not shame the punning invention of Frank Muir and Denis Norden. For example, a long-winded seafaring yarn is summarised by a travesty of the opening bars of 'Ah, Sweet Mystery of Life' as 'Ah, sweet Master Rae of Leith, I've gagged and bound thee; and the rats have gnawed the moorings of *de Gaulle*,' where the ship *de Gaulle* is skippered by Captain Rae who hails from Leith.

But in his ability to serve comedy in these respective arenas, Les Dawson never breaks faith with the querulous irksome monotone of his essential comic self. Nor are his north Manchester origins ever allowed to be forgotten as he treads his careworn path. As his feeble ambitions become remorselessly lost amid his joylessness, one sometimes thinks of that earlier northern Manchester comedian, the elder George Formby, his illusions of the good life ever breaking against the realities of his miseries.

This illustrates the immense store still set by regionalism in professional comedy. Perhaps this is a counterblast to the bland anonymity of much which from town hall, Whitehall or Brussels controls our existences with a charmless lack of individuality. It is a long-standing tradition. There have been the fast-talking, impudent cockney, the broad-humoured Yorkshireman, the gormless provincial, the garrulous and irrational Irishman, the sly, bucolic West Countryman, amongst others. With the arrival of West Indian comedians like Charlie Williams and Jock White, the mix grows even more variegated. The popular view of the regional persona is preserved as much by the comedians as by anything. It is interesting to observe that it is not only in comedy that this occurs. The BBC, particularly for its sports commentators, has followed some of these regional dictates.

The open culture of the seventies requires that such regional variations should at least have a douche of realism, even if they are not steeped in it. To be fair, the north-western tradition has not been lacking in this regard, and Les Dawson follows men like Robb Wilton, Norman Evans and Al Read in the presentation of careworn authenticity. Elsewhere the sentimentality of the comedy of London or Scotland is under attack. Most notably, Billy Connolly, part folk-singer as well as comedian, has hilariously demolished the white heather symbolism of the Scottish myth, associated with names like Harry Lauder, Will Fyffe and Andy Stewart. At the same time, he is creating another view, less misleading but still singular, of Scotland, just as Les Dawson angles his sombre assaults from a particular Lancastrian vantage-point, namely the concrete gruesomeness of its declining urbanism.

His hero is the jaundiced observer of another depression in another dispiriting place, the United States town life of the thirties. It is W. C. Fields, who himself spent several years on the British music-hall stage. Les Dawson shares with his idol two definitive traits. One is the flamboyant espousal of the English language, especially in describing the more seedy and mundane aspects of life. The other is the refusal to entertain pathos at any price, the consequence being a humour which is hard-hearted and stony-faced. Les Dawson may not appear as so devious or cruel as W. C. Fields, nor does he aspire to that air of gimcrack authority which made such a brave, if transatlantic, showing for the American as Micawber in the film of *David Copperfield*. Les Dawson slumps as if beleaguered by all the woes of the age, but he is never fooled by its pretences. The satirists of the sixties were never as hard-nosed as their American counterparts, astringent artists like Lenny Bruce or Mort Sahl who took grave personal risks in viciously offending their chosen targets. Our satire was much more circumspect and urbane than this, with, in the popular vein, Frankie Howerd scarcely approaching or wishing to approach such excesses.

But in the seventies Les Dawson and one or two other comedians can match the ruthlessness of W. C. Fields as he surveyed the Great Depression in the States. There may not be the reformist message of satire, but it is a sceptical, sometimes, for the tender, a callous humour. Bernard Manning, a fellow north Mancunian, is another who holds nothing sacred and is prepared to see humour anywhere. The conventional 'Englishman, Irishman, Scotsman' jokes have been replaced by ethnic gags of all descriptions, although the Irish, and to some extent the Jews, remain prime butts. The latest immigrant populations are the latest victims. Bernard Manning will say that in Bradford they must wait for snow before they can hold a census, or that when the police are called it's the Bengal Lancers who arrive. His showbiz colleagues are not exempt from this withering fire, and, while friendly jokes about rivals have always been part of the trading pattern, there is now a gleam of hostility. Morecambe and Wise do a little of this, and there is a hint of unkindness, simply because it sounds so true, as in their constant denigration of Des O'Connor, or when Eric Morecambe, watching *Opportunity Knocks* and hearing Hughie Greene cry 'Now it's make your mind up time', grunts 'I have' and curtly switches off. Bernard Manning goes further than this. Speaking on television about Max Bygraves's efforts to launch

Clockwise:
Les Dawson, basically a club comic – I'm not saying ... but ...'

Les Dawson's hero was W. C. Fields 'with his air of gimcrack authority', who spent some time on the British music-hall stage.

Successful club comedians, like Les Dawson, are Bernard Manning and Charlie Williams.

Les Dawson's abrupt, funereal style of humour shares the same realism with which Billy Connolly demolishes the white heather symbolism of the Scottish myth.

his son into show business culminating in a disastrous flop in Jersey, he commented, 'The people in Jersey said that, if it came to a toss-up, they'd rather have the Germans back.' Whatever else, there is no hypocrisy, no back-stabbing behind radiant smiles, in the typical humour of the seventies.

Les Dawson casts his sceptical eye neither on the racial question nor on the others in his profession. He is plainly preoccupied with his own troubles and ailments and with a life full of ghastly misfortunes and hideous relations. He is, then, cruel about himself and his nearest and dearest, rather than about those external to him. Whilst his self-mocking, embittered attitude is appropriate for the mournful glumness of the 1970s he preserved the northern drolls' obsession with the family.

No mother-in-law has been more cruelly savaged than Les Dawson's, that alarming bogy of comic mythology. It was he who coined the now well-known description: 'I'm not saying she's horrible, but she was sacked from the Gestapo for cruelty.' He narrates – sign of the times – not the horrors of Wakes Week in Blackpool but the discomforts of a package tour to the Costa Brava. The culminating fiasco is robbery at the hands of brigands who take their every last stitch. 'Don't worry,' his wife consoles him, 'I hid your wallet and our passports in my mouth.' 'It's a pity', is his laconic rejoinder, 'that we didn't bring your mother. We could have saved the luggage as well.' He begins another account as follows: 'There was a knock at the door. It was the wife's mother. I knew it was her because the mice started throwing themselves on the traps.' She has a mouth 'like a workhouse oven', and instead of tonsils she has a fan-belt. When she hangs out her vest to dry, an hour's daylight is lost. Like the janitor in one of those American horror-comic series like *The Munsters,* he dolefully relates the most macabre detail of a son-in-law's life.

He is brutal with himself. Friday Dawson he was christened: his father looked at him and said to his mother, 'Let's call it a day.' They took one look at him in the crib, held hands and ran off together. He was so ugly that they put shutters on his pram. His mother was so bewildered she talcum-powdered his face. 'God knows what she did with my dummy', he reflects morosely. There were so many babies that the wet nappies in the kitchen created a rainbow in the lobby. The house was very damp – 'three bedrooms and a jetty' – and instead of their father telling them tales he gave the children lifeboat drill. Les Dawson claims he shot his parents to go on an orphans' picnic. He is as unsparing with himself as with his much maligned mother-in-law.

A doomsday face, on a body in the doldrums: that physique, with its plaintive, cynical accompaniment, is fitting token to the seventies. Les Dawson sustains the lineage of comedians distracting us from the ills of the day by utilising the very idiom of those ills.

Ken Dodd

Programme

MAKE 'EM LAUGH

COMEDY'S EVANGELIST

'What a wonderful day it is for running down the road, sticking a green cucumber through the letter-boxes and shouting "the Martians are coming!" '

In the longer perspective, there is a sense in which the social history of society over the last fifty years has been unchanging. Its structure has remained solid enough, despite the vivid alterations in the superstructure, in its fashions, and mechanics and interests. After all, we are still living in a nation state, with a money economy, ruled by a form of parliamentary democracy, and with a mixture of public control and private influence. Robert Redford may reign instead of Rudolf Valentino, and sherry may be 'in' to the despair of the port wine trade. Pub talk may be about which model of motor car to purchase next, rather than whether to invest in a new pair of cycle clips. Shirt and hair lengths have, over half a century, ascended and descended with entertaining regularity, and the frozen fish-finger stalks a land which once knew but of cod in batter. Nonetheless, the underlying springs of national existence remain relatively untouched, and 'the more we change ...' is equally true of popular comedy. The peculiar quips and quiddities of individual comedians, often harmonising neatly and delightfully with the particular traits and tendencies of the short term, are, eventually, less important than their major similarities over an epoch in which society has remained (some would say, depressingly) similar.

Of the comedians I have described, the similarities are twofold. On the one hand has been or is their ability to move audiences, through one medium or several, to consistent and genuine laughter. Their tricks and devices – what John Milton might have called their 'quips and cranks' – have varied enormously, principally in response to the stimuli of their immediate time and its climate, but, very simply, they all make people laugh. Some may feel this is a low level of aspiration, hardly to be mentioned alongside the ecstatic joys of poetry or classical music or great paintings and literature. However, human kind, physiologically speaking, cries before it laughs, of which every newborn baby lustily reminds us. Theatrical records are littered with those who, were the aspiration low or high, could not achieve the difficult feat of stirring audiences from their gravity. However the springs of laughter are defined, whether in psychological or biological or spiritual terms, few doubt that laughter is a healthy, natural and normal reaction, much to be encouraged. If that may be accepted, without the tedious exploration of the several scholarly theories about why and how people laugh, then the successful comedian is an honourable public servant, as OBEs for Morecambe and Wise and Frankie Howerd would imply. Moreover, in that simple sense of straightforward laughter, many straightforward comedians would stand high in the ratings. If some form of laughometer could be applied to compare what, roughly, might be called classical and popular humour, the latter would probably fare rather well. Of course, the humour of Falstaff or

Don Quixote or Mr Pickwick, as well as the humour of Breughel or Tchaikovsky, has significant additional merit as it is the means of attaining a perhaps mightier end: in these cases making people laugh is an approach or method, rather than an objective, as it is with George Formby or Will Hay. But, concentrating on the actual laughter quotient, there cannot be many people who have not *laughed* more at one or other of this catalogue of comics than at the most beguiling characterisation of Bottom the Weaver or the happiest readings of *Tom Jones*. Comedians are professional mirth provokers, no more than that, but isn't that plenty?

The other chief similarity is the complement of this. Because their chosen art-form is the encouragement of laughter in its own right, they remain well within the province of the established regime. They may debunk and tease and, in so doing, send gusts of fresh air through the highways and byways of society, and that is wholesome and sometimes productive. But they never threaten. Even in the satiric sixties, comedians, as such, never menaced the bedrock of society. To use a phrase from the introduction, this means that comedians tend to be 'lightning conductors', diverting the pain and anxiety of life's problems, national or personal, and releasing the tensions. This is good or evil according to one's political assessment of the status quo, but, in our society, the revolutionary comedian is wellnigh a contradiction in terms.

This makes for an important conservationist component among comedians. It applies to their material. This is not said unkindly: it is the preservation of themes rather than actual gags which is meaningful. Sex frequently rears its hydra-head, but equally frequently it is the family and especially marriage which is the mainspring. The wife, to say nothing of that much-feared boggart, her mother, are constant butts. Comedians, moreover, are craftsmen who at best learn and at worst steal from those who have gone before. Because the needs and the approaches do not differ, the trade itself has not changed overmuch. Indeed, the comedian can trace his professional ancestry back to the court jester, except that in more democratic times the court is much more open to the public. Comedians are the people's jesters. They amuse and divert the court and, by pricking the bubbles of illusion, they relieve tension and reduce anxieties.

In mode and manner, comedians thus have a geography and a history. They must sharpen their God-given talent by reference to their sense of place and their grasp of inheritance. Ken Dodd is a valuable 'model' of this art-form, because his highly individualised comic flair is matched by his own diligent technical application. Message and medium, as in all art-forms, become one, and both are worthy of study, not least because Ken Dodd is a proficient investigator of humour in his own

right, one who encourages the disciplined appraisal of humour and a man who, in another incarnation, might well have chosen, he claims, social psychology for his metier.

He was born fifty years ago in the double-fronted house where he still lives, and, like several others described in these pages, he was born into the fringes of show business rather than, Judy Garland style, in a trunk, backstage. Billy Bennett, Jimmy James, Tony Hancock and Morecambe and Wise all had that proximity to show business which is perhaps sufficient to whet the appetite rather than cause indigestion. Even George Formby was deliberately held aloof by his father from the world of entertainment in the vain hope that he would seek fame elsewhere. Ken Dodd's father, Arthur, was a coal merchant (and the grimy, hefty trucks still lurch and wheel on the waste patch at the back of the house) who was also a saxophonist. Especially when, during the twenties, the coal trade was not too promising, he played professionally, including summers on the Isle of Man, and, along with the pineapple chunks each Sunday high tea, Ken Dodd heard the songs and patter of the variety stage. When he was eight, he began to develop a child ventriloquist act, a skill he still uses with Dickie Mint, the diddy doll. From that time onward, he began a ceaseless round of scout huts and church halls, graduating slowly to the dizzier range of masonics and clubs. He joined his father in the coal business, but he later floated a successful travelling hardware venture of his own, so much so that in his early twenties he had to choose between a prospering business with a lucrative sideline and the gamble of creating a career from a hobby. By this time, 'the wonder boy ventriloquist' was billed as 'Professor Yaffle Chuckabutty, Operatic Tenor and Sausage Knotter'. The ex-chorister of St Thomas's Church, Knotty Ash, had become a burlesque balladeer, and in 1954 he made his debut as a full-time professional at the Empire Theatre, Nottingham. He soon reigned triumphant, with his own television series following as early as 1959, and for twenty years he has remained consistently at the top of this arduous profession.

I first saw him in the late fifties at the Manchester Palace. It was *Aladdin,* with Norman Evans as a memorable Widow Twankey, and with Betty Jumel in pert support. They were no mean burlesque balladeers themselves, demolishing the 'Pipes of Pan', with Norman Evans as overweight soprano and Betty Jumel as pint-sized tenor. But the newcomer impressed with the two standards which still constitute the heart of his solo act. One was the 'Floral Dance', with Ken Dodd spiderlike and angular in tight-fitting black as he listened to the band with the curious tone. His adjustment of slight hand and feet movements to the phrasing of that old song was a piece of the most fluent clowning. It was matched by his 'Road to Mandalay', when, in garb reminiscent of one of Billy Bennett's rigs, he appeared in

Ken Dodd 'hits every stage with the same driving unstoppable dynamism' as Al Jolson whom he regards as 'the greatest showman of them all'.

khaki drill shorts and sun hat, plus the weirdest assemblage of camping equipment on his back, with a tailor's female dummy's leg particularly catching the eye. I have ever since been a devotee of his, and, with a live audience, I consider him to be the one comedian currently working who can rule, as the Prince of Misfits, over all and draw sustained and unrestrained laughter from audience after audience.

He is essentially a clown. The musical assaults on the style of ballad singers like Peter Dawson were highly visual, and despite his lengthy success as a radio comedian this remains at the heart of Ken Dodd's work. Of all the comedians described in this book, his appearance is the most *outré* and bizarre. He explodes on to stages wearing the garish hues of the fairground – bright pinks, vivid greens, glaring checks – and often carrying the Tickling Stick. Sometimes it is an enormous one, and he will reach out into the stalls in explorative fashion – 'Would you like a tickle, missus?' The Tickling Stick is in the great phallic tradition of the jester's slapstick or Mr Punch's truncheon, and its mop-head of coloured streamers is perhaps the only modern equivalent to such props. But even had he not invented that creator of havoc, the Tickling Stick, his physique would still write a clown's signature. The staring, gleeful eyes, the protruding rodent's teeth (did ever childhood bicycle accident prove more fruitful?), and the hair, malleable as black putty, amenable to the most ghastly instant sculpture – these features surmount a body of intricate knobs and angles. It is the hands, however, which are the most compelling. Ken Dodd's fingers signal with the jerky compulsion of old-time semaphore machines, each setting of the fingers a precise message to the onlooker.

Never forgetting the role of barker he played on the back of his ironmongery van, Ken Dodd assails every stage with the whizzbang gusto of Petticoat Lane. He is unashamedly the salesman, ever on the offensive, a Barnum and Bailey of a comedian, unresting in his efforts to draw and hold the crowds and leaving the crowds unrested as he spares nothing to dazzle and magnetise them. Where Jimmy James or Robb Wilton might steal up unawares and sap a corner of the fortress, Ken Dodd takes the citadel by storm. The barrage is laid through his 'what a wonderful day it is for ...' artillery. 'What a wonderful day it is for trooping the rentman'; or for 'grandad-baiting – stick a rabbit and a ferret in his trousers and see how long it is before his eyes cross'; for 'paying the rates'; for 'running down the road, sticking a green cucumber through the letter-boxes and shouting "The Martians are coming!"' The range is impressive, from the inverted surprise of paying the rates to the split-level gag of green cucumbers and Martians, which people may enjoy innocently or otherwise. He queries and cajoles: 'Would you like a moonlight dip, missus? You'll have to warm your hands first.' – 'Would you marry a man in a kilt and green socks – or would you wear a wedding dress?' Or, not without its irony, 'Stand up for yourselves: let them know you're British ... play on their sympathies.' Or the double question when he howls, 'Are you enjoying yourselves?' and then, in response to the affirmative shout, inquires frostily, 'Why, what are you doing?'

Predictably, he holds the record for non-stop gag telling. He erupts volcanically, the lava of his inexhaustible jokes flowing this way and that, eventually overwhelming the coldest auditor. I earlier tried to offer the theological contrast of Tony Hancock closeted in the confessional and Ken Dodd, a veritable Billy

Graham among comedians, calling for the repentance of the
soured and their conversion to laughter. Hours will literally
pass as he drives the faithful through frenzies of mirth, seeking
guffaws as hot gospellers seek souls. I watched his one-man
show *Ha Ha* at the Liverpool Playhouse in 1973. This
'Celebration of Humour' (the subtitle itself having sacramental
overtones) began at 7.30 and there was the usual interval: at
11.40 I had to leave, aching and fatigued, in order to catch my
last bus. I have watched him live many times and the result is
normally the same: a gasping, panting audience. I remember in
particular one night near Christmas during a winter season at
the Manchester Opera House. He appeared several times during
the evening, other acts intervened, and then Ken Dodd wound
up with a kind of Roman orgy of crackling jokes, sometimes
twenty a minute, so that he who, like the Ancient Mariner,
'stoppeth one of three' is doing better than par.

This fusillade means that, very soon, it is a case of laughter
continuous punctuated by gags from the stage, rather than the
reverse. One does not know which joke one is laughing at, or
whether one is laughing at several jokes at the same time. On
that occasion it really hurt: the adjective 'side-splitting' for, I
think, the only time in my theatre-going life came near to truth.
I felt bruised by laughter, stomach stitched and throat choked,
unable to bear it but wishing it to continue. The nearest similar
experience for me was Alan Bennett performing his sermon in
Beyond the Fringe, but that was only five or so minutes.

As with all great entertainers, Ken Dodd's sense of timing is
immaculate, his sensitivity to the living audience keen and
delicate. He uses his unpretentious love-songs, such as 'Tears',
as balm for the sore carcases of his watchers, relaxing them with
the warm, quiet sentiment of those melodies, the lull before
another hailstorm of wisecracks. Not that he is averse to
sending up these same popular ditties, changing 'Love is Like a
Violin' to 'Love is like a Set of Bagpipes – you don't know what
to do with your hands'. It was his exquisite sense of timing
which during his magnificent Palladium runs of 1965 and 1967,
Doddy's Here and *Doddy's Here Again,* caused John Osborne to
take the Royal Court Players, whilst in rehearsal, to watch him
several times.

Timing, obviously, is at the hub of great stage comedy, and
the question of audience rapport explains, almost entirely, the
difference between Ken Dodd in the theatre and Ken Dodd on
radio and television, where, despite prolonged achievements, he
has never quite attained the heights of his own theatrical
triumphs. Interestingly, his best telly performances seem to be
when, solo, he confronts the hugely predisposed gaiety of the
costumed *Good Old Days* audience. But it is in his theatre
performance that one can analyse the compound of flair and
technique, of art and craft, which makes him a champion comic.

In hectic conversations with him I have attempted such a learning process, anxious to grasp the historical roots of his comic gift and the geographic character of his careful technique. They seem to illumine not only his own work but that of popular comedy and its place in the social world over much of this century. Hectic conversations is right. My chief interview with Ken Dodd was one rainswept evening when I arrived to find him not yet returned from some mission, with his door being knocked by someone trying to persuade him to do a charity show in Worsley, prior to a long drive to Stratford-upon-Avon for a late night cabaret, and with several urgent phone calls in between times. And he very concernedly told me I looked tired and shouldn't overdo it! This was typical enough. He works fifty or fifty-one weeks a year dedicated to pressing at the frontiers of comedy. The religious commitment – it is little short of zealotry – is apparent again. Three months' work would probably provide him with his maximum income after tax, but that is not the issue. Nor is it a self-indulgent devotion to some egocentric view of comedy: the comedy has to work, that is audiences have to laugh energetically. Thus Ken Dodd studies and reads – he knows his Bergson and Freud – as he reaches towards the humour, hopefully, of the eighties. I once suggested to him that P. G. Wodehouse had defined humour as well as anyone with his 'the kindly contemplation of the incongruous'. Much as he admires the contemplative comic, Ken Dodd's answer was caustically to the point: 'He should try the Golden Garter Club in Wythenshawe on the Saturday night.' He went on to explain that the gentle, musing approach was a non-starter there and that the packed house, lubricated with alcohol and in sexual high spirits, were looking for what he called 'release' jokes, that is jokes which snap and liberate any remaining inhibitions, lubricants just like the alcohol.

Whence comes this inner compulsion and the accompanying talent, the one feeding the other to create this demonic comic passion? As a sceptical Mancunian, I remain unconvinced that this natural gift is involved with the myth of scouse humour; but Ken Dodd would disagree, pointing to the combine in Liverpool of northern objectivity and a Celtic proclivity for 'talking in pictures' provided by the Irish and the often underestimated Welsh influences in Liverpool culture. He is quick to compare the Diddymen with Manx pixies and illustrate the irreverence of Liverpool attitudes. There may be something in the cross-currents of cosmopolitan urban living which throws up a sharp-witted vein of humour (the cockney cheeky chappies from Sam Weller to Max Miller are instances), but is this exclusively a Merseyside phenomenon?

I harbour a suspicion that the reverse has happened, and that *because* of Ken Dodd Liverpudlians believe that they should be funny. I once watched Ken Dodd walk across Lime Street

Station and immediately all the porters started wisecracking at him, not unlike the arrival in Dodge City of the fastest gun in the West. Perhaps the Liverpudlian presents a persona of humour because he feels, in the shadow of Knotty Ash, that this is as expected of him as dourness from the Yorkshireman or musicality from the Welshman. Having lived nearly ten years in Liverpool I can testify personally to the occasional tedium of a city whose inhabitants feel obliged to be comical.

The myth is supported by reference to Liverpool's comedians. The affable bounce of Arthur Askey and the acute recall of Ted Ray are cases in point, but they were never quite top-class, while Tommy Handley managed only little stage success. The present shoal of Merseyside comedians hardly suggest any talent likely even to match Arthur Askey and Ted Ray, leaving the counter-argument very much in the personalities of Billy Bennett and Robb Wilton.

What is surprising is that, prior to their well earned climb to fame by the 1930s, it is almost impossible to name a nationally known Liverpool comedian. New Brighton's Hetty King apart, if one traces the tradition back to the golden age, there is no Merseysider in lights. Curiously, many Liverpool 'heritages' are remarkably modern; its labour militancy, for instance, scarcely predates 1911, and at the earlier watersheds of working-class history (such as the Chartist uprisings) it plays little or no part.

Liverpool, especially in these early decades, is no more impressive as a source for comedians than, say, the sturdy recruitment from the North-East with comedians like Jimmy James, Dave Morris and Wee Georgie Wood. The home counties contingent is noticeably an older vintage (Dan Leno, George Robey, Gus Elen), indicating the firm hold London held on the profession in former days. What is most surprising is the almost total absence of a midlands contribution with the inventive yet tragic figure of Sid Field standing alone.

What is interesting is the influences on his work which Ken Dodd would eagerly acknowledge. His major derivation is from the contemplative humorists, and 'droll' is a word constantly cropping up in any conversation with him. He is an admirer of the comic actors, and is quick to mention Alistair Sim and Cary Grant. Will Hay, master of the long double take and the disdainful sniff; Frankie Howerd, for being – in Ken Dodd's word – 'outrageous'; and, more latterly, for the exquisite deftness of his expertise, Jimmy James – these are some of the influences on Ken Dodd.

In the literary field it is not Lewis Carroll (whom, like so many, Ken Dodd found menacing as a child) but the transatlantic writers, Mark Twain and Stephen Leacock, who have influenced him. Ken Dodd's portmanteau phraseology (titifalarious, plumptuous) then bears only a superficial resemblance to Lewis Carroll: it is the understatement of the

Norman Evans, of 'Over the Garden Wall' fame, was a memorable Widow Twankey in Aladdin and, like Ken Dodd, a clever burlesque balladeer.

*other famous comedian born on
rseyside – like Ken Dodd as
ll as Billy Bennett, Robb
lton and Arthur Askey – was
d Ray.*

North Americans which attracts. Frederick Jackson Turner, American historian of *The Vanishing Frontier,* cited Mark Twain as 'a vital entertainer', that prototypical artist of transatlantic culture. Significantly, Ken Dodd regards another in that tradition – Al Jolson – as 'the greatest showman of them all'. Certainly Ken Dodd hits every stage with the same driving unstoppable dynamism. One recalls that a singer – G. H. Elliott – was also, for his gossamer-like fluency, a chief influence on Max Miller.

Although not so consciously integrated, there are subtle reminders of Billy Bennett in Ken Dodd's work, and, in his show *Ha, Ha,* he affectionately and splendidly presents the topsy-turveydom of the Bennett monologue, another aspect of comedy already explored. When one considers the oddities of the Bennett canon, one is bound to recall the surreal quality of Ken Dodd: compare his bizarre exploration of human mutations – the light on the finger for reading under the bedclothes; the ear under the arm (so that one can lift a threatening arm and say 'I beg your pardon, Madam'); the mouth on top of the head where one, when late, might stuff bacon butties, stick on a hat and rush to work.

But it is perhaps of Robb Wilton that Ken Dodd speaks most warmly, and he honours him with an impeccable and loving impersonation. Ken Dodd's tempo is brisker and more audacious than that of the 'Confidential Comedian'; he is, in his own expression, 'a fireworks comic'. But there is much of the same domestic commentary. The lugubrious Wilton's exasperated reply to his wife's suggestion that he wouldn't know who Hitler was if the Germans landed – 'I've got a tongue in my head, haven't I?' – is not too far removed from Ken Dodd's notion that, to discover the time during the night, one might bang a bass drum, on the grounds that someone is sure to yell 'Who the hell's banging a big drum at half past two in the morning?' It is the same dotty combine of the alien concept and the homespun rejoinder.

Maybe this precarious harmony of real and unreal is the true spring of Ken Dodd's comedy. It is educative to hear him ponder his patter to the ladies in the audience about their fantasies of 'continental Romeos'. 'You couldn't cope,' he upbraids them. And he will, in conversation, lovingly cherish the word 'cope' for its realistic appropriateness, and so on, as he thinks aloud about his ungallant suggestions that they would 'hide in the gas-cupboards' and 'feel one of their headaches coming on'. Here, then, is a nerve-touching assessment of the human dilemma – not, as is conventional, with a leisurely account, but with a vivid, incendiary assault. It is drollery with dynamite; contemplation at breath-taking pace.

This magnificent amalgam is highly individualistic, but, with indefatigable zest, Ken Dodd has probably invented the

Liverpool sense of humour and by the massive fact of his
national presence persuaded the country of its existence. Unlike
Billy Bennett and Robb Wilton, he 'places' his material
substantially in Liverpool – in Knotty Ash, where, indeed, he
still lives, despite the belief among many that it is a fictional
address like Gillie Potter's Hogsnorton. It is in the
establishment and sustenance of this superb national reputation
that the other side of the medallion – his careful grasp of
technique – may best be illustrated. Once known as 'the slide-
rule comic' because of his shrewd analysis of audience response,
Ken Dodd has, despite the stress of an unbelievably busy career,
remorselessly collated an astonishing record of how, night by
night, audiences react to what he terms his role as a 'catalyst
for laughter'. Many a noted author has scribbled ceaselessly in
his notebook and plenty of great painters have carried a sketch-
pad with them everywhere, but this enormous task of, so to
speak, action research is rare among comic entertainers. It
means, of course, that, when playing a return date, he is able to
check out audience styles and construct his act accordingly.
Such commitment to – such respect for – audiences has been the
springboard for his inexhaustible pushing at the borderlands of
his own talents: it determines the place of his singing and the
selection of ballads for his act; or the introduction of the
Diddymen, lovingly reminiscent of a favourite great uncle yet
owing a little, as he would gaily accept, to Lord Snooty and his
Pals in the *Beano*.

A typical extract from one of his log-books might run like this.
After the date, the season of the year, whether first or second
house, time on and time off, the size of the audience and
whether it was 'hard', 'slow', 'fast', or what, and the weather
conditions (another illuminating sidelight, this), there would be
a double column which might begin something like:

Joke cue	*Comment*
'Country'	went well, but try slower
'Docker'	v.g. (mimic voice and mime walk of policeman next time)
'Schweinhund'	ex., but re-phrase slightly
'H. Wilson (Scillies)'	political gags need punching more here

Ken Dodd generally built up this record himself, and, recalling
the salesman days of his pre-professional era and the stock-
taking it involved, he views it all as mundane common sense.

A cue-word for the gag, a mark-up of the reaction – but,
multiplied over many years, it gives him an encyclopedic
knowledge of British comic response. He is not solemn or over-
academic about it; he recognises only that, for him, it works,
and makes no superior claim for it. It is, by his criteria, possible
to observe the distinction as specifically as, say, playing Wigan

rather than Brighton. Wigan likes hearty vulgarity without too much overt sex, while Brighton fancies weird humour with a tinge of spice. Further, and now the refinements develop acutely, he deems it important to know in advance the venue, the size, the social composition, the time of assembly and the costume of the audience. Manners maketh the man, and an audience in evening dress becomes a different proposition from the same one in lounge suits.

It is interesting to compare Ken Dodd's summary and generalised comment on regional variation, not only in terms of his own unusual adaptability to it but in terms of other regional emphases to be culled from the adjoining table of comedians.

1 *Scotland*

English comedians must be quick-fire performers, replete with 'one-liners' *à la* Bob Hope. Fast-talking Stan Stennett made quite a hit at the Glasgow Empire – the 'House of Terror'.

2 *North-East*

Very class-conscious; a tradition of frustration and anti-pomposity, hence an affection for the dry and pensive. n.b. the success of Jimmy James.

3 *Yorkshire*

Friendly comedians are most popular. Observe this runs counter to the conventional dour image, but n.b. the success of Sandy Powell, Jack Pleasants, Albert Modley.

4 *Lancashire*

Warm-hearted, but with a more abrasive, cutting edge than (3), especially towards Manchester and Liverpool.
n.b. the success of George Formby senior, Norman Evans, Eric Morecambe, Les Dawson.

5 *Wales*

Wild, zany comedians are preferred; possibly it's the Celtic element. n.b. the success of the hilarious Tommy Cooper, born in Caerphilly.

6 *Midlands*

Here the preference seems to be for 'singing comedians'; maybe this links with the Midlands' lack of comedians. n.b. the success of Harry Secombe in the Midlands.

7 *London and the Home Counties*

The capital makes 'totems' of its comic entertainers (like Dan Leno, George Robey or Max Miller) and sometimes appears to like those with a Chaplinesque feature of pathos. n.b. the success there of Sid Field or Norman Wisdom.

8 *The South-West*

A liking for very honest and friendly comic entertainers. Bruce Forsyth made his early name in this part of the country and, while few would see him as an inventive comedian, none would doubt his superb capacity as a genial compère.

Remarkably, from the one specific source of his comic genius, Ken Dodd can imperceptibly adjust the angle of attack to suit

In Wales, zany comedians are preferred such as Tommy Cooper, born in Caerphilly. Suffering with/from him, at Television's 1952 Christmas Party, is McDonald Hobley.

all those situations in all their permutations. His majestic command in the live theatre means that he can subjugate an audience to his comic will until, invariably, the laughter is, and for once the cliché is accurate, uncontrollable.

One can, then, watch Ken Dodd develop an act historically and geographically. His broad canvas, over time, is that of the public entertainer. He is the universal clown, physically, sartorially and orally introducing a disruptive, anarchic but non-threatening element into mundane existence. There is the festive excitement of the circus about his performance, and, if one considers the arbitrariness of what we deem worthy of study and what we judge unworthy, it is interesting to observe how in Russia there are a thousand well equipped and properly organised circuses, drawing a hundred and fifty million people in crowds each year, and enjoying exactly the same status as opera and ballet.

Ken Dodd is clown and jester, but without the Pagliacci touch, eschewing that hint of pathos which is a ruination of popular comedy. Even Chaplin does not avoid that maudlin flavour in his more sentimental passages. Comedy is about real laughter at real issues, albeit tragic and cruel issues. At their height, all twelve of my favourite comedians face life squarely, even if it is from the rung of a window-cleaner's ladder. It is not that they are not escapist, but they invite you to escape by seeing the incongruous side of the ordinary rather than by sinking in the marshy ground of sentiment. Faced with problems, they never appeal for shallow sympathy, they demand full-throated support. Ken Dodd is a Jack Point unbeset by emotional quandaries.

From that foundation he built his act. A front-cloth comic, with an emphasis on burlesque, he was anxious to add the relaxed pleasures of the ballad to this, and persevered until this was taken seriously. The demand of radio – shows like *Blackpool Night* – called for the development of rapid-fire oral material, while since early in his career he has had to adjust again to television and the need, not always successfully met, to evolve the technique of the sketch. Les Dawson and Frankie Howerd may seem less successful when not solo, and of course television consumes an enormous volume of material. The Diddymen were introduced when, faced with early evening listeners and viewers, Ken Dodd realised that children must be catered for, and as a consequence Diddy products – dolls, books, keyrings, puppets – are sold all over the country. Although comedy remains his priority, he has been an important recording artist, topping the charts for eight weeks with 'Tears', one of Britain's best-selling records. His brash attack could have been ready-made for clubland, where he proves to be a sensational draw, and as Malvolio in a Liverpool Playhouse production of *Twelfth Night* he followed in the tradition of George Robey's Falstaff and

Frankie Howerd's Bottom. In his lengthier solo performances, he will sometimes include one of Malvolio's speeches, and a John Betjeman poem. Thus, cinema apart, he encompasses every outlet of entertainment.

The geography of humour – the Ken Dodd map of British laughter – is aligned with this temporal evolution. It paid in his early variety days for, as theatre managers quickly learned, he required no induction period but was, first house Monday night, ready for the worst Sunderland (where according to Ella Shields, 'they eat their young') could offer. Songs were plugged more in the Midlands, sarcasm emphasised in Lancashire, and so on. Ken Dodd draws an interesting distinction between the tales he tells at a stag night, which husbands will carry home to relate to their wives, and those he will tell at a ladies' night direct to those wives.

All in all, Ken Dodd personifies the chief characteristics of professional comedy. It is, initially, intensely professional. Out of respect for his craft and the paying public, he grafts assiduously at the sheer technology of his business. Some might call it manipulative, but we expect the same assiduity from our surgeons and bridge builders. The splendid match of his comic gift with this grasp of historic roots and geographic spread makes for a final and integral example of the harmony of comedian with society; in Ken Dodd's case it is universal, then national, then as specific as Bolton or Brentford.

As Ken Dodd pursues his sincerely held philosophy of promoting 'happiness' in the sense of a mood of sheer exuberance, he accepts an onerous responsibility. The fine balance of his supreme talent and his delicately sophisticated technique gives him a sway over massed assemblies which many actors, preachers and orators might envy. Fortunately, his philosophic approach has no ulterior motive. He remains embarked on the dedicated and single-minded examination of ever more extensive modes of evoking glee or, as he terms it, 'wahoo' for the mutual satisfaction of his audience and himself. He likes to feel that his appeal is to what he calls the 'trilogy': mum and dad guffawing hugely at his verbal excesses, and the child, not only enjoying his physical clowning, but watching the merriment of the parents and basking in the security of their pleasure.

It may, to some, appear an unpretentious, even sentimental, approach, but W. S. Gilbert (who might well have enjoyed Ken Dodd's penchant for 'ingenious paradox') would probably come to his defence. He might offer, in fact, the foremost justification of this my self-selected First Team for the game of laughter. When d'Oyly Carte remonstrated with him, remarking that he earned more than the prime minister, Gilbert replied curtly: 'I give more pleasure.'

Ken Dodd – 'unashamedly the salesman, ever on the offensive, a Barnum and Bailey of a comedian'.

Acknowledgements for illustrations

The author and publishers wish to thank the following for the use of copyright material and photographs:

Radio Times Hulton Picture Library: Oxford 'Electric' Theatre, p. 19; Billy Bennett, p. 28; George Formby senior in 1921, p. 35; Gracie Fields, pp. 38, 39; Wartime Blackpool, p. 43; Sandy Powell, p. 45; George Formby in 1943, p. 50; Will Hay in stage sketch, p. 55; in *The Goose Steps Out* (1942), p. 63; 'Mr' Gillie Potter, p. 61; The Marx Brothers, p. 68; Leslie Henson, p. 69; ITMA, pp. 78, 79; Charlie Chester, p. 81; *Much-Binding-in-the-Marsh,* p. 81; Sid Field, p. 97; Dave Morris, p. 98; Max Miller, pp. 106, 108–9; with Western Brothers, p. 113; Al Read, p. 117; *Educating Archie,* p. 132; *The Goons,* p. 133; Burns and Allen, p. 168; Al Jolson, p. 196

BBC Copyright Photographs: Charlie Cairoli, pp. 20–1; Albert Modley, p. 45; Jimmy Edwards, p. 66; *Merry-go-Round,* p. 80; Arthur Lowe, p. 82; John le Mesurier, p. 82; Jimmy James, p. 93; Larry Grayson, p. 100; Roy Castle, p. 101; Tony Hancock, p. 125; Tony Hancock and Sid James, pp. 128–9 (both); *Steptoe and Son,* pp. 136–7; *The Likely Lads,* pp. 136–7; *Porridge,* pp. 136–7; Frankie Howerd, pp. 142–3, 147, 153; *That Was the Week that Was,* p. 150; *Beyond the Fringe,* p. 150; *Up Pompeii!* pp. 152–3; Morecambe and Wise, pp. 162–3; Les Dawson, pp. 176–7; Bernard Manning, p. 189; Charlie Williams, p. 189; Billy Connolly, p. 189; Norman Evans, pp. 200–1; Tommy Cooper, p. 203

The Raymond Mander and Joe Mitchenson Theatre Collection: Albert Whelan, p. 21; Billy Bennett, p. 23; Gus Elen, p. 24; Marie Lloyd, p. 25; Harry Tate, p. 26; George Formby senior in 1919, p. 34; George Formby in 1940, p. 37; Flanagan and Allen, p. 47; Arthur Lucan and Kitty McShane, p. 51; The Western Brothers, p. 60; Ronald Frankau, p. 60; Claude Dampier, p. 61; Robb Wilton, p. 80; Billy Russell, p. 85; Will Fyffe, p. 96; Jack Pleasants, p. 104; G. H. Elliott, p. 106; Bob Hope, p. 118; Wilson, Keppel and Betty, p. 119; G. S. Melvin, p. 154; Dan Leno, p. 155; Wilkie Bard, p. 155; Morecambe and Wise, p. 158; Revnell and West, p. 169; Jewel and Warriss, p. 169; Scott and Whaley, p. 169; Ted Ray, pp. 200–1

EMI Films Ltd/National Film Archive Stills Library: George Formby in *Come on George* (1939), pp. 32–3; in *Spare a Copper* (1941), *Turned out Nice Again* (1941) and two stills from *Come on George* (1939) pp. 40–1; Will Hay in *The Ghost of St Michael's* (1942), pp. 56–7, 62–3; in *My Learned Friend* (1944) p. 63; Stills by Courtesy of EMI Films Ltd and the National Film Archive Stills Library

The Amalgamated Press and Howard Baker Ltd: Excerpts from 'Will Hay, the Master of Mirth and the Boys of St Michael's' from *The Jolly Comic* in *Tiger Tim's Own Comics Collection,* p. 54 ff

Rank Film Distributors Ltd/National Film Archive Stills Library: Will Hay in *Good Morning Boys* (1936), pp. 56–7; In *Oh! Mr Porter* (1938) pp. 62–3; Stills by Courtesy of Rank Film Distributors Ltd and the National Film Archive Stills Library.

D. C. Thomson & Co. Ltd: Hotspur's Red Circle School, p. 65

Liverpool Empire: Robb Wilton, pp. 72, 74, 86; with Florence Palmer, p. 85

Keystone Press Agency Ltd: Home Guard, p. 82; Laurel and Hardy, pp. 172–3; W. C. Fields, p. 189

Mr James Casey: Jimmy James, p. 89 (both)

Mr Ellis Ashton: 'Happidrome', p. 99; Max Miller, p. 110; Murray and Mooney, p. 167

Royal Court Theatre: The Entertainer, p. 115

Times Newspapers Ltd: Look Back in Anger, p. 123

Mr Danny La Rue: Danny La Rue, p. 155

Mr Les Dawson: Les Dawson, p. 180

Nottingham Playhouse/Mr Gerald Murray: The Comedians, p. 185

Ms Shirley Hill: Les Dawson, p. 189

Mr Ken Dodd: Ken Dodd, p. 194

Kaye Photography: Ken Dodd, p. 205

Index of Entertainers

207